61

37,95

CONNECTING CIVIC EDUCATION & LANGUAGE EDUCATION

The Contemporary Challenge

CONNECTING CIVIC EDUCATION & LANGUAGE EDUCATION

The Contemporary Challenge

SANDRA STOTSKY
with
Barbara Hardy Beierl
John W. Cameron
Jeanne S. Chall
Lisa Ede
Dorothy Henry
Richard A. Katula

Teachers College, Columbia University
New York & London

Published by Teachers College Press, 1234 Amsterdam Avenue
New York, NY 10027

Library of Congress Cataloging-in-Publication Data

Stotsky, Sandra.
    Connecting civic education & language education : the contemporary
challenge / Sandra Stotsky with Barbara Hardy Beierl . . . [et al.].
        p.   cm.
    Includes bibliographical references and index.
    ISBN 0-8077-3081-5 (alk. paper)
    1. Civics—Study and teaching (Secondary)—United States.
2. Civics—Study and teaching (Higher)—United States.   3. Language
arts (Secondary)—United States.   4. English language—Study and
teaching (Higher)—United States.   5. Interdisciplinary approach in
education—United States.   I. Beierl, Barbara Hardy.   II. Title.
III. Title: Connecting civic education and language education.
H62.5.U5S76   1991
320.4'071'073—dc20   91-2222

ISBN 0-8077-3081-5

Printed on acid-free paper

Manufactured in the United States of America

98 97 96 95 94 93 92 91   8 7 6 5 4 3 2 1

To
Sharon and Rick
Ellen and Yitzhak
Steven and Sue
Janet, and Warren.
And especially to
Bruce, Amy, Ariel, Ronen, Sara, and Jay.

Contents

PART II   Writing and Speaking: The Expression of a Civic Ethic

Foreword

RICHARD L. LARSON

In discussing the achievements of retiring Supreme Court Justice William Brennan, President George Bush (as quoted by Anthony Lewis in his *New York Times* column for August 3, 1990) remarked, Brennan's "powerful intellect, his winning personality, and, importantly, his commitment to civil discourse on emotional issues that at times tempt uncivil voices, have made him one of the great figures of our age." Thus did the President remind readers that successfully confronting the central issues faced by our society requires of us all the civilized conduct of civic discourse. That, fundamentally, is the need addressed in this book. It shows how teachers of English can help students—citizens who will soon be voting and participating in public discussions of important social and political issues—to present their views in informed and responsible discourse, with voices at once forceful and considerate.

It was the responsibility for teaching effective public discourse that energized the work of the first teachers of composing in Western civilization: the rhetoricians of Greece and Rome, such as Aristotle, Cicero, and Quintilian. They envisaged public discourse—which was mainly oral—as falling into three classes: that which evaluates public acts or the behavior of persons; that which is concerned with judicial or legal decisions; and that which is concerned with policy (future-directed) decisions. Their advice about public discourse has been read attentively over the centuries, and as recently as thirty years ago it was recalled to the attention of teachers at all levels by such scholars as Edward P. J. Corbett, Richard Hughes, and P. Albert Duhamel. But in the last two decades teachers of written composition have tended to focus attention, not on developing in students the qualities of character and mind and the powers of language needed for public discourse, but on eliciting autobiographic and introspective pieces, and on instructing students in composing "processes" and rhetorical techniques. Few would deny that writing can be an important activity for assisting a student's growth as a person, but such growth is only one, most often private, purpose for writing. When students learn what is usually identified as "the writing process," they often do so without much concern for addressing readers or for achieving, by their writing, a public purpose (e.g., moving readers to an informed judgment, encouraging wise action). And when—as happens regrettably often in our writing courses these days—students practice writing using fossilized rhetorical categories or traditional "plans of organization," they frequently do so with little attention to substance, value, or force of reasoning.

Current instruction in writing, that is to say, tends to neglect the public purposes and public forums for which writers may write, even though the student moving through a school or college is a citizen—not just a future farmer, factory worker, salesperson, nurse, or teacher—and may therefore have to write or speak during discussions of public or private actions. What's more, whether or not that student will later write about public questions, he or she will regularly have to confront the analyses, arguments, and exhortations—sometimes in bewildering profusion—of those who would change the minds of citizens or would move them to significant actions. To discuss public questions, orally or in writing, is good practice for responding to such appeals.

If the findings of a large national study of *college* writing programs that I recently conducted for the Ford Foundation can be extended, even hesitantly, to programs in the schools, there is abundant evidence to suggest that programs in language education today are not preparing students adequately for their roles as citizens. It is important for civic writers and speakers to know how to gather information about how issues arise, and to know how to analyze such issues incisively, formulate cogent ideas, and support assertions convincingly; yet I could find little in many of the programs I examined to suggest that they are helping students develop these abilities. The emphasis in such programs falls, instead, on having students work through many drafts to produce well-ordered, grammatically correct writings, just to demonstrate that they can produce such writings. Responsible citizenship requires of citizens the ability to gather and interpret information, recognize and judge the generalizations of others, and shape and limit their own generalizations; few of the programs I studied demonstrated that they are helping students develop these cognitive abilities. Participating in civic discourse requires speakers and writers to work their way from data to inferences to conclusions; yet there was little evidence that the programs are helping students develop that ability, though the syllabi for many programs do include construction and evaluation of syllogisms and avoidance of fallacies. Only in some advanced courses in writing and in some courses in disciplines *other than* composition and reading, are students thoughtfully guided in these activities.

Instruction in carrying on literate civic discourse must teach such acts of thought and rhetoric, but it must also teach much more: it must teach ethical behavior in discussion. If citizens are to help make decisions and influence policy on public issues, they must develop just standards for evaluating ideas and actions, and must learn how to advocate positions without sacrificing fairness and considerateness of tone. The speaker's *ethos,* as classical rhetoricians remind us, is an important form of argument.

Connecting Civic Education & Language Education urges teachers of language to help students meet the responsibilities of public discourse by enacting the needed ethos—an ethos based on fairness, and, as Richard Katula suggests in the final chapter, on willingness to try to walk a "narrow ridge" with those whose views differ from one's own. It is by such courtesy in using language, the book affirms, that human beings negotiate the progress of their society. Dr. Stotsky and her colleagues urge teachers of language to take responsibility for helping students, whatever their personal interests or opinions, learn to engage in reasoned negotiation through language—to be informed, thoughtful, sensitive, and fair-minded citizens.

Preface

The chapters in this book are based chiefly on papers presented at a one-week interdisciplinary Institute on Writing, Reading, and Civic Education, which I have organized and directed at the Harvard University Graduate School of Education for the past four summers. The institute stems to a large extent from my academic interests. For almost two decades, I have been exploring the connections between reading and writing, the uses of writing for learning, and the social contexts for writing. But the institute and this book have also grown out of my civic activities in the town I have lived in for almost 30 years—a town whose institutions and facilities reflect an extraordinarily rich history of civic benevolence by its citizens in years past, and whose form of government still permits a remarkable degree of civic participation by large numbers of citizens.

I have often, only half-jokingly, described myself as an "unreconstructed Jeffersonian." Like Jefferson, I believe that New England town government is the best form of government ever devised. I am currently serving a third three-year term as a trustee of the public library and as a town-meeting member, both elected offices. A long-term member of the League of Women Voters, I recently helped to found the Brookline Civic Association, an organization concerned about the quality of candidates for local government offices and the future of the town's public institutions, especially its schools, parks, and libraries. The reader and writer as citizen has long been a familiar role to me. In fact, I sometimes think I spend as much time reading local news, scribbling ideas for speeches, writing letters to editors, and working on studies or reports for the organizations to which I belong as I spend on my own academic research. But I don't begrudge one minute of that time. What I have learned from my experiences with self-government may not be exactly what John Stuart Mill or James Bryce had in mind. But it has been morally and intellectually stimulating.

Several years ago, I became particularly interested in the frequency with which political considerations and ethical principles seem to collide rather than coincide in a town composed of citizens who consider themselves highly civic and very high-minded. I began to note how often many of these citizens deliberately use erroneous facts and "red herrings" to misinform and distract voters, make unsupported charges, fail to seek out and consider all relevant information on controversial issues, label those who uncover problems they do not wish to see uncovered as "divisive," accuse their opponents on an issue of using the unethical strategies that they are actually using themselves, call their opponents names and personalize issues rather than consider their opponents' ideas, view themselves and their opponents as stereotypical members of special-interest groups rather than as individuals, and are unwilling to seek common ground or to consider the common good in resolving public issues. And these are frequent problems in a community where, ironically, most active citizens are academic and professional people who would undoubtedly consider these to be highly inappropriate professional behaviors. As a result of my observations, I became deeply concerned about what I perceived as serious deficiencies in the moral framework for public discourse and behavior, in my own community and elsewhere.

I began to ponder the nature of civic education and to do extensive research in a variety of academic and professional disciplines on the meaning, philosophical origins, and manifestations of a civic ethic in this country. Although, as I discovered, civic education in the schools is the official responsibility of social studies educators, it has always been an implicit responsibility of other teachers as well, especially English teachers. The result of my thinking was the institute and now this book.

This work has two major purposes: to indicate some of the challenges that secondary and college-level English teachers now face in developing in young Americans the moral framework for public discourse and public behavior in this country, and to suggest how these teachers might best address these challenges in the context of their regular academic programs. Each chapter focuses on the social, theoretical, pedagogical, and research issues in a particular area of the English language arts, and then suggests how a civic ethic can be enhanced in that area.

It has never been easy to cultivate the civic virtues. But today, for a variety of reasons, it is clearly more difficult than ever for teachers to encourage in their students independent moral thinking about the common good; a motivation to participate in public life; an obligation for public service in the local community; an insistence on the observance of ethical principles in public life; support for the principles and procedures that make self-government in a free society possible; and a sense of membership in their civic communities that transcends differences in social status, ethnicity, race, religion, and gender.

I intend this book to serve chiefly as a means for helping educators in this country to find ways to develop the civic sensibilities of the most diverse group of young Americans the schools have ever had. However, in light of the fragmenting forces in contemporary life in other multi-religious and multi-ethnic countries as well as in our own, I believe it may also be useful to educators in other societies who seek to develop citizens capable of independent moral thinking about the common good. Although a possibly unique blend of individualistic and communitarian values underlies responsible participation in public life in this country, autonomous moral thinking sustains responsible participation in any republican form of government.

I would be remiss if I did not acknowledge the assistance that the reference librarians in the Brookline Public Library gave me in locating information and in obtaining all the articles and books I needed for my research. They were paragons of efficiency, helpfulness, and courtesy, and are among the most dedicated public servants I have ever encountered.

Sandra Stotsky
Brookline, Massachusetts

Introduction

SANDRA STOTSKY

The ethical framework that should guide the behavior of Americans as citizens is complex. It integrates three distinct ethical strands: an ethic based on a respect for majority rule, an ethic based on a regard for individual rights, and an ethic based on a concern for the common good—the civic ethic. Until recently, these three ethical strands have been of almost equal strength in shaping our behavior as citizens. However, in the past several decades, the civic ethic has seriously eroded. Its erosion has been as evident in our public discourse as in our public behavior. In large measure, this erosion reflects a decline in our civic identity—our sense of individual membership in our civic communities. Indeed, for many of us, our identity as members of various religious, ethnic, economic, racial, and gender groups may be far stronger than our civic identity today.

Different scholars have suggested different causes for the decline in our sense of responsibility for our civic communities, ranging from a self-centered individualism and an outright denial of responsibility for others to a lack of civic self-esteem. But regardless of the social or intellectual trends that may account for its decline, a civic ethic remains a necessary source of moral values for shaping public discourse and public behavior in a ''civic'' culture—a culture that depends on many voluntary and obligatory acts of citizenship, especially in the local community. The revitalization of a civic ethic and the strengthening of civic identity and civic self-esteem are of particular importance in a multi-ethnic society whose people have no common religious values or historical memories.

Although there are many settings in which a civic identity and a civic ethic can be nurtured—in the home, for example, or in organized youth groups like the Scouts—for most young Americans today they are probably cultivated most directly in school. Remarkably, civic education in the schools—which includes the development of all three ethical strands—has been the official responsibility of only social studies educators since the second decade of this century. It is most visible in the secondary school curriculum in courses in American government or civics, although it has always been the rationale for courses in United States history.

Because civic education in the schools is the responsibility of only social studies educators, concentrated thinking about the way in which we prepare students for their role as citizens in a republican form of government takes place only within the context of the social studies. Rarely do educators in other disciplines discuss how their subjects contribute to the development of the moral framework for public discourse and public behavior in this country. Yet English or humanities teachers, as well as teachers in other subject areas, have also been responsible, if only implicitly, for cultivating the distinctive ways of thinking required for a republican form of self-government. What students gain from their study of English or the humanities has as much to do with the growth of their civic sensibilities and their ability to understand and take part responsibly in public affairs as what they gain from their social studies.

What are those distinctive qualities that sustain republican self-government and promote a sense of individual responsibility for the common good? Among the many values, ideals, and beliefs that define our civic character and civic identity, I would stress independent thinking, honesty, fairness, a willingness to seek out and consider all points of view on issues, an obligation for public service, a tolerance of different points of view, a sense of responsibility for one's own learning and behavior, a commitment to the principles and procedures that make self-government in a free society possible, an appreciation for an intellectually demanding liberal education, a respect for moral and civic law, a willingness to seek common ground in discussions of controversial issues, a view of people as unique individuals of equal moral worth rather than as representative members of variously defined and privileged groups, and a regard for all human beings as sharing a common humanity and capable of engaging together in rational discourse. All these habits of the mind and heart underlie responsible public discourse and public behavior. Unfortunately, there are a number of limitations today in public life, the academic world, and the school curriculum that strongly affect the ability of English and humanities teachers to develop or regenerate a civic ethic in their students.

This book grows out of a perceived need for a text that explores some of the challenges now facing teachers of English or the humanities in their efforts to shape those ways of thinking that contribute to their students' capacity for promoting the common good. To my knowledge, this book is the first collection of essays in which scholars in English literature, composition teaching, reading, and speech communication examine the conditions in public life, the academic world,

world, or the school curriculum that seriously affect the development and expression of a civic ethic.

The immediate purpose of this collection is to indicate the challenges these scholars believe language educators face today in connecting civic education and language education and to suggest how teachers might guide the development and expression of a civic ethic through their regular academic programs despite these limiting conditions. The chapters in this volume present a vision of the English or humanities teacher's responsibilities that has possibly never been articulated before. But I believe most teachers would recognize the validity of this vision. I also believe they recognize the seriousness of the problems we face today in American public life that requires an articulation of these responsibilities.

The larger purpose of this collection is to stimulate educators to engage in interdisciplinary discussions about how the entire curriculum can contribute to the formation of civic character, the strengthening of civic identity, and the revitalization of the civic ethic. The need for school-wide discussion, and cogent discussion within and beyond each professional discipline, is perhaps urgent now as the public schools enroll a growing population of students from countries without a tradition of responsibility for the common good or of obligation to participate in public life to help determine the common good. But the children of native Americans as well as of new Americans are equally in need of a revitalized introduction to the ethical components of public discourse and public behavior if they are to participate responsibly in the civic life of this country.

This book is based primarily on papers that have been presented at a week-long institute on writing, reading, and civic education held at the Harvard Graduate School of Education for the past four summers. The thrust of the institute, which is funded by the Lincoln and Therese Filene Foundation, is to help administrators and teachers in English, the humanities, history, and the social studies examine ways in which their curricular programs could contribute better than they now do to the development of the ethical framework for public discourse and behavior in this country, particularly in the local community. The essays authored or co-authored by Jeanne Chall, Dorothy Henry, Barbara Hardy Beierl, Richard Katula, and myself have been given as papers at the institute, although in a different form. The essay by Lisa Ede and the annotated reading list by John Cameron were invited for this publication because of their obvious relevance to its subject.

Chapter 1 provides the historical background and contemporary context for the book, beginning with a brief history of the way in which the civic tradition has been manifested in domestic affairs in this country. I offer many possible causes for the decline in the ethic of individual responsibility for the common good that has historically been such an outstanding characteristic of the American people. In the conclusion, I discuss the meaning of civic identity and suggest why its development is central to the effort to regenerate a civic ethic.

The chapters in Part I examine the challenges that language educators face with respect to the role of reading, literature, and the research assignment in the development of a civic ethic. What students read can help them to learn about the ethical values of their local, state, and national communities and to participate more responsibly in public life. They can develop a sense of membership in their national community through direct study of the seminal civic documents expressing its basic principles and values. The development of their civic identity is also influenced by the newspapers, articles, and other kinds of informational material they may read to keep abreast of public affairs. However, an inability to read our basic civic documents and much general public information is a serious obstacle for taking advantage of one's rights and for understanding and fulfilling one's civic responsibilities.

Chapter 2 by Jeanne Chall and Dorothy Henry discusses the results of several recent national assessments of literacy from this perspective. They present a readability analysis of several key historical documents (the Preamble to the Constitution, the Declaration of Independence, and Lincoln's Gettysburg Address) and survey the research literature on the readability of general public information. As their data and their survey show, most of our seminal civic documents and general public information require at least upper level, high school reading skills. But according to these recent assessments of reading, a majority of high school students and young adults in this country cannot read these historic texts on their own, nor can they read with ease much general public information of importance to them as citizens and as consumers. Chall and Henry discuss the implications of this state of affairs for defining an acceptable level of literacy in this country. They also recommend several ways to close the gap between our students' current reading abilities and the reading level of the material they need to be able to read if they are to exercise both the rights and responsibilities of American citizenship and to see themselves as integral members of their civic communities.

Literature programs can assist in the development of a civic ethic in several ways. They can expose students to the intellectually and morally significant works of literature in the history of their communities. They can also help students see that they share a common humanity with all those who inhabit their civic communities, re-- gardless of differences in religion, race, gender, class, and cultural interests. Nevertheless, while some of the literature they read may stimulate positive feelings toward society, much twentieth-century American literature may also influence their attitudes toward their society in negative (although subtle) ways, a concern voiced by Howard Mumford Jones in *Jeffersonianism and the American Novel*. It is not clear how the contemporary American literature our students now read in the schools shapes their image of this country or affects their sense of membership in it. Although some prominent scholars and educators have advocated a common core of literary readings for developing a shared language and a common cultural identity, such a core will not necessarily contribute to the development of civic sensibilities if it consists largely of contemporary literature. Much depends on what is taught and on how it is taught.

In Chapter 3, written with Barbara Hardy Beierl, I suggest several reasons why a common core of twentieth-century American literature in the schools today might not develop the intellectual and moral values that sustain responsible participation in a republican form of government. I then discuss a number of ethical questions for educators to consider in selecting literary works for classroom study and in evaluating pedagogical goals and learning strategies used for literary study today. Chapter 3 concludes with some practical strategies for developing students' awareness of the possible anti-civic and anti- social effects created by the literature they read. In particular, I offer a series of questions for classroom discussion that can call students' attention to the nature of a civic community in their literary texts and to the ways in which literary authors may lessen or enhance students' capacity for civic self-esteem and their concern for the common good. In an appendix, John Cameron provides an annotated reading list of contemporary literary works that in his judgment offer a ''balanced understanding of the human heart and . . . renew our faith in the human spirit.''

The research-based writing assignment is probably the most important vehicle teachers have for fostering open-ended inquiry, inde- pendent reading, and critical thinking—intellectual habits that are basic to informed and responsible public discourse. Yet, academic researchers have just begun to pay attention to the thinking processes involved in doing research at all educational levels, and we seem to know very little about how teachers might best guide their students in undertaking open-ended inquiry. Before more studies are carried out, both teachers and researchers need to be aware of the findings and limitations of existing research in this area so that future studies can be as pedagogically informative as possible. They also need to be aware of the particular problems that students encounter in doing independent reading, thinking, and writing for a research paper.

Chapter 4, on the research assignment, has several purposes. It provides a critique of the few existing empirical studies on the research process. After examining the fit between the findings of this small body of research and current theoretical and pedagogical thinking about the composing process, I offer a series of guidelines for further studies on the research process. I also point out the problems with the research assignment that teachers mention in their own published articles, noting how many of these problems are located in the generative phases of the research process, the phases where students should be engaged in open-ended inquiry, independent reading, and the use of both primary and secondary sources. Since these habits of the mind are crucial for responsible public discourse, I suggest that research on the local community, its government, and history can provide one of the best means for developing these abilities and skills.

The reading that students do for their English or humanities classes plays a major role in their civic education in yet another way. What they read and how well they read powerfully affects the development of their writing ability, a competence that is as instrumental to citizenship as the ability to read; hence the focus in Part II on writing.

Writing has been as much a part of the history of democracy, and as essential for democratic self-government, as reading. In this country, as local self-government developed, so did the kind and amount of writing that people needed to do as citizens, both for maintaining democratically run citizen boards and other voluntary political or civic groups and for communicating with other citizens or public officials. What citizens write or say in their public discourse can influence other citizens and their public officials and helps shape public policy, for better or for worse. As Congressman Morris Udall of Arizona once wrote in a newsletter to his constituents, ''On several occasions, a single, thoughtful, factually persuasive letter did change my mind or cause me to initiate review of a previous judgment.''

Writing is also a vital support for the most direct way that citizens can express themselves and participate in public life—as public speakers. Public speaking was the primary medium for participation in public affairs at the birth of democracy in ancient Athens, and even today, public dialogue or argument is for most citizens the chief means for participating in public life.

The chapters in Part II address the challenges that educators face in helping students learn how to express themselves orally and in writing as responsible citizens. In their writing and speaking assignments, students can learn to observe the ethical scruples that should guide their intellectual development as well as the public expression of their thinking. If public policy is to be shaped in a way that advances the common good, these moral scruples need far more explicit attention than teachers and textbooks have given them, to judge by the relative lack of attention—in writing theory, research, and instructional material—to a writer's ethical responsibilities to the reader.

In Chapter 5 on teaching writing as moral and civic thinking, I discuss the different ways in which academic writing cultivates the moral reasoning responsible civic discourse should exhibit. I group the varied obligations of academic writers into four categories: (1) those relating to other writers, (2) those relating to the complexity and integrity of the subject of their research, (3) those relating to the integrity of the reader, and (4) those relating to the nature and purposes of academic language itself. For example, students can learn as part of doing research and writing research-based papers that responsible writers do not quote other writers' ideas out of context; seek information on all points of view about a question and evaluate the quality of the information that is gathered; do not assume their readers will agree with their point of view without being given reasonable evidence; and present the results of their inquiry in a way that respects all possible readers. Throughout, I offer examples from contemporary published academic writing or curriculum materials to illustrate the different moral responsibilities that developing writers must learn to observe in both academic and public discourse.

Too often public dialogue or argument is little more than polarized, or polarizing, debate, with neither side genuinely listening to and learning from the other. Chapter 6 by Lisa Ede and Chapter 7 by Richard Katula focus on the development of strategies for constructing effective and ethical arguments—arguments that can promote a rational understanding of controversial issues and the possibility of finding common ground. Ede comments on both the negative and positive strategies she finds in an analysis of a group of letters to the editor on a controversial issue concerning the local school curriculum, helping us to see what would-be writers should avoid doing or try to do. Public policy, she suggests, is ill served by public argument in which participants show little or no attempt to understand each other's positions or to find shared values as the basis for a common ground. Ede also offers writing teachers practical advice for helping students learn how to construct arguments that increase, not close off, genuine communication.

In Chapter 7, Katula makes a case for teaching argumentation in the schools, not as formal debate but as a learning dialogue or as a way to gain knowledge about all perspectives on an issue. He is concerned with the teaching of argument as method, not as result. Stressing the value of public talk throughout the history of Western civilization, Katula advocates training in oral communication in every classroom. He proposes a philosophical rationale for the teaching of thoughtfully reasoned argumentation that is based on the metaphor of "the narrow ridge" developed by Martin Buber. The narrow ridge is a position between two extremes; the walker must remain alert and open to learning in order to maintain balance as he or she walks it. Katula contrasts this model of argument with a model he calls the "Morton Downey" model, a form of argument that is unfortunately too common in public and academic life today. Katula then suggests how the metaphor of the narrow ridge can be applied to help students develop a balanced perspective on controversial issues. He describes a series of writing and speaking assignments for secondary or postsecondary teachers to use in developing rational argumentation. These assignments, which move students from the personal and subjective to the analytical and objective, lead them to attend to opposing views and to weaknesses in their own positions. By this means, Katula suggests, students learn to walk the narrow ridge. They learn to construct arguments that advance, not polarize, the understanding of an issue. And by learning to construct arguments that respect the truth; demonstrate an understanding of, if not sympathy with, alternative positions; and bring out common values as well as points of difference, students learn the moral thinking that helps to resolve social conflict.

While this book is directed chiefly to teachers of English and the humanities in the secondary school and in undergraduate college courses, it should be of interest to educators in all disciplines. Indeed, it should be of interest to everyone who is concerned about the role of the schools in preserving what President Benno Schmidt of Yale University referred to, in his baccalaureate address to the senior class in 1988, as "a republic of virtue." For if a new generation of young Americans does not develop independent moral thinking—a way of thinking that transcends differences in religion, wealth, ethnicity, race, or gender—and a sense of individual membership in our civic communities, a republican form of self-government cannot survive.

1 The Decline of a Civic Ethic

SANDRA STOTSKY

Although a moral education is not necessarily a civic education, a civic education is always a moral education. The various goals of a civic education usually include giving students an understanding of a nation's political process and helping them develop the skills needed for participation in it. The central goal of a civic education is the cultivation of an ethical framework for acting as a citizen in that nation. This framework, consisting of a specific set of moral principles and political values, is expected to shape both personal and public behavior and, in essence, create the moral character of a people.

THE ETHICAL FRAMEWORK

The ethical framework that should guide an individual's behavior as a citizen of this country is complex. It integrates several distinct and sometimes conflicting ethical strands: a consideration of the greatest good for the greatest number, a respect for individual rights, and a concern for the common good—or, to use the terms that Michael Sandel does in *Liberalism and Its Critics* (1984), a utilitarian ethic, a rights-based ethic, and a communitarian, or civic republican, ethic. The utilitarian ethic rests on principles embodied in the Constitution of the United States, primarily the principle of majority rule; its roots on this continent lie in the political institutions developed by the first English settlers in colonial America.[1] The rights-based ethic also rests on principles embodied in the Constitution but evolved from the liberal political thinking of the Enlightenment. The communitarian, or civic republican, ethic, often referred to as simply the civic ethic, designates the moral code of citizens in a republican form of government; it also has its roots on this continent in the first English settlements in colonial America, although its conceptual origins can be traced to ancient Greece and Rome (see, for example, the discussion in Wood, 1969).

The utilitarian ethic is reflected in a willingness to accept the decisions made by the majority of those voting (or by those elected or appointed by the majority of those voting) and to abide by those decisions peacefully (or at the most to protest nonviolently) until they are changed by legal means. Most public policy decisions are made on the basis of majority vote. However, because the principle of majority rule is constrained by constitutional protection for the rights of individuals in a numerical minority, the utilitarian ethic has always been modified in our nation's moral thinking by the rights-based ethic.

The rights-based ethic values personal freedom and autonomy, tolerates differences in thinking and behavior that do not harm others, encourages critical inquiry, and sanctions individual initiative guided by self-interest alone. The rights-based ethic also cherishes free and unimpeded debate on controversial issues, culminated by an expression of the will of the majority. Finally, the rights-based ethic seeks to enhance personal development and respects an individual's right to choose not to participate in public life; it views the achievement of self-chosen purposes as the highest form of development.

On the other hand, the civic ethic emphasizes individual responsibility for the common good, public service, observance of moral standards in personal and public life, the moral equality of all citizens, and obedience to the laws created by one's civic communities—those communities in which one may claim the rights of citizenship and to which one must discharge the obligations of citizenship. The civic ethic also values fairness and the seeking of common ground in the resolution of public issues. In contrast to the rights-based ethic, the civic ethic seeks to enhance the quality of public life and considers active participation in public life as an obligation of citizenship; it views advancement of the common good as the highest form of personal development.

Overall, the rights-based ethic stresses responsibility to and for oneself; the civic ethic, responsibility to and for others. Together, all three ethics constitute the moral code that should guide participation in public life in this country, enabling a diverse citizenry to promote both the public interest and its individual needs (Himmelfarb, 1988). All three are indispensable to the life of a free and peaceful society.

Until recently, the rights-based ethic and the civic ethic have been of almost equal strength in our moral thinking as citizens. However, in the past several decades, the civic ethic has seriously eroded. Indeed, a number of scholars who have studied contemporary public life, such as Robert Bellah and his associates (1985), have commented on the marked decline in the ethic of civic responsibility that has historically been so prominent a feature of American community life. This decline warrants serious concern inasmuch as a civic ethic continues to be as necessary a source of moral values for shaping participation in public life today as it has been through the years.

A civic ethic drives such basic acts of citizenship as voting, paying taxes, and serving on juries and in the military. It also stimulates the myriad forms of public service that are still essential for local self-government and community life in this country. No other country of remotely comparable size depends as we do to this day on the voluntary work of millions of citizens in over 70,000 local political units for setting policy regarding such basic public services as schools, libraries, police and fire protection, parks and recreational facilities, and sanitation, and for determining the level and nature of public expenditures. In fact, only three other democracies in the world (Switzerland, Canada, and West Germany) have a larger proportion of total tax receipts under local control than we do (Lijphart, 1984). And for some essential local services, such as emergency medical services and firefighting, we depend heavily on local volunteers. According to Kenneth Perkins (1987, 1989), volunteer fire departments, an indigenous American institution like free public libraries, provide protection to three-fourths of the geographical area of the United States; as of reports through 1985, he notes, 91 percent of all firefighters in this country are volunteers and 84 percent of all departments are voluntary organizations. A civic ethic also motivates support for the public institutions that enrich the quality of life across different levels of government, such as our public universities, and state and national parks. The revitalization and strengthening of a civic ethic are thus of considerable importance to a "civic" culture (Almond & Verba, 1963)—a culture that depends for its existence on both voluntary and obligatory acts of citizenship by all its citizens, especially in the local community.

How English language arts programs in both private and public schools can help revitalize a civic ethic is the subject of the other chapters in this collection. The primary purpose of this chapter is to suggest the sources that may account for the decline in a civic ethic. The chapter concludes with a discussion of the meaning and value of civic identity—one's sense of individual membership in one's civic communities—and suggests why the development of the civic character that constitutes our civic identity is central to the effort to regenerate a civic ethic. We begin by noting briefly how a civic ethic has historically been manifested in domestic affairs in this country, especially in the local community.

THE HISTORICAL MANIFESTATION OF A CIVIC ETHIC

The Seventeenth and Eighteenth Centuries

A sense of responsibility for the common good was not just a geographical necessity as small groups of English settlers began to spread over a vast continent in the seventeenth and eighteenth centuries. Although most settlers were members of colonies ruled by governors appointed by the King of England or by proprietors (only settlers in Connecticut and Rhode Island elected their governors), they brought with them deeply rooted attitudes about local autonomy.[2] In the New England area, small groups of settlers regularly incorporated themselves as independent towns from the 1620s on, as soon as they felt they were large enough in number to assume the financial burden of local self-government. For example, the inhabitants of what became the town of Brookline, Massachusetts, asked Boston officials in 1686 for a school of their own (History Committee of the Brookline Education Society, 1897). They were told they might choose their own public officers and not pay taxes to the town government of Boston if they would support a school, keep their roads in repair, and take care of their poor people. The first Brookline town meeting, held the next year, voted to provide the revenue for maintaining the schoolmaster. It also chose a town clerk and three men to manage the community's affairs. The townspeople's petition for incorporation as a separate town, with about 50 families, was finally granted in 1705. As in other towns, a responsibility for a civic community, as distinct from a religious or ethnic community, developed directly from the experience of making joint decisions about the management and objectives of public expenditures.

English settlers also brought with them political principles that created widespread involvement in political decision making in the local community. In the Middle Ages, according to Edward Jenks (1898), England had worked out a solution to the problem of concentrated political power in the local community. The solution, which was unique among European countries, was to divide the exercise of authority. As Jenks notes, a shire—the local unit—was an executive unit, a military unit, a judicial unit, and a police unit, with a different person responsible for each function, each person independent of the others (p. 175). English settlers in colonial America applied the principle of divided authority as extensively as they could in local government. In the New England states, a small group of men, eventually called a board of selectmen, did much of the administrative work, but many other public officials or public boards had both administrative and legislative powers. Other local officials with independent policy-making responsibilities might have included assessors, tax collectors, constables, town clerks, treasurers, highway surveyors, school committeemen, fire wardens, fence viewers, sealers of weights and measures, and measurers of wood and bark— many of which positions can still be found in New England communities today, as well as newer ones. Town meetings, which all free, land-holding men could attend, had final control of the budget, a power that embodied the principle of fiscal autonomy in the local community.

In other parts of the country, local bodies worked within the political boundaries of counties or townships, but usually with the same fragmentation of local authority and mixture of legislative and administrative powers as in the New England towns. Similar to the situation in New England towns, positions on these bodies were usually responsible, directly or indirectly, to a local electorate.

Public positions were of necessity unpaid or at best supported by modest fees for work rendered. The positions tended to be part-time so that men would also have time to manage their own domestic affairs. Undoubtedly, men were motivated to participate in local affairs by their interest in the way in which their own tax money was spent and by the desire for power or status inherent in a public position. But it is unlikely that these motives alone would have been sufficient to sustain steady attendance at public meetings and many hours of unpaid and often tiresome work dealing with local personalities as well as local issues. Hence, public service and participation in local government had to be seen as a civic responsibility in order for local self-government to exist at all.

As new local tax-supported institutions came into being, or old ones developed to provide better services to the local community, local pride served to enhance a sense of civic responsibility. During the seventeenth and eighteenth centuries, important dates in a community's history might have centered around the building of its school house or meeting house, the purchase of land for a town cemetery, or the formation of a volunteer fire company, which, Perkins (1987) notes, was often the main source of a community's identity. A community's contribution to the Revolutionary War in men, material, or money was always noted. Writing in the early part of the nineteenth century, Alexis de Tocqueville was sufficiently impressed by the "municipal spirit" he found in America to devote several pages in *Democracy in America* (1835–40/1969) to the subject and to deplore its general absence in Europe. He attributed this civic spirit to two sources: local fiscal and political autonomy and the degree of participation required by the structure of local government, especially in the New England states.

The Nineteenth and Twentieth Centuries

During the nineteenth and early twentieth centuries, the civic impulse, enriched by ideas emanating from the Enlightenment, found its expression in the establishment of free (or very low-cost) public schools, universities, kindergartens, libraries, zoos, water supplies, hospitals, museums, parks and forests, and recreational and health facilities, and the design of new forms of local government (such as the council-manager and commission form of city government and the representative town meeting) to address the problems of growing towns and cities. Local pride in municipalities across the country was enhanced by such events as the establishment of a high school, post office, public library, or police force; the laying out of major streets and parks; the introduction of electric lighting and telephone lines; the development of a municipal water supply and sewer systems; or the building of a town or city hall, public library, public high school, municipal fire station, or public bathhouse. In some cases, the civic spirit was expressed by the establishment of educational and cultural institutions open to the public but privately financed and administered.

The civic spirit of the nineteenth and early twentieth centuries was motivated by more than a desire to improve the qualify of life for all. The men and women who worked to establish publicly financed educational and cultural institutions in their local communities believed that the preservation of a republican form of government depended on the civilizing influences of such institutions. They were confident that these institutions could transform growing numbers of illiterate or semiliterate rural migrants or immigrants from countries with no traditions of democratic self-government into citizens capable of dealing with the complexities of an increasingly industrial and urban society. For example, in a discussion of the social and intellectual context of the work of Frederick Law Olmsted, the designer of most of our major urban parks, Albert Fein (1972) describes these institutions as "innovative responses to the social problems of an industrializing and urbanizing nation" (p. 18). Fein notes that Thomas Jefferson's philosophy dominated American intellectual circles, and that his followers wanted Americans to develop a "distinctively superior, yet homogeneous and harmonious, civilization to serve as an example for the divided and warring continent of Europe" (p. 19). Without social or physical planning to provide for such basic needs as education, recreation, and a healthy and pleasant environment, Fein writes, they feared that the processes of industrialization and urbanization would permanently undermine individual freedom and dignity.

Although the public schools were seen as the major resource for developing an intelligent and moral citizenry, the free public library was also considered an important resource for intellectual and moral development. The free public library had had a place in Jefferson's thinking as a means of civic and general education "for those lacking better opportunities." In a reply to a letter asking his advice regarding a newly founded library, he wrote: "I have often thought that nothing would do more extensive good at small expense than the establishment of a small circulating library in every county. . . . These would be such as would give [the people] a general view of other history, and particular view of that of their own country" (Honeywell, 1931, p. 24). But Jefferson's educational priorities during his years of public service in Virginia were public education and the University of Virginia, so he never did more than submit one bill, which was defeated, to establish a public library. Although a few free public libraries were established in the first half of the nineteenth century, their major development began with the founding, in 1854, of the Boston Public Library. In an essay discussing in part the philosophical origins of the free public library, Richard Harwell and Roger Michener (1974) describe its founders as philosophical descendants of the Framers of the Constitution who believed that democratic self-government should be sustained by an educated people. An expression of the philosophy motivating supporters of free public libraries can be found in an appeal to the citizens of Brookline, Massachusetts for donations to their newly established library, written in 1857 by their first elected board of trustees.

> The benefits derived from the establishment of a free Public Library are not remote but immediate, they are not fitful but constant, not temporary but permanent, not partial but universal—they reach the young and the old, the rich and the poor, the learned and the unenlightened. Those, therefore, who have to give, will not only find here a safe depository, but one of immediate, constant, and permanent utility to all classes of society.
>
> With the limited means placed at their disposal, the Trustees have

been able to purchase only about one thousand volumes. These books have been selected with care, and with the view, as far as practicable, of gratifying the public taste. . . . We ask the rich to contribute liberally, and the poor to cast in their mite. We know the times are unpropitious; yet it is an hour for reflection, an hour for associate action, an hour to think and act for one another—pre-eminently the time to study our social, intellectual, and moral advancement. (Board of Trustees, 1857)

The founders and supporters of these public institutions also believed that, in a democratic country founded on notions of equal worth, antagonisms created by differences in social status and wealth could be reduced if citizens from all walks of life had common interests *and* common meeting grounds in their schools, libraries, parks, and playgrounds. Fein (1981) comments in a discussion of the American environmental tradition that, for the supporters of public parks, "the common good depended in part on the creation of common lands." Olmsted himself wrote that his major urban parks were the only places in those cities where one could find "coming together, all classes largely represented, with a common purpose" (Fein, 1981, p. 102). And in a description of the fight for Central Park in New York, Ian Stewart (1981) points out that one of the central arguments made on behalf of public parks was their use as devices "for lessening class antagonisms" (p. 97).

This argument was used to support not only the public schools but also the public libraries. In one of the major histories of the public library movement in this country, Sidney Ditzion (1947/1971) commented that librarians in the nineteenth century, too, saw that one of the public library's functions was "to blunt the edges of [class] differences" and to reduce "divisive tendencies, having their origins in prejudices of race, section, nationality, creed and class" (p. 137). According to these scholars, the thousands of citizens in towns and cities across the country who agreed to additions to their local tax burden to support these public institutions did so in large measure because they believed these institutions could help create the intellectual and moral character on which a republican form of government depended—a character based on independent and moral thinking.

INDICATIONS OF THE DECLINE OF A CIVIC ETHIC

A half century to a century later, a number of scholars believe that we have lost much of the civic spirit that supported the development and maintenance of public institutions. Based on interviews with dozens of Americans on the East and West Coasts, Robert Bellah and his co-authors Richard Madsen, William Sullivan, Ann Swidler, and Steven Tipton suggest in *Habits of the Heart* (1985) that most Americans no longer have the sense of responsibility they once did to their civic communities. Other scholars see more tangible evidence. Referring particularly to our "parks, public buildings and squares, monuments, libraries, schools and grand public works . . . that we inherited from the era before the Great Society," Mark Lilla (1985) claims that we now live in an "age of public affluence and civic squalor" (p. 79). This civic property, he notes, is everywhere in disrepair, and almost nothing has been added to it since the middle of the century.

Other indications of a decline in a civic ethic can also be found. Numerous articles (e.g., Kemp, Reckers, & Arrington, 1986; Dubin, Graetz, & Wilde, 1987) comment on the increase in tax evasion in the past decade, although they note that it is not clear what the actual decline in tax compliance is and what its exact causes are. Even the sense of obligation to vote seems to have diminished. The proportion of registered voters voting in national elections has declined almost steadily in the past two decades, despite passage of the amendment to the Constitution in 1971 giving 18-year-olds the right to vote. Willingness to report for jury duty, too, may be declining. Data from the Administrative Office of the United States Courts, based on questionnaires distributed to the courts in 1981 and 1987, indicate that the percentages of questionnaires and summonses sent out that are returned undeliverable increased slightly during the six-year period, and that the percentage of questionnaires that are not returned also increased somewhat; however, in 1987 many courts may have been using more incorrect addresses than the courts in 1981 because of the way in which lists of names and addresses of potential jurors are provided to the courts (David Williams, Senior Programs Specialist, Court Administration Division, personal communication, August 2, 1989).

There are also some indications that volunteerism may be declining. In a report on the characteristics and survival potential of volunteer nonprofit emergency medical service corporations, whose members make up 65 percent of the emergency medical service labor force in the United States, Kenneth Perkins and Terry Wright (1989) note that many of these volunteer corporations are experiencing "severe human resource shortages" (p. 1), with, for example, many counties in Virginia reporting a perceived decrease in the level of volunteerism. The survivability of the volunteer fire department is also being threatened. Robert Boorstin (1987) and Lindsay Gruson (1987) suggest in newspaper articles that rural communities especially are facing growing difficulties in recruiting volunteers; while there may still be more than one million volunteer firefighters in the United States, about the same number as 20 years ago, their percentage in the total population is down.

SOURCES OF THE DECLINE IN A CIVIC ETHIC

The Fragmented Community

A decline in the sense of responsibility to a local community can be attributed directly to several specific trends in contemporary life. Today, fewer people work or live in the community where they grew up, and more people live and work in two different communities and frequently change where they live and work. Moreover, there has been a dramatic increase in family fragmentation, in childless households, and in the population density of suburban towns and cities. Because of the increase in both family mobility and fragmentation, young people are apt to have fewer opportunities to develop a sense of responsibility to even the network of relatives or neighbors that close family life and stable neighborhoods tended to foster. Single working mothers probably have even less time to give local community affairs than two working parents do. Thus, for several reasons, young people are less apt to see, in their immediate families, models of active civic behavior with respect to their local community. An increase in childless households also has an impact on community ties; young childless adults are apt to have little interest in the network of local community institutions that serve families or the specific needs of children. Finally, the sheer size of most towns and cities today means that fewer people develop a sense of responsibility for their local community by participating directly in its governance.

Individualism

Several intellectual and social trends in the past few decades may be responsible for the general weakening of a civic ethic at all levels of community. Some scholars have attributed the general weakening of the civic ethic to changes in fundamental social values. William Sullivan argues in *Reconstructing Public Philosophy* (1982) that the civic ethic has been overwhelmed by an unbridled entrepreneurial spirit and an asocial individualism that he believes are characteristic of the liberal political tradition. In a related argument in *Habits of the Heart*, Bellah and his associates (1985) attribute our loss of a sense of community and a lack of commitment to a particular community to the increasing dominance of an individualism that they characterize as a preoccupation with self-expression or self-advancement. The current strength of this individualism, they believe, interferes with the development of communal ties and obligations. Further, they think that its dominance has caused us to lose the very language in which we have expressed and justified commitment to our communities or to others in our public lives—the language of civic republican thinking.

There is much to be said for these explanations. A philosophy of individualism that is interpreted to signify only, or primarily, a narcissistic focus on the self or an all-consuming drive for success and material comfort, may not be very hospitable to a civic ethic. However, individualism in this country can mean, and has meant, something other than self-centeredness or fiercely competitive acquisitiveness bordering on greed. As Richard Vetterli and Gary Bryner note in *In Search of the Republic: Public Virtue and the Roots of American Government* (1987), "individualism was at the core of the American concept of virtue" (p. 79). As individualistic ethic stressed the positive values of self-reliance, resourcefulness, personal autonomy, and independent, nonconformist thinking, especially on political and religious matters. And this individualism, which antedates the economic or "expressive" individualism of the nineteenth and twentieth centuries and has its roots in Protestantism, the settling of the American continent, and British and European political philosophy of the seventeenth and eighteenth centuries, was not, and is not, antithetical to a sense of responsibility to a civic community or to the notion of community interdependence. Indeed, throughout American history, an individualistic ethic and a civic ethic have flourished together. Nor have entrepreneurial activity and individual ambition in themselves necessarily precluded public service or civic largesse. In an essay on the relationship between ethics and politics in American life, Martin Diamond (1986) stresses that commercial activities and "bourgeois" values such as hard work, prudence, moderation, frugality, tranquility, and order have been, and are, quite compatible with civic virtue and communal responsibility. Thus, it does not seem accurate to claim that individualism is in or by itself responsible for the decline in a civic ethic. However, a corrupted form may have accompanied or contributed to the decline.

The Dysjunction of Rights from Responsibilities

The weakening of a civic ethic may also be, in part, a subtle side effect of the specific social concerns of the past decades, reflecting not so much a change in values as the failure to emphasize certain values. Lawrence Mead argues in *Beyond Entitlement: The Social Obligations of Citizenship* (1986) that in the effort to secure individual rights and full citizenship for disadvantaged or handicapped groups of people—an effort strongly motivated by a sense of social obligation—we have de-emphasized, if not ignored altogether, the social obligations of citizenship as the moral counterpart of individual rights and as a condition for receiving the entitlements provided by many social programs in the past several decades. Mead does not explore the effects of these social concerns on society as a whole. But it is possible that this dysjunction of the concept of rights from the notion of civic responsibility in the rhetoric of those advocating the rights of the disadvantaged or handicapped has contributed to the general decline of a civic ethic.

William Donohue, too, in *The New Freedom: Individualism and Collectivism in the Social Lives of Americans* (1989), believes we have uncoupled a concept of rights from a concept of responsibilities. Like Sullivan and Bellah and his associates, Donohue sees an asocial individualism as the cause of our lack of civility and community. But in contrast to their view that this malignant individualism is inherent in the liberal political tradition, Donohue argues that this asocial individualism has been fostered by an exclusive stress on an "individual liberty without limits"—a fraudulent conception of freedom, he believes, and not inherent in the liberal political tradition.

Education

Like Mead and Donohue, Morris Janowitz (1983) also believes that we have failed in recent decades to emphasize the notion of civic responsibilities as the counterpart of individual rights. However, he sees the source of the problem in the schools. In *The Reconstruction of Patriotism: Education for Civic Consciousness*, a book that advocates national service for all young adults in this country, Janowitz argues that the weakening of a civic ethic can be attributed in large part to an imbalanced approach to civic education itself. Tracing the development of citizenship in this country from the time of the American Revolution to the present, Janowitz suggests that students no longer receive a balanced view of the rights and obligations of citizenship.

Evidence to support Janowitz' argument can be found in school texts and in the curriculum itself. For example, the 1985 edition of the leading high school textbook on American government, *Magruder's American Government* (McClenaghan, 1985), contains two full chapters on civil rights, thus orienting students to some of the basic values of the rights-based ethic. But such terms as "civic," "civic responsibilities," or "responsibilities of citizenship" do not appear in the index, and there seems to be no discussion anywhere in this 650-page text of the concept of citizenship as one entailing responsibilities, even in the section that describes juries and the selection of jurors. In this textbook, as good as it may be in other respects, the civic republican tradition does not exist.

The decline in stories about American history in elementary school social studies programs as well as reading programs may also constitute evidence supporting Janowitz's argument. Diane Ravitch (1987) notes that in the late nineteenth and early twentieth centuries, history in the primary grades was taught mainly through stories, biographies, legends, and folktales. But a new curriculum, called the "expanding environments" curriculum, was developed in the 1930s, and, according to Ravitch, the historical part of the social studies curriculum was dropped and replaced by a sociological and economic emphasis on home, school, and community.

Basal reading series published from 1900 to 1970 show a decline not only in stories about American history but also in stories that express, as Charlotte Iiams (1980) puts it, "pride in the American nation." In recent readers, there seems to be little mention of any national holiday except the Fourth of July. Even nonhistorical civic content has diminished. Today, stories about children that are meant to emphasize good citizenship usually depict right conduct in everyday life, not activities on behalf of a civic community. Moreover, few stories present the workings of government—people paying taxes, serving on juries, voting, or becoming citizens—or show public service employees other than police officers or firefighters. On the other hand, Iiams found that elementary readers now contain stories about a variety of ethnic or racial groups—an important part of American history that previously had been badly neglected. Such stories imply that we are a country that not only tolerates but willingly embraces a diversity of people from every part of the globe—a message that strengthens the development of the rights-based ethic. However, it is doubtful that children or adults in these ethnic communities play important roles in their civic communities or interact with others for the benefit of a civic community, since Iiams found so few examples altogether of genuine civic activity. It is thus possible that lessened exposure to American history and to models of basic civic behavior in their reading materials may have left young Americans with a diminished sense of national identity, few heroes and heroines, and a limited understanding of the nature of basic civic behavior at all levels of government.

The Media

The attention given by the media in recent years to the lack of personal ethics in public figures who should otherwise command respect, if not emulation, has also left young Americans with few clear models of moral behavior in contemporary public life. Citizens today may know more about the sexual escapades or marital infidelities of George Washington, Benjamin Franklin, Franklin Delano Roosevelt, Dwight Eisenhower, John Fitzgerald Kennedy, and Martin Luther King (as well as of various presidential candidates and members of Congress in recent years) than they know about their political philosophy and accomplishments. In addition, the media have also given extensive publicity in recent years to the unethical public behavior of a large number of highly placed public officials, ranging from a president and vice-president of the United States and members of the president's cabinet to a speaker of the House of Representatives and other members of Congress. By exposing or publicizing the unethical behavior of public officials in the performance of their official responsibilities, the media have performed a significant public service. They have clearly made citizens more aware of the significance and nature of ethical behavior in public office. Nevertheless, the number and prominence of these public officials, most of whom have had to resign from their office, have been dismaying, and there has undoubtedly been a diminution of faith in the ethics of any public official and the integrity of any government program.

Academic Scholarship

It is also possible that a civic ethic has been eroded, in part, by the even more subtle effects of a recent and highly negative interpretation of American history based on an analytical framework derived from European thinking and experience—a framework postulating that economic interests determine a society's political and social institutions. A number of scholars in various academic disciplines have proposed that the establishment or expansion of such public institutions as parks, schools, libraries, and playgrounds in the nineteenth and early twentieth centuries should be seen as a reflection of class interests, not as an expression of Enlightenment liberalism and civic republican concern for the moral and intellectual character of a self-governing citizenry. They view the latter account of the origins and purposes of these institutions as too idealistic and benign. Instead, these scholars claim that the institutions were founded or expanded by well-to-do professionals and businesspeople to inculcate certain values in immigrants or the poor that would preserve the political and social dominance of these professionals and merchants and maintain the "social order" necessary for their economic activities. For example, in an analysis of the forces causing the expansion of education in mid-nineteenth-century Massachusetts, Alexander Field (1976) argues that universal public schooling came about primarily because of the need for "social order." He suggests that both professionals and manufacturers viewed schools primarily as agencies of social control (p. 548).[3] We find a similar interpretation in a history of the movement between 1880 and 1920 to establish supervised playgrounds in cities across the country. Dominick Cavallo (1981) suggests that the playground became "a vehicle of political socialization" by "play organizers" (p. 8), who sought to encourage cooperative team playing among city children as a way to reduce ethnic conflicts and to inculcate values useful for industrial work and urban life.

The development of our public parks and public libraries has been interpreted in a similar way. In an essay on the social context of the work of Frederick Law Olmsted, Geoffrey Blodgett (1981) sees the designer of many of our major municipal parks not as a Jeffersonian or a utopian socialist but as a member of a "gentlemanly, cosmopolitan elite which tried . . . to impose its will on American political and cultural development" after the Civil War (p. 112). To Blodgett, Olmsted is an example of those "profoundly conservative" reformers who, "deprived of grass-roots political power, learned to assert their authority in public life through specific technical expertise in the higher echelons of urban governance" (p. 122). And in a self-characterized revisionist interpretation of the history of the American public library, Michael Harris and Gerard Spiegler (1974) describe the founders of the Boston Public Library as "authoritarian elitists" who believed that the public libraries might contribute to a "general effort directed at controlling and moderating the behavior of the 'dangerous classes' in society" (p. 264). In Harris and Spiegler's judgment, "one reason the public library has proven so inhospitable and cold for the man on the street is that it was designed to control him and not to liberate him" (p. 264).

In sum, recent scholarship suggests that the effort to promote civic values and social cohesion was in essence an attempt to preserve the "status quo"; that the notion of public service by the well educated was in actuality a form of elitism; and that the undertaking of "conservative reform" to reduce if not eliminate racial and ethnic divisiveness had as its underlying purpose the stabilizing of society for economic activity and growth. The development or expansion of these public institutions was, according to much of this scholarship, a deliberate substitute for addressing the pressing economic and social needs of the immigrants or the poor, and was not intended as a means for helping them.

It may well be that the founders and supporters of the public schools, parks, libraries, playgrounds, and other public institutions of the nineteenth and early twentieth centuries were motivated largely or wholly by a concern for preserving their values and political power rather than by republican morality, a fear of the destructive effects of industrialization and urban life on Americans, or a concern for maintaining a form of government that required at least a moderately virtuous citizenry. But it is also possible that an interpretation of the development of American institutions in European terms is not valid, for, as Tocqueville noted, the strong civic spirit he found in America in the early nineteenth century was missing in Europe. Moreover, the nineteenth-century concern for moral character and social responsibility in America was, according to some scholars, an effort to *counter* the spirit of aggressive ambition and individual aggrandizement in this country: Social ills were seen as resulting from lapses in private morality rather than from structural features of a particular economic and political system or, more generally, of society itself. That is why, Anne MacLeod (1976) suggests, "docility" was emphasized in mid-nineteenth-century children's literature, which was read primarily by the children of professionals or merchants; parents, ministers, and teachers hoped to counteract the "selfishness" that led to social problems. As MacLeod notes, the word *docility* in the mid-nineteenth century did not mean "passivity" or "flaccid obedience to authority"—as many scholars today fail to appreciate— but encompassed the notion of "personal and social responsibility to others." Thus, an analytical framework based on European experience may be inherently inappropriate for understanding the American experience and incapable of detecting the presence of a civic imperative. Theories borrowed from one context for use in another may prove to be seriously flawed conceptual tools in the new domain.

Nevertheless, regardless of whether this negative interpretation of the motives of those who developed or expanded public institu-

tions is valid, it is important to consider the way in which this interpretation of American history may have affected our attitudes today
toward our public institutions and toward belief in a civic ethic itself.
A portrayal of institutions serving the whole community as instru-
ments for socializing immigrants, the working class, or the poor into
an undesirable social order rather than as ways to integrate and benefit the whole community clearly makes them seem less deserving of
broad public support. Worse yet, a portrayal of ostensibly public-
spirited citizens as consciously or subconsciously serving class interests tends to breed cynicism about the sincerity of a civic ethic. It
implies that a civic ethic is fundamentally a bogus moral code, advancing class interests rather than the common good. As a consequence,
it demoralizes by casting doubt on the validity of a republican form
of government.

The influence of scholarship on public institutions. The effects of
these intellectual trends in the academic world on the strength of a
civic ethic may be more indirect than direct. That is, their major
impact on the general public may be through the work of those in
other fields whose professional responsibility requires them to be
alert to developments in contemporary scholarship and to reflect such
developments in their own work. A case in point is the attempt by the
National Museum of American History in Washington, DC to portray
American history with greater candor than it may have been presented
in earlier years. In an exhibit entitled "A Nation of Nations," museum
officials tried to explain how the many different peoples who came or
were brought to this country became one nation. Near the entrance to
the exhibit, one of the explanatory scripts written by the museum staff
reads as follows: "America was the place where a man could hope for
fair return from his labor. America was where you could be successful,
happy, and free. These dreams lured millions of immigrants in the
years following the Civil War. But the reality was often very different.
America turned out to be—the place where you were expected to become an American." The jolting ending implies not only that becoming
an American often meant *not* becoming successful, happy, and free but
also that immigration to America meant being socialized into an undesirable form of citizenship.

Similar themes run through other scripts for this exhibit. For
example, near a display of a schoolroom in Cleveland, Ohio, in the
early years of the twentieth century, a script reads as follows: "Immigrant children were Americanized and taught English in the free
public schools. A good dose of patriotism and Yankee social values

were [sic] administered along with the 3 Rs. For how else were all these new Americans going to learn what it means to be an American?" Here, the sarcasm in the question implies that the public schools snared unsuspecting immigrant children into learning English, developing a commitment to this country, and acquiring "Yankee social values," although we are not told what these possibly undesirable values were.

A faithful reflection of these recent intellectual trends in academia, this museum exhibit is undoubtedly trying to correct a presentation of American history that may have ignored the exploitation, prejudice, and belittlement that many immigrants experienced. Nevertheless, an interpretation of American history that makes the verb *Americanize* appear manipulative, that gives the word *American* a negative connotation, and that portrays our public schools as patronizing, self-serving, and antipluralistic might well leave visitors to the exhibit, which has been in place since 1976, with the feeling that an allegiance to this country by all its citizens is not deserved and that the obligations of American citizenship need not be taken seriously.

The influence of scholarship on textbooks and the social studies. These intellectual currents in academia also seem to have influenced the publishers of the textbooks that teachers use, thus affecting the development of a civic ethic in the schools. To begin with, social negativism now appears in school texts at very early grade levels, and it is often highlighted. For example, the Scott, Foresman social studies textbook for grade 5 (Berg et al., 1979) opens its discussion of the Constitutional Convention by noting the absence of women (as well as "Black people and American Indians") at the Convention. One may debate whether such discussions should omit (as they usually do) the fact that women did not receive the right to vote nationwide in any country until 1893 (New Zealand), over 100 years after the Convention, and that the enfranchisement of women was not a controversial issue at the time of the Convention. Nevertheless, the effect of such prominent faultfinding at this grade level, especially when it is isolated from a full discussion of the whole issue of women's right to vote, is to reduce respect for an achievement (and ultimately for the institutions created by the Constitution) that Americans traditionally have wanted their young people to view with pride.[4]

Social negativism may also receive a great deal of space in textbooks. In the Scott, Foresman textbook, for example, of the nine pages in the chapter dealing with the creation of the Constitution, *two* focus primarily on the absence of women at the Convention.

Perhaps the failure of the Framers to give women the right to vote warrants much more attention than slavery, which is not mentioned at all as such in this chapter (and which was a highly significant issue at the time). Nevertheless, the effect of devoting so much text space to the limitations of the franchise in 1791 is to overshadow the many different achievements of the Constitutional Convention simply by leaving fewer pages for discussing them.

In an essay on the state of American history and social studies textbooks, Gilbert Sewall (1988) points to a particularly disturbing feature of this social negativism: It seems to give a "sinister cast to the majority culture." For example, the 1984 curriculum guide for high school social studies in the Boston Public Schools lists as one of the priority objectives for study in United States history courses, "Describing the American voter at the end of the 18th century, and describing who cannot vote" (Boston Public Schools, 1984, p. 133). The suggested teaching activity is: "Write a short description of 'The American Voter,' and outline the strategies used by White Protestants to keep Blacks, Catholics, women, and other groups from voting and holding office" (p. 133). For eighth-grade history, the curriculum guide suggests that students describe "the way in which Native American, African, Hispanic, and other 'minority' cultures have been treated by Europeans in the United States, citing instances of prejudice, discrimination, and oppression" (p. 126). Whether the complexity of the truth should be reduced to incorrect generalizations in order to make students aware of the history of discrimination and prejudice in this country, the effect of such a negative approach to American history is to pit the descendants of non-European groups against those of both the original settlers and other European immigrants, and to elicit a sense of hostility, rather than obligation, from each group toward the other.[5]

Has the attempt to give students a realistic portrayal of the experiences of various ethnic and racial groups in this country gone beyond academic boundaries and is it, instead, arousing resentment in African-American or American Indian students toward students whose ancestors came from European countries for discriminatory or exploitative acts committed by some of their ancestors? Further, is it also creating hostility in students whose ancestors came from European countries toward African-American and "Native American" students for a lack of understanding of the hardships and exploitation many of their own ancestors experienced here and for having all their ancestors lumped together indiscriminately in a category called "Europeans," stereotyped, and collectively accused of prejudice, dis-

crimination, and oppression? Clearly, educators and other public officials need to explore whether the reported increase in racial, gender,
and ethnic animosities at college campuses around the country is
being stimulated or even caused by the use of such oversimplified
and inaccurate curricular materials in the high school.

The possible influence of scholarship on civic participation by the young.
In *Democracy and Its Discontents: Reflections on Everyday America*, Daniel
Boorstin (1975) writes that in our schools "the story of our nation has
been displaced by 'social studies'—which is often the story only of what
ails us" (p. 45). Boorstin thus also implies that students have been offered only a one-sided, and negative, account of the American experience. That this imbalance is both real and pervasive is indirectly acknowledged in James Shaver's (1986) reflective essay about his own
work in civic education. Shaver raises a question about the appropriate
educational level for social criticism in the social studies, implying that
a negative, faultfinding stance toward this country, its history, and its
values has perhaps been introduced too early, and without a corresponding emphasis on its strengths. Although no one has directly examined the effects on young Americans of a persistent, unrelenting
negative view of their own society, Shaver is clearly not unmindful of
the results of the studies of citizenship and social studies done by the
National Assessment of Educational Progress in the late 1960s, middle
1970s, and early 1980s (Mullis, 1978, 1983). These studies indirectly
suggest that the effects of social criticism on the civic behavior of young
Americans have been the opposite of what curriculum developers had
hoped. Instead of an increase in political involvement, there has been
stasis or even decline.

For example, when students were asked, in the 1969 and 1975
assessments, about their ability to participate meaningfully in government, less than half of the 13-year-olds in both 1969 and 1975 felt that
they could influence decisions of local government. Moreover, the
percentage of 17-year-olds feeling that they could have such influence
dropped considerably from 1969 to 1975, from 73 to 56%. On a similar
question concerning the national level, the percentage of 17-year-olds
in 1975 feeling that they could have an influence rose from 39% in
1969 to 52% in 1975. However, despite the institution of the 18-year-
old vote in 1971, actual participation in political activities by 17-year-
olds declined from 1969 to 1975. Fewer 17-year-olds had signed petitions or written letters to government officials, while the percentage
having participated in a public election campaign declined from 18%
in 1969 to 9% in 1975. Political participation was not included in the

1982 assessment, so we do not know whether there has been a reversal of this decline.

It is unlikely that this decline in civic participation was simply a reflection of a change in national issues once the war in Vietnam was over. Issues arousing political passion regularly occur at the local and state level; moreover, they are the ones with which precollege students are apt to be most familiar. If the newer curricula introduced in the 1960s and 1970s to develop critical thinking and to encourage participatory behavior were influencing the students exposed to them, it is quite possible that they may have subtly reinforced—or even created—the feeling of alienation that they were often designed specifically to help overcome. Although educators were undoubtedly trying to help students learn how to think critically about public issues, and to stimulate their interest in participatory activities, an emphasis on the social problems of society, with little or no attention to its strengths or virtues, may have inhibited the development of students' sense of membership in it and contributed to their apathy about participating in public life.

The influence of scholarship on the curriculum as a whole. A civic ethic has undoubtedly been weakened by a failure to shape the ethical framework for our behavior as citizens in a balanced way within the social studies curriculum. But it may also have been weakened by a failure to conceptualize the overall curriculum from the perspective of its basic civic function—to develop in young Americans a sense of individual responsibility for their civic communities, the motivation and skills to participate in determining the common good, and a commitment to those principles and practices that promote freedom, justice, and peace. Indeed, overall institutional neglect may have done as much damage as excessive social faultfinding at an early age or a lack of attention to civic values within the social studies curriculum or the reading curriculum.

For example, many educators in recent decades have seemed to suggest that the primary purpose of the public schools is to develop the basic skills students need for participation in the work force. Much of the motivation behind the "basic skills" movement has, of course, been a legitimate concern that graduates of the public schools be self-sufficient and employable. The building of vocational high schools and the development of occupational resource centers as part of a comprehensive high school clearly reflect this concern. However, although employability may be one reasonable educational goal, a basic skills orientation may have encouraged students to believe that learning how to make a good living was the major aim of education. The effects of such an orientation may also have worked against the development of a civic ethic by its unintentional slighting of the significance of voluntary community activity.

At the other extreme, some educators, particularly in English and language arts, have advocated personal growth as the only defensible end of education. After the Dartmouth Conference in 1966, a conference on the teaching of language and literature attended by American and British educators, John Dixon (1967), a British educator, wrote an influential book called *Growth Through English*, which urged a model for curriculum development based on personal growth rather than on mastery of skills or on knowledge of a cultural heritage. Dixon believed that the latter two models were outdated and inappropriate to students' real needs.

It is not clear that this assumption was correct then, or that it is now. The curriculum that Eliot Wiggenton (1985) developed around the student-produced journal called *Foxfire* in an Appalachian mountain community in Georgia in the 1960s is an enduring and remarkably successful example of an emphasis on both basic skills and a cultural heritage. Based almost completely on John Dewey's philosophy about the value of experiential learning guided by clear academic objectives, Wiggenton's project-oriented curriculum is unquestionably humane; yet it has never placed personal growth at its center. Most student learning has been based on research into the folklore and folk customs of the region rather than on formal study in school textbooks. Self-esteem and individual development have been by-products of students learning about their heritage and acquiring academic skills.

Other influential educators in English and the language arts besides Dixon have also urged a focus on the student's personal needs, interests, and experiences, particularly for the writing curriculum. Clearly, personal development is as worthy a goal of an educational program as employability. However, it is possible that an overemphasis on self-defined needs and interests in the English language arts curriculum has also contributed to a self-absorbed individualism and inhibited the development of a civic self.

Changes in Family Values

Although the intellectual trends in the academic world in the past several decades may have had a strong negative influence on the development of a civic ethic in young Americans through their effects on school curricula, the schools and their curricula cannot be held any more responsible for the decline in a civic ethic in the young than can the students' own parents. The moral and civic behavior of the young is fundamentally shaped by the home, and many educators attribute the weakening of a civic ethic particularly to changes in family values. Regardless of socioeconomic level, students seem increasingly to come from homes that do not model or encourage socially responsible behavior. Deficiencies in parental values and behavior may be reflected in various forms of antisocial behavior by the young in and outside of school, ranging from school absenteeism, smoking, alcohol and drug abuse, and teenage pregnancy, to stealing, vandalism, and other forms of criminal activity. Any truly effective programs to reverse the decline in our students' sense of individual responsibility toward their civic communities and toward each other will clearly depend on the involvement and cooperation of their parents.

CIVIC IDENTITY AS THE BASIS FOR A CIVIC ETHIC

Clearly, teachers in every area of the school curriculum need to help young Americans learn that, as citizens, they have civic responsibilities as well as rights. But preaching to students that they have civic responsibilities, mandating their "voluntary" participation in community service projects, and/or stimulating their active involvement in social and political issues are unlikely to instill a deeply felt and self-imposed sense of individual responsibility toward their local, state, and national governments and all the people who live in them. In order to develop the ethical framework that supports responsible participation in a republican form of government and a concern for the common good, the schools must, above all, revitalize their efforts to help all young Americans acquire a civic identity—a sense of individual membership in their local, state, and national communities.

The Meaning of a Civic Identity

A civic identity is much more than a feeling of belonging to a particular political entity that can be defined by specific principles and processes. In part, it is a feeling of kinship with all those who live within the boundaries of that political entity, regardless of economic, intellectual, ethnic, racial, gender, or religious differences. In a passage describing the varied shades of meaning of "identity" in *Identity and the Life Cycle*, Erik Erikson (1980) suggests that the term *identity* refers to something in an individual's core that is an "essential aspect of a group's inner coherence." An identity signifies a "persistent sharing of some kind of essential character with others" and facilitates the "maintenance of an inner *solidarity* with a group's ideals and identity" (p. 109). This feeling of kinship undergirds a sense of responsibility for all those who share one's civic communities. At the same time, a civic identity is a view of the self as an individual citizen, not as a representative member of a special interest group. Thus, civic identity makes possible a critical stance on public issues that does not destroy a sense of obligation to one's civic communities.

If citizens have no civic identity, their participation has no necessary moral base and may be little more than self-serving, manipulative, or cynical. Without a civic identity, they are unlikely to arrive at self-interest or special group-interest properly understood, or to transcend self-interest or special group-interest for the sake of the common good. The common good can emerge only when all participants in a political conflict believe that they share some essential values despite individual or group interests. For if citizens in a republican form of government do not share some common values, then public policies cannot be advocated or defended on moral grounds. That is why, R. Freeman Butts (1988) suggests, educators need to emphasize those values—or, in Erikson's words, the "essential character" and group "ideals"—that should be common to all citizens, rather than those that link some individuals to others on the basis of "race, ethnicity, religion, class, party, or life-style" (p. 165).

What are these essential attitudes, values, and ideals that constitute our civic character? As suggested in the Introduction, these values include independent thinking, honesty, fairness, a willingness to seek out and consider all points of view on issues, a tolerance of different points of view, a sense of responsibility for one's own learning and behavior, the importance of an intellectually demanding liberal education, a respect for moral and civil law, an obligation for public service, a concern for the common good, a respect for the principles and procedures that make self-government in a free society possible, a view of people as unique individuals rather than as representative members of variously defined groups, and a regard for all human beings as sharing a common humanity and capable of engaging together in rational discourse.

Unfortunately, in recent years some educators have suggested that students should not be taught that any particular values are better than any others. For example, in a review entitled *"Education*

for Democracy Does Not Advance the Debate'' in *Social Education*, a
professional journal for social studies educators, William Fernekes
(1987), a social studies teacher, criticizes *Education for Democracy*, a
pamphlet published by the American Federation of Teachers in 1987,
for suggesting that democratic forms of government are superior to
nondemocratic governments. The effect of such a relativistic stance is
to eliminate the philosophical basis for a republican form of government. A republican form of government is based on the belief that
adults are capable of making rational and moral choices, and that
human beings grow morally by having to make choices about the
common good. As J. G. A. Pocock (1971) notes in an essay on civic
humanism, citizenship acquires a moral definition only when it concerns the determination of the common good. To claim that all values
are relative is to deny the intrinsic value of moral growth and the
political means for achieving it—a form of government that allows
people to make choices they perceive as meaningful.

Unless students are taught that there is greater value in making
choices about the common good than in accepting decisions about
the common good made by public officials who govern without the
consent of the governed or who, even if ostensibly elected, have not
had to explain and defend their own policies and criticize alternative
policies, they are unlikely to value participation in public life. They
clearly will be incapable of understanding the momentous events that
have taken place recently in Eastern Europe and China. And unless
they are taught that there is greater value in defining themselves
primarily as unique, autonomous members of their civic communities
rather than as stereotypical members of permanently defined subgroups, they will be incapable of determining the common good and
inhibited in their moral growth. For they will believe that they should
not or cannot engage in independent critical thinking.

The Benefits of a Civic Identity

Because it is an identity that is distinct from, and superordinate
to, an identity based on accidents of birth with respect to gender,
ethnicity, religion, race, or social status, a civic identity serves several
significant functions. It protects individuals from intimidation and
coercion by self-appointed spokespersons who claim to represent
them as members of groups to which they may not necessarily choose
to belong (insofar as they have not voluntarily chosen to be dues-
paying members of these groups). A civic identity safeguards the
right of individuals to choose those groups to which they wish to

belong and to criticize those groups with which they disagree, even if they appear to belong to the groups. Indeed, there is probably no more important bulwark than a civic identity for safeguarding the right to self-identification and the right to dissent from the views of associations based on social status, gender, religion, ethnicity, race, or language—associations or communities that have as long a history of intolerance and narrow-mindedness as many civic communities have had.

A civic identity also counteracts the diminution or denigration of individual worth that results from the implicit or explicit classification of individuals in groups defined by involuntary traits. The stereotyping that commonly accompanies such classifications does much more than deny individual uniqueness. It tends to imply that the activities or thinking of individuals can be understood only as a reflection of the social contexts and accidents of their birth rather than of their individual uniqueness; in short, it denies self-definition and self-responsibility.

Finally, because a civic identity supersedes all other chosen or ascribed identities, it provides a neutral higher ground amidst the frequently conflicting loyalties that arise from the overlapping characteristics of ethnicity, race, gender, religion, and social status. Thus, paradoxically, a civic identity safeguards intellectual diversity and personal freedom at the same time that it motivates a sense of responsibility for the common good.

Threats to a Sense of Individual Responsibility for the Common Good

Acts of civic virtue—voluntary acts of service to one's civic community—take place within a moral framework of what one owes one's community as an autonomous individual with self-imposed obligations. As Pocock (1971) states in his exploration of civic republican thinking: "The only truly virtuous and indeed human being . . . was defined in terms of his independence of the government in which he participated" (p. 93). Thus, the greatest threat to the working out of the common good that moral and political philosophers could conceive was not "individualism" but, as Pocock notes, the corruption of intellectual and moral autonomy.

The special interests that have historically corrupted a citizen's autonomy have been economic, religious, linguistic, or ethnic in nature. Special economic interests constantly pose a threat to the working out of the common good, but some of the other special interests in this country today loom as a greater force for corrupting intellectual and moral autonomy than they ever have before. Despite the good intentions that may have motivated it, the increasing official (and more frequently unofficial) categorization of members of our civic communities into a variety of differing ethnic, racial, or gender groups for a variety of public purposes would appear to negate the concepts of individual uniqueness, self-responsibility, and independent moral thinking that form the ethical basis for a republican form of government. Adults or their children have been classified in varying categories for the federal census, for municipal employment, for public school assignment, and even for competency testing or an annual street listing. For example, adults living in Boston in the past 10 years had to identify themselves for the federal census in 1980 as white, black or Negro, Japanese, Chinese, Korean, Philippino, Vietnamese, American Indian, Asian Indian, Hawaiian, Guamanian, Samoan, Eskimo, Aleut, or other. For municipal employment in Massachusetts, they had to identify themselves as white, black, Hispanic, Asian, Pacific Islander, Native American, Alaskan, or Cape Verdean. They had to identify themselves on their local residence form in 1987 as white, black, Asian, Pacific Islander, American Indian, of Hispanic/Latino origin or descent, or other. For public school assignment, their children were labeled white, black, Native American, Oriental, or Hispanic. For the Massachusetts Basic Skills Test in 1986, their children had to identify themselves as white, black, Hispanic, or unknown.

When students and their parents are officially given permanent primary identifications with subgroups that extend across civic boundaries, they are unlikely to acquire a sense of individual membership in their civic communities, and, thus, a sense of responsibility for the common good. Worse yet, racial, ethnic, and gender classifications may inhibit the very development of those qualities of individual initiative and self-responsibility that will enable these students and their parents to improve their lives by their own efforts and to feel self-respect. Shelby Steele, in his book *The Content of Our Character: A New Vision of Race in America* (1990a), comments movingly on the adverse psychological effects of the form of black identity that has accompanied official and unofficial preferential racial policies in the past two decades. In a short essay highlighting some of the book's major points, he suggests that this "adversarial," "victim-focused identity" is a repressive identity for black Americans that "generates a victimized self-image, curbs individualism and initiative, diminishes our sense of possibility, and contributes to our demoralization and inertia'' (1990b, p. 2). He notes that by ''simply living as an individual in America—with my racial identity struggle suspended temporarily—I discovered that American society offered me, and blacks in general, a remarkable range of opportunity if we were willing to pursue it,'' despite ''racial insensitivity and some racial discrimination'' (p. 1). A separation of race/ethnicity and state is as urgently needed today as the separation of church and state was needed several hundred years ago.[6]

It is ironic that perhaps the greatest challenge that teachers in all subjects and schools face today in revitalizing a civic ethic is how to help their students acquire a civic identity that is at least as strong as their ethnic, racial, gender, or religious identity in the face of official government policies and practices that seem to undermine the very basis for republican self-government and that might well be viewed as unethical, even if legal. But, then, there are ample precedents in this country's history for coping with unethical but legal policies in order to realize the ideals of republican self-government.

CONCLUSION

As the Framers of the Constitution knew, a republican form of government depends on more than the pursuit of self-interest or group interest for determining the common good. It also requires a morally responsible citizenry. Although the moral character of a citizenry may first be developed by the family and religious institutions, it must also be shaped by public institutions. In classical democratic theory, the moral development of a citizenry takes place publicly through participation in the activities of self-government. An often quoted passage in John Stuart Mill's *Considerations on Representative Government* (1861/1966) perhaps best articulates the educative value of participation in public life.

> It is not sufficiently considered how little there is in most men's ordinary life to give any largeness either to their conceptions or to their sentiments. . . . Giving him something to do for the public, supplies, in a measure, all these deficiencies. If circumstances allow the amount of public duty assigned to him to be considerable, it makes him an educated man. . . . He is called upon, while so engaged, to weigh interests not his own; to be guided, in case of conflicting claims, by another rule than his private partialities; to apply, at every turn, principles and maxims which have for their reason of existence the common good; and he usually finds associated with him in the same work minds more

familiarized than his own with these ideas and operations, whose study
it will be to supply reasons to his understanding, and stimulation to his
feeling for the general interest. (pp. 196–198)

The moral development of a people also takes place in its
schools. The philosophy that education should serve civic ends supported Thomas Jefferson's vision of universal public education, with
free instruction in the elementary school. Jefferson recommended the
teaching not only of reading and writing but also of history and
geography, for both informational and civic purposes; citizens of the
first nation created in history needed to know who they were as a
people and why their country existed. Most Americans no longer live
in the small, homogeneous rural communities that Jefferson saw as
the basis for a republican form of government. Nevertheless, the civic
mission of the schools has not changed since Jefferson's time; for
students to value the participatory culture that defines and unites us
as a people, they still need to learn how and why we came into
being as a people and why American citizenship is worthwhile. A
republican form of government can be preserved as long as all citizens see each other first and foremost as unique members of their
civic communities.

The forces that are contributing to the weakening of a civic ethic
in this country are multiple, complex, and deeply intertwined with
each other in subtle ways. Indeed, because these forces seem to be so
strong and pervasive, the growth of a self-obsessed individualism
may more likely be the result than the cause of the decline in a sense
of obligation to participate in public life, to give public service, and to
consider the common good. A revitalized civic education not only
may serve to inhibit the growth of a self-centered individualism and
the elevation of private identities over a civic one, but may also reme-
diate some of the psychological damage many students have suffered
in recent years as a result of being encouraged to see themselves as
disenfranchised or oppressed victims of their society. Rather than
teaching them critical thinking and empowering them as citizens,
such approaches are more likely to have alienated them from the
political process and undermined their will to shape their futures in
morally acceptable ways.

At the same time, we would gain little if we sought to strengthen
a civic ethic by devaluing, as several prominent scholars have done
in recent years, the liberal political tradition, the rights-based ethic,
and the concept of self-responsibility that lies at the root of true individualism. A civic education that stresses individual responsibility

for one's own behavior as well as for one's civic communities is fundamental to intellectual and moral maturity. As John Gibbs and Steven Schnell (1985) comment in a critique of moral developmental and socialization theories, a theory of socialization that emphasizes feelings and a sense of membership in a social community is not incompatible with a theory of moral development that emphasizes independent thinking and the individual; the theories are complementary and interdependent. Indeed, the full development of the individual self and the civic self results precisely from their interdependence.

Today's students need to understand why, in Mary Follett's words, we "can never be citizens of the world until we learn how to be citizens of America or England or France" (1918, p. 348). But they also need to understand that community interdependence and a commitment to a specific form of government do not preclude individual autonomy and critical inquiry, and that civic pride can co-exist with an unblinded eye toward social inequities and injustice. In his conclusion to *The Spirit of Modern Republicanism*, a reinterpretation of the moral vision of the Framers of the Constitution, Thomas Pangle (1988) suggests how teachers might frame the intellectual approach to this daunting task.

> The questioning of what America stands for is not un-American; it is, paradoxically, part of the very core of what it means to be a patriotic American. To a degree rarely seen in history we are asked to love our country while at the same time purifying or rarifying our ardor by cultivating an awareness that our country may not be the best, certainly not the best conceivable, political order. This it seems to me can and ought to be a source of reasonable pride. For we may rightly assert that what distinguishes American patriotism, in the sense of setting it apart from and above most previous forms of patriotism, is the sternness of its challenge to the *minds* of citizens old and young. American life does not impose moral tests as harsh as those imposed by earlier, and in many ways nobler, republics; it does not require as frequent or as regular sacrifices of life, property, private liberty, and ease; but it calls each and all of us to an intellectual probity, to an education in the great texts of political philosophy, to a quest for self-knowledge as a people, that is perhaps unprecedented. (p. 279)

Over the past 200 years, the emphasis in our public schools on the development of civic character has helped various immigrant groups, including the first settlers, to overcome the religious, racial, economic, and ethnic animosities that they often brought with them from the "old country" and that still exist today in the "old country" (whether in Europe, Asia, or South America). The centrality of our civic identities in public life has helped us become a model for other countries struggling with religious, racial, and/or ethnic strife, despite the remnants of these older animosities that we still need to deal with, and despite newer animosities not unexpectedly arising between recent and older religious, ethnic, and racial groups, such as the continuing conflict between black Americans and Korean–Americans in the New York City area. As our schools continue to absorb the children of immigrants with little or no understanding of the democratic process or the civic republican tradition, English language arts teachers can make a significant contribution to the preservation of a republican form of government through readings, discussions, and activities in literature, composition, and speech programs that develop both students' civic characters—their sense of membership in their local, state, and national communities—*and* their capacity for independent moral thinking. For the goal of a civic education in this country is, simultaneously, the transcendence (not negation) of individual and group identity and the celebration of intellectual and moral autonomy.

NOTES

1. The early Puritan communities are usually portrayed as having attempted to make decisions by consensus (sometimes coerced), the implication being that the vote of a numerical majority was not used for decision-making in these early communities. To judge by the bylaws adopted in 1649 by the Puritan town of Springfield, Massachusetts, however, it is likely that the use of majority rule on matters of public policy was a common practice in early New England town meetings. The Springfield Bylaws spell out that "for the better carrying on of town meetings . . . though there be but nine of the inhabitants assembled. . . . what the major part of the assembly there met shall agree upon, it shall be taken as the act of the whole town and binding to all" (Morris, 1876, pp. 58–63, cited in Vaughan, 1972, p. 196).

2. Jenks (1898) noted that England, unlike most European countries, left to local control such basic services as police, roadmaking, sanitation, and education. Moreover, local communities even in the Middle Ages controlled the fiscal needs of the crown by their control of taxation through the members of parliament whom they themselves chose (Maddicott, 1981).

3. The influence of this interpretation of the expansion of public education in America can be seen in many of the objectives in the 1984 guide for

high school social studies in the Boston Public Schools. One priority objective is "identifying school reform [in the nineteenth century] as an attempt of the middle class to recreate their [sic] values of family, work and citizenship for everyone" (Boston Public Schools, 1984, p. 140). The suggested teaching activity is: "Read from the reports of Horace Mann and the letters and diaries of students and/or teachers, and compare their goals, experiences, and values with your own" (p. 140).

4. In contrast, Richard B. Morris' latest text on the Constitutional period (1987) amply discusses the absence of women at the Constitutional Convention and the failure of the Framers to enfranchise them, but in a concluding section of a chapter entitled "A Cautiously Transforming Egalitarianism."

5. For example, the Quakers were "White Protestants" but did not oppress the "Native Americans" they encountered; property qualifications prevented many "White Protestants" from voting at the time of the founding and were not designed as a "strategy" to exclude cultural minorities; and many European and Middle Eastern groups, such as the Irish, Italians, Jews, and Armenians, were systematically discriminated against for many years.

6. In the Fall 1991 issue of *Issues & Views*, editor Elizabeth Wright noted that a forthcoming article in the Winter issue would examine a growing movement of blacks and Asians in Great Britain who are trying to "prevent a duplication of U.S. affirmative action policies." According to Wright, they are "lobbying Parliament to abolish all preferential race legislation in England, and to pass a bill that will make it illegal to ever institute government-mandated laws biased in favor of particular groups" (Wright, 1990, p. 3).

REFERENCES

Almond, G., & Verba, S. (1963). *The civic culture: Political attitudes and democracy in five nations*. Princeton, NJ: Princeton University Press.

Bellah, R., Madsen, R., Sullivan, W. M., Swidler, A., & Tipton, S. M. (1985). *Habits of the heart: Individualism and commitment in American life*. Berkeley: University of California Press.

Berg, R., et al. (1979). *Social studies, grade 5*. Glencoe: IL: Scott Foresman.

Blodgett, G. (1981). Landscape design as conservative reform. In B. Kelly, G. T. Guillet, & M. E. W. Hern (Eds.), *Art of the Olmsted Landscape*. New York: New York City Landmarks Preservation Commission, 111–123.

Board of Trustees, Public Library of Brookline. Proceedings of April 11, 1857.

Boorstin, D. (1975). *Democracy and its discontents: Reflections on everyday America*. New York: Vintage Books.

Boorstin, R. (1987, July 13). Rural New York: A time of ferment. *New York Times* (national ed.), pp. 14, 81.

Boston Public Schools. (1984). *High school social studies curriculum objectives*. Boston: Boston School Committee.

Butts, R. F. (1988). The moral imperative for American schools: ". . . Inflame the civic temper . . .". *American Journal of Education, 69*, 162–194.

Cavallo, D. (1981). *Muscles and morals: Organized playgrounds and urban reform, 1880-1920*. Philadelphia: University of Pennsylvania Press.

Diamond, M. (1986). Ethics and politics: The American way. In R. Horwitz (Ed.), *The moral foundations of the American republic* (3rd ed.). Charlottesville: University Press of Virginia, 75-108.

Ditzion, S. (1971). Democratic strivings. In M. H. Harris (Ed.), *Reader in American library history* (pp. 135-137). Washington, DC: NCR Microcard Editions. (Original work published 1947)

Dixon, J. (1967). *Growth through English*. London, England: Cox & Wyman.

Donohue, W. (1989). *The new freedom: Individualism and collectivism in the social lives of Americans*. New Brunswick, NJ: Transaction Publishers.

Dubin, J., Graetz, M., & Wilde, L. (1987). Are we a nation of tax cheaters? New econometric evidence on tax compliance. *American Economic Review, 77*, 240-246.

Erikson, E. (1980). *Identity and the life cycle*. New York: Norton.

Fein, A. (1972). *Frederick Law Olmsted and the American environmental tradition*. New York: George Braziller.

Fein, A. (1981). The Olmsted renaissance: A search for national purpose. In B. Kelly, G. T. Guillet, & M. E. W. Hern (Eds.), *Art of the Olmsted Landscape*. New York: New York City Landmarks Preservation Commission, 99-109.

Fernekes, W. (1987). *Education for democracy* does not advance the debate. *Social Education, 51*, 396-406.

Field, A. (1976). Educational expansion in mid-nineteenth century Massachusetts: Human-capital formation or structural reinforcement? *Harvard Educational Review, 46*, 521-552.

Follett, M. P. (1918). *The new state: Group organization the solution of popular government*. New York: Longmans, Green.

Gibbs, J., & Schnell, S. (1985). Moral development "versus" socialization. *American Psychologist, 40*, 1071-1080.

Gruson, L. (1987, April 19). Ranks of firefighters grow thinner. *New York Times*, Section 1, pp. 14, 20.

Harris, M., & Spiegler, G. (1974). Everett, Ticknor, and the common man; The fear of societal instability as the motivation for the founding of the Boston Public Library. *Libri, 24*, 249-275.

Harwell, R., & Michener, R. (1974). As public as the town pump. *Library Journal, 99*, 959-963.

Himmelfarb, D. (1988). Freedom, virtue, and the Founding Fathers. *Public Interest, 90*, 115-120.

History Committee of the Brookline Education Society. (1897). Selections from *A guide to the local history of Brookline, Massachusetts* in *Town of Brookline: 1632-1976, Bicentennial Commemorative map and guide to local history*. Brookline, MA: Town of Brookline.

Honeywell, R. (1931). *The educational work of Thomas Jefferson*. Cambridge, MA: Harvard University Press.

Iiams, C. (1980). *Civic attitudes reflected in selected basal readers for grades one through six used in the United States from 1900–1970.* Unpublished dissertation, University of Idaho, Caldwell.

Janowitz, M. (1983). *The reconstruction of patriotism: Education for civic consciousness.* Chicago: University of Chicago Press.

Jenks, E. (1898). *Law and politics in the Middle Ages.* New York: Henry Holt.

Kemp, R., Reckers, P., & Arrington, C. E. (1986). U.S. tax reform: Tax evasion concerns. *Business Economics, 21,* 55–58.

Lijphart, A. (1984). *Democracies: Patterns of majoritarian and consensus government in twenty-one countries.* New Haven: Yale University Press.

Lilla, M. (1985). What is the civic interest? *Public Interest, 81,* 64–81.

MacLeod, A. (1976). Education for freedom: Children's fiction in Jacksonian America. *Harvard Educational Review, 46,* 425–435.

Maddicott, J. R. (1981). Parliament and the constituencies, 1272–1377. In R. G. Davies & J. H. Denton (Eds.), *The English Parliament in the Middle Ages.* Manchester, England: Manchester University Press, 61–87.

McClenaghan, W. (1985). *Magruder's American Government.* Newton, MA: Allyn & Bacon.

Mead, L. (1986). *Beyond entitlement: The social obligations of citizenship.* New York: Free Press.

Mill, J. S. (1966). *Considerations on representative government* (World's Classic ed.). London: Oxford University Press. (Original work published 1861)

Morris, H. (1876). *Early History of Springfield.* Springfield, MA.

Morris, R. B. (1987). *The forging of the Union: 1781–1789.* New York: Harper & Row.

Mullis, I. (1978). *Citizenship/social studies achievement trends over time, National Assessment of Educational Progress.* Paper presented at the Annual Meeting of the American Educational Research Association, Toronto.

Mullis, I. (1983). *Citizenship and social studies achievement of young Americans: 1981–82 Performance and changes between 1976 and 1982* (No. 13–CS–01). Denver, CO: National Assessment of Educational Progress. (Reprinted December 1984)

Pangle, T. (1988). *The spirit of modern republicanism.* Chicago: University of Chicago Press.

Perkins, K. (1987). Volunteer fire departments: Community integration, autonomy, and survival. *Human Organization, 46,* 342–348.

Perkins, K. (1989). Volunteer firefighters in the United States: A descriptive study. *Nonprofit and Voluntary Sector Quarterly, 18,* 269–279.

Perkins, K., & Wright, T. (1989, February). *Characteristics and survival potential of volunteer nonprofit EMS corporations: A Virginia sample* (Professional Paper No. 13). Blacksburg: Virginia Tech, Center for Volunteer Development.

Pocock, J. G. A. (1971). Civic humanism and its role in Anglo-American thought. In *Politics, language and time: Essays on political thought and history.* New York: Atheneum, 80–103.

Ravitch, D. (1987). Tot sociology, or what happened to history in the grade schools. *The American Scholar, 56,* 343–354.

Sandel, M. (Ed.). (1984). *Liberalism and its critics*. New York: New York University Press.

Sewall, G. T. (1988). American history textbooks: Where do we go from here? *Phi Delta Kappan, 70*, 553–558.

Shaver, J. (1986). Reflections on citizenship education and traditional social studies programs. *Georgia Social Science Journal, 17*, 1–15.

Steele, S. (1990a). *The content of our character: A new vision of race in America*. New York: St. Martin's Press.

Steele, S. (1990b). Letting go of our victim image: It's time for blacks to shift from a wartime to a peacetime identity. *Issues & Views, 6*, 1.

Stewart, I. (1981). Fight for Central Park. In B. Kelly, G. T. Guillet, & M. E. W. Hern (Eds.), *Art of the Olmsted landscape* (pp. 85–97). New York: New York City Landmarks Preservation Commission.

Sullivan, W. (1982). *Reconstructing public philosophy*. Berkeley: University of California Press.

de Tocqueville, A. (1969). *Democracy in America* (J. P. Mayer, Ed.; G. Lawrence, Trans.). New York: Doubleday. (Original work published 1835–40)

Vaughan, A. (Ed.). (1972). *The Puritan Tradition in America: 1620–1730*. Columbia: University of South Carolina Press.

Vetterli, R., & Bryner, G. (1987). *In search of the republic: Public virtue and the roots of American government*. Totawa, NJ: Rowman and Littlefield.

Wiggenton, E. (1985). *Sometimes a shining moment: The Foxfire experience*. New York: Anchor Press Doubleday.

Wood, G. S. (1969). *The creation of the American republic: 1776–1787*. Chapel Hill: University of North Carolina Press.

Wright, E. (1990). Speaking out on affirmative action in Great Britain. *Issues & Views, 6*(4), 3.

Part I

READING
and the Development
of a Civic Ethic

2 Reading and Civic Literacy

Are We Literate Enough to Meet Our Civic Responsibilities?

JEANNE S. CHALL
DOROTHY HENRY

The central concern of this chapter is whether the literacy levels of high school students and young adults allow them to take full advantage of their civic rights and meet their civic responsibilities. To address this concern, we examine three questions: How literate are American high school students and young adults today? What level of literacy is needed for full civic participation? Do the literacy levels of our high school students and young adults match the literacy requirements for full participation in public life? These questions will be examined from the viewpoint of educational research and practice in the field of reading.

When one makes judgments about whether a level of literacy is or is not sufficient for certain ends, two factors must be considered—the reading ability of those who are expected to use written materials and the difficulty of the materials. Reading ability implies knowledge, language, and cognitive abilities, as well as reading skills. Difficulty of materials is based also on language, knowledge, and the complexity of thinking required. Both factors can be placed on a continuum. For example, the materials can be rated from easy to hard; the reading ability of individuals, from low to high. Essentially, then, the question about whether the level of literacy of young adult Americans is sufficient for their civic responsibilities is a question of fit—whether those Americans who "need" to read certain materials to meet their civic responsibilities and to take advantage of their rights are able to read and understand them.

In this chapter we first present information from the most recent nationwide assessments on the reading abilities of American high school students and young adults, and discuss what these abilities mean in cognitive and linguistic terms. Next, we examine several selected civic texts and public documents in terms of the level and nature of the reading ability needed to comprehend them. Finally, we make some recommendations concerning what can be done to lessen the gap between the level of literacy of many young Americans and the difficulty level of the material they need to read for civic purposes.

READING ABILITY AND ITS PRACTICAL SIGNIFICANCE

Reading Abilities of High School Students and Young Adults

The National Assessment of Educational Progress (NAEP) is often referred to as the nation's report card. It is a congressionally mandated project that collects data over time and reports on the academic achievement of young Americans. Assessments are conducted approximately every four years on the performance of students in grades 4, 8, and 12 (9- , 13- , and 17-year-olds) attending public and private schools. The assessment in reading is based on sampling students' ability to read various types of printed matter over a wide range of difficulty—textbooks, poems, newspaper articles, and such commonly encountered public documents as telephone bills and public transportation schedules. Students are required to respond on several levels of understanding, from simple identification of the information that is stated in the material to interpretation of such information in writing.

Mullis and Jenkins (1990) recently summarized the national trends in reading achievement for 9- , 13- , and 17-year-olds based on data from the five NAEP studies conducted from 1971 to 1988. Their data are reported on a scale of five levels, anchored to numerical ratings from 0 to 500. The scales make it possible to compare results across age groups and among student populations. Levels of reading difficulty are ranked as Rudimentary (150), Basic (200), Intermediate (250), Adept (300) and Advanced (350+). Figure 2.1 contains the five levels with brief descriptions (Mullis & Jenkins, 1990, p. 23).

The studies showed that although an increasing percentage of students had achieved Basic and Intermediate reading skills over the years, only 10 percent of 13-year-olds and 42 percent of 17-year-olds could perform at the Adept level—a level that is roughly equivalent to the ability to read high school texts. Only 5 percent of the 17-year-olds attained proficiency on an Advanced level—a level equivalent to college reading. Black and Hispanic students show substantial gains since 1971, but their 1988 performance still lags behind that of white

Figure 2.1   A Description of the Levels of Reading Proficiency Used in the National Assessment of Educational Progress

Rudimentary (150)

Readers who have acquired rudimentary reading skills and strategies can follow brief written directions. They can also select words, phrases, or sentences to describe a simple picture and can interpret simple written clues to identify a common object. *Performance at this level suggests the ability to carry out simple, discrete reading tasks.*

Basic (200)

Readers who have learned basic comprehension skills and strategies can locate and identify facts from simple informational paragraphs, stories, and news articles. In addition, they can combine ideas and make inferences based on short, uncomplicated passages. *Performance at this level suggests the ability to understand specific or sequentially related information.*

Intermediate (250)

Readers with the ability to use intermediate skills and strategies can search for, locate, and organize the information they find in relatively lengthy passages and can recognize paraphrases of what they have read. They can also make inferences and reach generalizations about main ideas and author's purpose from passages dealing with literature, science, and social studies. *Performance at this level suggests the ability to search for specific information, interrelate ideas, and make generalizations.*

Adept (300)

Readers with adept reading comprehension skills and strategies can understand complicated literary and informational passages, including material about topics they study at school. They can also analyze and integrate less familiar material and provide reactions to and explanations of the text as a whole. *Performance at this level suggests the ability to find, understand, summarize, and explain relatively complicated information.*

Advanced (350)

Readers who use advanced reading skills and strategies can extend and restructure the ideas presented in specialized and complex texts. Examples include scientific materials, literary essays, historical documents, and materials similar to those found in professional and technical working environments. They are also able to understand the links between ideas even when those links are not explicitly stated and to make appropriate generalizations even when the texts lack clear introductions or explanations. *Performance at this level suggests the ability to synthesize and learn from specialized reading materials.*

Source: Ina Mullis & Lynn Jenkins, *The Reading Report Card, 1971–88.* The National Assessment of Educational Progress. Washington, DC: Office of Educational Research and Improvement, U.S. Department of Education, 1990, p. 23.

students (it is unclear whether the data for other racial/ethnic groups were included in the latter category). At age 17, only 26 percent of black students and 24 percent of Hispanic students showed reading proficiency at or above the Adept level. The report concluded: "Whether they are in or out of school, 17-year-olds who have not developed Adept reading skills and strategies would appear to be at risk as they become adults in a society that depends so heavily on the ability to extract meaning from varied forms of written language" (Mullis & Jenkins, 1990, p. 35).

To broaden the picture of the status of national literacy and help clarify whether illiteracy is a major problem in the United States, a survey of young adults was conducted. In 1985, NAEP surveyed the literacy skills of young adults aged 21 to 25 (Kirsch & Jungeblut, 1986). Roughly one-fourth of the adults reported being enrolled in school and almost half (45%) held postsecondary degrees.

A goal of the study was to be able to compare the performance of young adults with that of in-school, 17-year-olds, so sample exercises from the reading scale administered to the school group were included in the assessment. Performance was linked statistically to the NAEP reading scale, permitting comparison with the performance of the in-school population. The skills for three types of literacy tasks were examined: prose literacy tasks, such as those one would typically encounter in reading newspaper articles, magazines, and books; document literacy tasks, which required the identification and use of information in forms, tables, schedules, and so on; and quantitative literacy tasks, which required a combination of reading and numerical operations on materials such as menus and sales advertisements.

The levels of difficulty for the prose tasks ranged from locating information in the text (easy), to interpreting information and making generalizations (difficult). Document literacy tasks were assessed as easy if there were few categories or features in the document that had to be located. The level of difficulty increased to moderate if there were several distracting features in the document. If the information asked for in the document was obscure, the document was considered most difficult—challenging and complex. Examples of document tasks representing the range from easy to difficult, for example, were locating the expiration date on a driver's license; filling out a job application; determining employee benefits from a table; and reading a bus schedule (Kirsch & Jungeblut, 1986, p. 28).

The report on young adults aged 21 to 25 showed that most could read at some level, but it was a very low level, equivalent to the Rudimentary and Basic levels in the NAEP study (Kirsch &

Jungeblut, 1986). Few could read at moderately difficult or complex levels, which would be roughly equivalent to the Advanced Level in the NAEP study. "Only a relatively small percentage of this group is estimated to perform at levels typified by the more complex and challenging tasks" (p. 4).

The reading abilities of blacks and Hispanics were significantly lower than those of whites, and the gap became greater with increasing complexity of the reading tasks. Thus, the report noted that at a level considered by most to correspond to the reading difficulty of high school materials, "fewer than four in 10 adults are estimated to attain this level—about 4 in 10 white, 1 in 10 black, and 2 in 10 Hispanic young adults" (Kirsch & Jungeblut, pp. 15–18). Since the report did not include data on the reading performance of dropouts, the results reported may well have been underestimates.

The Development of Reading Ability

What does it mean in cognitive and linguistic terms to be able to read at these different levels of difficulty? To understand this, let us examine one theory of how reading ability develops. Chall (1983) proposes six stages of reading development and discusses what it means to read at lower and higher levels and what is required to advance on the continuum of reading ability. Figures 2.2 and 2.3 illustrate the characteristic changes required as the learner develops from prereading to highly advanced, skilled reading.

Figure 2.2 contains brief excerpts from books that range in difficulty from approximately a first-grade to a college level, which helps give a quick picture of the increasing difficulty as one progresses from beginning reading to advanced reading. If one reads down, one can see that, as the selections become increasingly more difficult, they contain more words and concepts that are specialized, technical, and abstract, and that the sentences become longer and more complex. For example, the selections in Stages 1 and 2 are concrete and contain words that are most common in the English language. The meanings would be known by most children in the first and second grades and the sentences are short. Beginning with Stage 3, the words become less familiar and the sentences become longer and more complex. Further, the content becomes less concrete and more removed in time, place, and ideas.

Figure 2.3 gives a brief overview of the linguistic, cognitive, and reading demands of each stage. It indicates that as one proceeds from lower to higher reading levels, one moves from being able to identify

Figure 2.2 Reading Samples Showing Increasing Range of Difficulty

Stage 1	"May I go?" said Fay. "May I please go with you?"
Stage 2	Spring was coming to Tait Primary School. On the new highway big trucks went by the school all day.
Stage 3A	She smoothed her hair behind her ear as she lowered her hand. I could see she was eyeing *beauty* and trying to figure out a way to write about being beautiful without sounding even more conceited than she already was.
Stage 3B	Early in the history of the world, men found that they could not communicate well by using only sign language. In some way that cannot be traced with any certainty, they devised spoken language.
Stage 4	No matter what phenomena he is interested in, the scientist . employs two main tools—theory and empirical research. Theory employs reason, language, and logic to suggest possible, or predict probable, relationships among various data gathered from the concrete world of experience.
Stage 5	One of the objections to the hypothesis that a satisfying after-effect of a mental connection works back upon it to strengthen it is that nobody has shown how this action does or could occur. It is the purpose of this article to show how a mechanism which is as possible psychologically as any of the mechanisms proposed to recount for facilitation, inhibition, fatigue, strengthening by repetition, or other forms of modification could enable such an after-effect to cause such a strengthening.

Source: Jeanne S. Chall, *Stages of Reading Development.* New York: McGraw-Hill, 1983, p. 39.

and "sound out" words whose meanings are generally familiar, to knowing the meanings of less common, technical words and to understanding texts of increasing difficulty at more complex cognitive levels.

Chall's six-stage progression of reading difficulty can be reduced to three broad levels of development—learning to read, reading to learn, and advanced literacy. The first level—learning to read—involves the ability to read simple signs, labels, instructions, and very easy books. This level usually does not entail the learning of new information or ideas from printed materials. One generally finds children in grades 1 to 3 at this level. Adults who read at this level are considered to be reading below a functional literacy level.

The next broad level of literacy is reached by most children in grades 4 to 8. Among adults, this level is often called functional literacy and refers to the ability to read simple application forms, signs and labels, easy instructional materials, the local news of a daily newspaper, and the simpler articles in a magazine such as *The Reader's Digest*, which is generally estimated to be at an eighth-grade reading level. For children, it means the ability to read chapter books and textbooks in science and social studies, and to learn from them. The major task for adults and children at this level is to learn to use their reading skills as a tool for acquiring knowledge, information, and other skills.

The third broad level, advanced literacy, is required for the reading of most high school textbooks, news magazines such as *Time*, and *The New York Times*, generally estimated to be at an average reading level of twelfth grade. It requires advanced linguistic abilities; an extensive vocabulary, including abstract, technical, and specialized terminologies; advanced cognitive development for critical reading; and a broad background of knowledge.

To move from one of these broad literacy levels to the next higher one takes considerable development and change in the individual's language, knowledge and experience, cognition, and reading skills. Perhaps the greatest transition is from level 1 to 2, which usually comes at about a fourth-grade reading level. A pre-grade 4 reading level can be said to represent the "oral tradition," in the sense that text rarely goes beyond the language and knowledge that the reader already has acquired from listening, direct experience, or watching television. Reading beyond fourth-grade level can be viewed as comprising the literary tradition—when reading matter goes beyond what is already known. Thus, grade 4 reading level can be seen as the beginning of a long progression in the reading of texts that are increasingly more complicated, literary, abstract, and technical, and that require more knowledge and more sophisticated language and cognitive abilities if readers are to be able to engage in the interpretations and critical reactions expected for such materials.

Stages of Reading and the NAEP Results

The NAEP study found that 86 percent of 17-year-olds were able to read on an Intermediate level—which corresponds roughly to Chall's Stage 3 (see Figure 2.3). This stage indicates the ability to read and understand materials on a fourth- to eighth-grade level, the most difficult of which are represented by articles in *The Reader's*

Figure 2.3 Stages of Reading Development: An Outline of the Major Qualitative Characteristics and How They Are Acquired

1 STAGE DESIGNATION	2 GRADE RANGE (AGE)	3 MAJOR QUALITATIVE CHARACTERISTICS AND MASTERIES BY END OF STAGE	4 HOW ACQUIRED	5 RELATIONSHIP OF READING TO LISTENING
Stage 0: Prereading, "pseudo-reading"	Preschool Ages 6 months–6 years	Child "pretends" to read, retells story when looking at pages of book previously read to him/her; names letters of alphabet; recognizes some signs; prints own name; plays with books, pencils, and paper.	Being read to by an adult (or older child) who responds to and warmly appreciates the child's interest in books and reading; being provided with books, paper, pencils, blocks, and letters.	Most can understand the children's picture books and stories read to them. They understand thousands of words they hear by age 6 but can read few if any of them.
Stage 1: Initial reading and decoding	Grade 1 & beginning Grade 2 (ages 6 & 7)	Child learns relation between letters and sounds and between printed and spoken words; child is able to read simple text containing high frequency words and phonically regular words; uses skill and insight to "sound out" new one-syllable words.	Direct instruction in letter-sound relations (phonics) and practice in their use. Reading of simple stories using words with phonic elements taught and words of high frequency. Being read to on a level above what child can read independently to develop more advanced language patterns, knowledge of new words, and ideas.	The level of difficulty of language read by the child is much below the language understood when heard. At the end of Stage 1, most children can understand up to 4000 or more words when heard but can read only about 600.
Stage 2: Confirmation and fluency	Grades 2 & 3 (ages 7 & 8)	Child reads simple, familiar stories and selections with increasing fluency. This is done by consolidating the basic decoding elements, sight vocabulary, and meaning context in the reading of familiar stories and selections.	Direct instruction in advanced decoding skills; wide reading (with instruction and independently) of familiar, interesting materials which help promote fluent reading. Being read to at levels above their own independent reading level to develop language, vocabulary, and concepts.	At the end of Stage 2, about 3000 words can be read and understood and about 9000 are known when heard. Listening is still more effective than reading.

Stage	Grade (age)	Reading is used to... / Materials	Relationship of listening and reading
Stage 3: Reading for learning the new	Grades 4–8 (ages 9–13)	Reading is used to learn new ideas, to gain new knowledge, to experience new feelings, to learn new attitudes; generally from one viewpoint.	At beginning of Stage 3, listening comprehension of the same material is still more effective than reading comprehension. By the end of Stage 3, reading and listening are about equal; for those who read very well, reading may be more efficient.
Phase A	Intermediate, 4–6	Reading and study of textbooks, reference works, trade books, newspapers, and magazines that contain new ideas and values, unfamiliar vocabulary and syntax; systematic study of words and reacting to the text through discussion, answering questions, writing, etc. Reading of increasingly more complex fiction, biography, nonfiction, and the like.	
Phase B	Junior high school, 7–9		
Stage 4: Multiple viewpoints	High school, grades 10–12 (ages 15–17)	Reading widely from a broad range of complex materials, both expository and narrative, with a variety of viewpoints. Wide reading and study of the physical, biological, and social sciences and the humanities; high quality and popular literature; newspapers and magazines; systematic study of words and word parts.	Reading comprehension is better than listening comprehension of material of difficult content and readability. For poorer readers, listening comprehension may be equal to reading comprehension.
Stage 5: Construction and reconstruction	College and beyond (age 18+)	Reading is used for one's own needs and purposes (professional and personal); reading serves to integrate one's knowledge with that of others, to synthesize it and to create new knowledge. It is rapid and efficient. Wide reading of ever more difficult materials, reading beyond one's immediate needs; writing of papers, tests, essays, and other forms that call for integration of varied knowledge and points of view.	Reading is more efficient than listening.

Source: Jeanne S. Chall, *Stages of Reading Development.* New York: McGraw-Hill, 1983, pp. 85–87.

Digest. However, the NAEP data also indicate that fewer than half of all 17-year-olds in school and young adults have achieved the Adept and Advanced levels, which correspond to Chall's third broad level of advanced literacy. When looked at separately, even fewer black and Hispanic 17-year-olds and young adults have achieved these levels of proficiency.

CIVIC DOCUMENTS AND PUBLIC INFORMATION

Civic literacy implies knowledge of the principles and processes of government and an understanding of one's rights and responsibilities as a citizen (Remy, 1980). To take full advantage of their civic rights and to fulfill their responsibilities as informed citizens, Americans must be able to read certain civic documents and various forms of public information.

Civic Documents

What are the civic documents all Americans should be able to read? Mortimer Adler (1982) makes our task simpler by stating clearly and emphatically that the ''minimal essentials'' of civic literacy are understanding and repeated rereading of our founding documents— the Declaration of Independence; the U.S. Constitution, particularly its Preamble; and Lincoln's Gettysburg Address. These documents, he holds, must be read and studied and, like the Bible, read over and over again. If one agrees with Adler (and he presents a compelling view), what kind of reading task would these documents present? Are most American high school students and young adults up to this task?

To answer these questions we undertook several readability analyses of some historic documents as well as samples of public information. Readability measurement has been widely used over the past 70 years to estimate the difficulty levels of various print materials. Readability formulas are essentially predictive. That is, they predict how readable a particular piece of written material will be in terms of the ability required to read and understand it (Fry, 1989; Klare, 1963). The validity of readability measures has been well documented (Bormuth, 1968; Chall, 1958; Klare, 1984; Zakaluk & Samuels, 1988).

Most readability measures, similar to most reading tests, express results quantitatively in terms of grade levels. Thus a readability score of grade 10 for a particular text suggests that at least a tenth-grade reading ability is likely to be needed to read and comprehend the material. Readability measures also use various qualitative descriptions, such as "very easy," "easy," "standard," and "advanced," which resemble those used by the NAEP studies.

We used two readability formulas for the analysis of the documents, the new Dale–Chall (in press) and the Fry (1972). Both are based on counts of vocabulary features (word difficulty or word length) and syntax. The Fry measures word difficulty on the basis of the number of syllables in a sample passage. The Dale–Chall bases its measure of word difficulty on the number of unfamiliar words in 100-word samples of text; their unfamiliarity is determined by reference to a list of 3000 words familiar to 80 percent of fourth graders. Syntactic difficulty in both formulas is measured by the average number of words in each sentence in the sample passage, that is, average sentence length.

A third measure used to analyze the documents was the Holistic Assessment of Texts Scales (Chall, Bissex, Conard & Harris, in press), a qualitative analysis based on judgments and comparisons with exemplars. The exemplars are graded passages of increasing difficulty in four content areas—traditional literature, popular fiction, science, and social studies. They offer a quick means of qualitatively matching material and reader.

These measures were applied to samples from the Declaration of Independence, the Constitution (the Preamble was assessed separately), and the Gettysburg Address. The sample passages are presented in Figure 2.4, with "unfamiliar words" underlined, and followed by the results of the three readability analyses.

The analyses show that both the Declaration of Independence and the Constitution are written on readability levels usually found in texts for college students—an advanced level—and, according to the NAEP results (Mullis & Jenkins, 1990), above the level of all but about 5 percent of 17-year-olds. Figure 2.4 also shows that the Constitution is certainly as difficult as the Declaration. Even though the Preamble is often thought to be less difficult than the body of the Constitution, analysis shows that they may be equally difficult.

Lincoln's Gettysburg Address is easier, according to the readability check. Generally, one would expect this since a text written to be given as a speech is usually lower in difficulty than a text written only to be read by others. But although the Gettysburg Address is considerably easier than the Declaration of Independence and the

Figure 2.4 Sample Passages, with Difficult Words* Underlined: Selected Historic Documents

THE DECLARATION OF INDEPENDENCE

Sample 1:

We hold these truths to be self-evident, that all men are created equal, that they are endowed by their Creator with certain unalienable rights, that among these are life, liberty, and the pursuit of happiness.

That to secure these rights, governments are instituted among men, deriving their just powers from the consent of the governed. That whenever any form of government becomes destructive to these ends, it is the right of the people to alter or to abolish it, and to institute new government, laying its foundation on such principles and organizing its powers in such form as to them . . .

Sample 2:

He has excited domestic insurrections amongst us, and has endeavored to bring on the inhabitants of our frontiers, the merciless Indian savages, whose known rule of warfare is an undistinguished destruction of all sexes and conditions.

In every stage of these oppressions we have petitioned for redress in the most humble terms. Our repeated petitions have been answered only by repeated injury. A prince, whose character is thus marked by every act which may define a tyrant, is unfit to be the ruler of a free people.

Nor have we been wanting in attentions to our British brethren. . . .
- -
THE CONSTITUTION OF THE UNITED STATES

Sample 1: Preamble

We the People of the United States, in Order to form a more perfect Union, establish Justice, insure domestic Tranquility, provide for the common defence, promote the general Welfare, and secure the Blessing of Liberty to ourselves and our Posterity, do ordain and establish this Constitution for the United States of America.

Sample 2: Section 3, Article I

The Senate of the United States shall be composed of two Senators from each State, chosen by the Legislature thereof, for six Years: and each Senator shall have one Vote.

---

*According to the New Dale–Chall Formula

Figure 2.4 *Continued*

Immediately after they shall be assembled in Consequence of the first Election, they shall be divided as equally as may be into three Classes. The Seats of the Senators of the first Class shall be vacated at the Expiration of the second Year, of the second Class at the Expiration of the fourth Year, and of the third Class at the Expiration of the sixth Year, so that one third . . .

Sample 3: Section 9, Article I

The Migration or Importation of such Persons as any of the States now existing shall think proper to admit, shall not be prohibited by the Congress prior to the Year one thousand eight hundred and eight, but a Tax or Duty may be imposed on such Importation not exceeding ten dollars for each Person.

The privilege of the Writ of Habeas Corpus shall not be suspended, unless when in Cases of Rebellion or Invasion the public safety may require it.

No Bill of Attainder or ex post facto Law shall be passed.

No Capitation, or other direct, Tax shall . . .

- -

THE GETTYSBURG ADDRESS
November 19, 1863

Fourscore and seven years ago our fathers brought forth on this continent, a new nation, conceived in liberty, and dedicated to the proposition that all men are created equal.

Now we are engaged in a great civil war, testing whether that nation, or any nation so conceived and so dedicated, can long endure. We are met on a great battlefield of that war. We have come to dedicate a portion of that field, as a final resting-place for those who here gave their lives that that nation might live. It is altogether fitting and proper that we should do this.

- -

Results of Readability Analysis

	Holistic Assessment	New Dale-Chall Formula	Fry Formula
Declaration of Independence	13–15	13–15	College +
Constitution	13–15	13–15	College +
Preamble alone	13–15	16 +	College +
Lincoln's Gettysburg Address	9–10	9–10	9

Figure 2.5   Sample Passage, with Difficult Words Underlined:
Ronald Reagan, January 24, 1987

STATE OF THE UNION ADDRESS

But whether delivered in person or in writing, these annual messages
represent one of our nation's basic historical texts—a body of writings that
show our development from a fledgling Republic to a great bastion of freedom; that present our Presidents as individual men, struggling as best they
could with the issues of their day; that in our time—our own time—provide
continuity, a sense of the proud history that we as Americans have inherited.

In 198 Presidential messages to Congress certain themes reappear. National security—there is Washington's urging that the Republic remain
strong; for, in his words . . .

Results of Readability Analysis

	Reading Grade Level
New Dale–Chall Formula	9–10
Fry Formula	12
Holistic Assessment of Texts Scales	9–10

From: Public Papers of the Presidents, Ronald Reagan, 1987. U.S. Document 1010.

Constitution, it is on an Adept level, and is thus still above the reading ability of most young adults and in-school 17-year-olds, according
to the most recent national assessments of reading and literacy. As
noted earlier, fewer than half of the young adults and in-school 17-
year-olds tested on an Adept level—one that permits reading with
understanding of materials that are found in textbooks with reading
levels from grades 9 to 12 (Kirsch & Jungeblut, 1986, p. 39). The
words and ideas in the Gettysburg Address are quite difficult, requiring considerable prior knowledge, which one usually acquires only
in school and/or from wide reading.

What about similar texts written today? Would they be less difficult to comprehend, since language has become less formal over the
past 100 years? Not necessarily so, it seems. Figure 2.5 contains a
readability analysis of President Reagan's State of the Union Address
of 1987. According to the Dale–Chall and Fry formulas, the passage
from Reagan's State of the Union Address appears to be at the ninth-
grade level of difficulty, about the same level as Lincoln's Gettysburg
Address.

Figure 2.6 Sample Passage, with Difficult Words Underlined:
Information on Ballot

SUMMARY OF QUESTION 1

This question asks Newton voters to decide whether to override (increase) next year's property tax levy limit by $5 million. The additional revenue would be used to support educational and municipal services for the fiscal year beginning July 1, 1990 and ending June 30, 1991.

This question is presented to Newton voters in accordance with the state law known as Proposition 2 1/2. This law limits the annual increases in real estate and personal property taxes a municipality can levy. This is called the annual levy limit. Consistent with Proposition 2 1/2, a municipality may annually increase the amount it raises through taxes . . .

Results of Readability Analysis

Dale–Chall Formula Reading Grade Level	11–12
Fry Formula Reading Grade Level	College

From: Newton Election Commission, Sample Ballot. City of Newton, City Hall, Newton, MA, 1990.

General Government Documents and Public Information

In order to understand their public benefits and to fulfill their civic responsibilities, Americans need to read a variety of general government documents—from application forms for food stamps and loans for housing to census and tax forms. There is considerable evidence suggesting that the levels of difficulty of these writings are also poorly matched to the reading ability of those who need to use them (Chall & Conard, 1982; Kirsch & Jungeblut, 1986; Sticht, 1977). Analyses have shown that many of these forms and documents are inaccessible to those with average or lower reading abilities (Kirsch & Jungeblut, 1986); they often require an Adept level of reading proficiency (ninth to twelfth grade). Figure 2.6, for example, shows the results of a readability analysis of a passage of information for voters on the ballot for a local election. The information requires an Adept level of reading proficiency. In sum, there is a gap between the reading ability of many individuals in society and the essential materials they must read to fulfill their responsibilities and to benefit from their rights as citizens.

Other written communications that can be considered ''public information'' and that all individuals need to be able to read in order to function as citizens include such materials as notices from utility companies, operating and assembling instructions for household appliances, and inserts in medicine packaging. These forms of public information may also be difficult for most Americans. For example, Powers (1988) used the Fry readability formula to analyze medical educational materials generated commercially or by hospitals for patients in the emergency department of a large hospital. He noted that many were written on an eighth- to thirteenth-grade level, while most patients who needed to use them were estimated to read at an eighth-grade level or below.

One of the authors of this chapter has served as an expert witness in several class action suits for groups of people having limited education and reading ability who suffered because important information for them was written on a high school or college level while they could read only on an eighth-grade level. One of these suits, which was successful, claimed that food stamp recipients had been denied renewal of their benefits because they could not read the instructions. Another suit concerned the failure to renew a housing contract because the contract was written in language too difficult for the homeowners to read and therefore they could not know what was in it. Public information that is written on a level requiring Advanced or Adept reading skills can be unfairly penalizing to individuals whose reading level precludes them from reading and using the information.

Realizing that many government documents with vital information regarding individual rights and responsibilities are not readable to large numbers of the population, the U.S. Department of Education and other federal government agencies have sponsored efforts to make these documents more readable (Boyce, 1982; Felker & Rose, 1981; Felker, Pickering, Charrow, Holland, & Redish, 1981; Prochaska, 1988). The government, for instance, has spent a considerable amount of money to make tax forms more readable, and the Food and Nutrition Service of the Department of Agriculture has produced and disseminated guidelines on simplifying text and designing documents to make them more easily readable by adults with limited reading skills (Prochaska, 1988).

Nontextual materials, such as forms and documents that require readers to follow directions in order to fill in information or answer questions, present a somewhat different task than textual materials. Kirsch and Mosenthal (1990) have studied the factors involved in reading and understanding non-textual materials. They have identified variables specific to a broad variety of documents from the 1985

NAEP literacy assessment in an attempt to determine what makes the documents easy or difficult to read. Their aim is to provide a theoretical basis for instruction in reading and understanding non-textual documents and to develop a model that can be used by document designers to improve the usability of non-textual documents. Their work could lead to instructional approaches in the special skills that readers need for non-textual documents and forms.

BRIDGING THE GAP: SOME RECOMMENDATIONS

How can we bridge this gap between the reading ability of many individuals and the essential materials they must read to fulfill their responsibilities and benefit from their rights as citizens? One solution to closing the gap between the reading difficulty of materials and the reading ability of many Americans lies in continuing efforts to make government documents and public information more readable and understandable to larger numbers of people. This effort is particularly needed on such important concerns as voting, welfare eligibility, and food stamps, since those who most need to use information of this kind usually have lower levels of literacy. It has been amply demonstrated that such information is needlessly difficult to read and understand.

To some extent, our historic documents can also be "rewritten" so that their content is more comprehensible to newcomers to the United States, to new citizens, and to those who are preparing to become citizens. Rewritten or simplified historic documents can also be useful for adults attending literacy classes.

Unfortunately, it takes great effort, concern, and skill to write more simply and readably. Writers must be trained not only to write simply but also to appreciate the knowledge, needs, and literacy skills of readers (Klare & Buck, 1954; Redish, 1983). Consequently, rewriting documents cannot be the only solution or even the major one for reducing the gap.

The chief way to bridge the gap between reader and material is to improve our educational efforts. The reading abilities of our children must be improved to make it possible for them to read newspapers and news magazines and thus be informed about local, national, and world affairs as well as their civic rights and responsibilities.

Of course, television helps communicate difficult ideas more simply. But it does not really solve the problem of the gap. Spoken communication requires knowledge, language, and thought similar to that needed for reading. The correlation between listening and reading comprehension is generally high (Sticht, Beck, Hauke, Kleiman, & James, 1974). And as Walter Cronkite noted many years ago, it is not possible to be informed only by watching TV news. It is too spotty and does not permit the kind of analysis that can be offered in newspapers, magazines, and books. Students have an advantage when they can read at advanced levels. A look at Column 5 in Figure 2.3 shows the relationship of reading to listening in the different stages of reading development. Note that at the advanced stages of development, reading becomes more efficient than listening.

To make better readers, literacy needs to be conceived more broadly—as a way to develop language, knowledge, and thought as well as reading and writing skills. If some students have difficulty advancing, they should be given special help. Otherwise, they will not achieve the level of literacy they are capable of and need for civic purposes.

One of the goals of education should be to have more Americans reach an advanced reading level—a high school level or higher. Although the average American adult today reads better than the average adult 50 years ago, the current reading levels are not sufficient in a world that is more complex and technical and requires higher levels of literacy for work and for making choices as citizens.

One of the major ways that teachers can help students improve their reading is to focus on vocabulary development. Since each teacher after the primary grades is both a teacher of content and a teacher of reading, teaching vocabulary as well as concepts within the context of particular subject matter is essential. Indeed, knowledge of the meanings of words is the first component of reading that increases at a less than normal rate among low-income children after the primary grades: in the primary grades, these children learn vocabulary at a normal rate. (Chall, Jacobs, & Baldwin, 1990). And as the knowledge of word meanings decelerates, so do reading comprehension and writing skills. It is particularly important, then, for content area teachers to provide instruction in vocabulary to children from low-income families. Numerous techniques have been developed for teaching students vocabulary in the content areas (Estes & Vaughan, 1978; Herber, 1970; Herber & Nelson-Herber, 1984).

Another way in which teachers can help students develop their reading ability is to present them with challenging reading materials. The study by Chall et al. (1990) showed that those children who were exposed to a variety of reading materials, much of which was challenging, improved in word meanings. Although students generally need to be matched to the level of reading material that they are capable of handling on their own, the use of challenging material should not be ignored. Challenging levels of reading materials that improve vocabulary knowledge enhance reading development. Thus, books on the student's reading level or somewhat higher, for which the teacher provides instruction, may produce better gains than books below the student's reading level.

CONCLUSIONS

This chapter has focused mainly on the relationship between the current reading abilities of young adults and high school students and the reading difficulty of our nation's historic civic documents and printed public information. We have looked specifically at the literacy levels of young Americans as determined by recent NAEP assessments, and we have examined the levels of literacy required to read and understand a few selected civic documents and forms of public information.

Although our examination of the difficulty level of selected civic documents and our survey of research on the difficulty level of government documents and public forms are limited in scope, it appears that there is a considerable gap between the literacy levels required to read and understand these documents and forms and the reading abilities of most young people and adults in America today. Our historic documents and much public information that all citizens must be able to read seem to require a level of literacy that is higher than that attained by most adults and young people.

Clearly, efforts are called for to make the public communications that need to be read by all Americans as close to the reading levels of most citizens as possible. However, we must also work toward raising the reading levels of our children, young adults, and even older Americans. And, in order to develop reading ability in students, we do need to use challenging material. To help all high school students achieve an Advanced literacy level (twelfth grade and above) is necessary as well as challenging. This level requires an extensive general and specialized vocabulary, considerable knowledge, and the ability to reason and to think critically. But it allows an individual to use reading to solve problems as well as to gain information.

Improvements have been made and are still being made in raising the literacy levels of children and adults. Efforts are also being made to write public documents at a reading level sufficiently low so as to make them accessible to a larger percentage of the general population than they now are. Both efforts—lowering the difficulty levels of important documents and raising the literacy levels of students at all ages—will contribute to a better fit between the reading level of our historic documents and various forms of public information, and the ability of the general public to read and understand them. More Americans may then be better able to participate in public life, to fulfill their responsibilities as citizens of this country, and to become integral members of their civic communities.

REFERENCES

Adler, M. (1982). *The paideia proposal: An educational manifesto*. New York: Macmillan.
Bormuth, J. R. (1968). Cloze test readability: Criterion reference scores. *Journal of Educational Measurement, 5*, 189–196.
Boyce, M. R. (1982). *Guidelines for printed materials for older adults*. East Lansing: Michigan Health Council.
Chall, J. S. (1958). *Readability: An appraisal of research and application*. Columbus: Ohio State University, Bureau of Educational Research.
Chall, J. S. (1983). *Stages of reading development*. New York: McGraw-Hill.
Chall, J. S., Bissex, G., Conard, S., & Harris, S. (in press). *The holistic assessment of text scales*. Boston: Houghton Mifflin.
Chall, J. S., & Conard, S. (1982). *Analyses of food stamp notices*. Unpublished paper, Harvard Graduate School of Education, Cambridge, MA.
Chall, J., Jacobs, V., & Baldwin, L. (1990). *Families and literacy*. Cambridge, MA: Harvard University Press.
Dale, E., & Chall, J. S. (in press). *Readability revisited and the new Dale–Chall readability formula*.
Estes, T. H., & Vaughan, J. L. (1978). *Reading and learning in the content classroom*. Boston: Allyn & Bacon.
Felker, D. B., Pickering, F., Charrow, V., Holland, V. M., & Redish, J. C. (1981). *Guidelines for document designers*. Washington, DC: Document Design Center, American Institutes for Research.
Felker, D. B., & Rose, A. M. (1981). *The evaluation of a public document* (Technical Report No. 11). Washington, DC: Document Design Center, American Institutes for Research.
Fry, E. B. (1972). *Reading instruction for classroom and clinic*. New York: McGraw-Hill.
Fry, E. B. (1989). Reading formulas—maligned but valid. *Journal of Reading, 32* (4), 292–296.
Herber, H. L. (1970). *Teaching reading in the content areas*. Englewood Cliffs, NJ: Prentice-Hall.

Herber, H., & Nelson-Herber, J. (1984). Planning the reading program. In A. Purves & O. Niles (Eds.), *Becoming readers in a complex society* (pp. 174–208). Eighty-Third Yearbook of the National Society for the Study of Education. Chicago: University of Chicago Press.

Kirsch, I., & Jungeblut, A. (1986). *Literacy profiles of America's young adults.* National Assessment of Educational Progress. Princeton, NJ: Educational Testing Service.

Kirsch, I., & Mosenthal, P. B. (1990). Exploring document literacy: Variables underlying the performance of young adults. *Reading Research Quarterly, 25* (1), 5–30.

Klare, G. R. (1963). *The measurement of readability.* Ames: Iowa State University Press.

Klare, G. (1984). Readability. In P. D. Pearson (Ed.), *Handbook of reading research* (pp. 681–744). New York: Longmans.

Klare, G., & Buck, B. (1954). *Know your reader.* New York: Hermitage House.

Mullis, I. V., & Jenkins, L. B. (1990). *The reading report card, 1971–88.* National Assessment of Educational Progress. Washington, DC: Office of Educational Research and Improvement, U.S. Department of Education.

Powers, R. (1988). Emergency department patient literacy. *Annals of Emergency Medicine, 17* (2), 124–126.

Prochaska, S. (1988). *Guidelines: Writing for adults with limited reading skills.* Washington, DC: U.S. Department of Agriculture, Food and Nutrition Service, Office of Information.

Redish, J. (1983). The language of the bureaucracy. In R. Bailey & R. Fosheim (Eds.), *Literacy for life: The demand for reading and writing* (pp. 151–174). New York: Modern Language Association.

Remy, R. (1980). *Handbook of basic citizenship competencies.* Alexandria, VA: Association for Supervision and Curriculum Development.

Sticht, T. (1977). Comprehending reading at work. In M. A. Just & P. A. Carpenter (Eds.), *Cognitive processes in comprehension* (pp. 221–245). Hillsdale, NJ: Erlbaum.

Sticht, T. G., Beck, L. J., Hauke, R. N., Kleiman, G. M., & James, J. H. (1974). *Auding and reading.* Alexandria, VA: Human Resources Research Organization.

Zakaluk, B., & Samuels, S. J. (1988). *Readability: Its past, present and future.* Newark, DE: International Reading Association.

3 Teaching Contemporary American Literature

A Professional Dilemma

SANDRA STOTSKY
with Barbara Hardy Beierl

Literature programs in both private and public secondary schools in this country may serve several broad purposes. First, they may expose students to literary texts of aesthetic, intellectual, and moral worth, regardless of the cultural origins of these texts. In so doing, literature programs serve the humanistic goals of a liberal education. School literature programs may also acquaint students with some of the significant literary texts in the cultural and political history of their local and national civic communities, a corpus that includes literature, in English, about the ethnic, religious, and racial groups in these communities. In so doing, these programs serve the civic goals of a liberal education. They not only help provide all students with common cultural information and a common cultural language, but they also help give all students a civic identity—a sense of individual membership in their civic communities and a feeling of kinship with all those who live in these communities, regardless of religious identity, socioeconomic status, intellectual ability, ethnic background, or gender.

Literature Programs in the Nineteenth and Early Twentieth Centuries

In the nineteenth and early twentieth centuries, literature programs in both elementary and secondary schools in this country contributed consciously and considerably to the development of students' civic identity and their sense of common membership in their national community. A major task facing this country in the early days of the republic was the building of a national identity. Most Americans at that time had much stronger identities with their local or state governments than with their new national government, a situation that continued until well after the Civil War. Proud of what the American Revolution had accomplished, many citizens of this new country did not want their entire school curriculum to continue being simply an imitation of a British or European one. Thus, it is not surprising that, as Ruth Windhover (1979) notes, school readers in the first decades of the nineteenth century began to offer more literature composed by Americans, and between 1820 and 1840 especially, featured selections lauding the virtues of the new republic.

By the middle of the century, Windhover observes, speeches by great public orators, particularly Daniel Webster and Edward Everett, appeared frequently in school readers. Webster's speeches addressed issues like the preservation of the Union and reminded students about their responsibilities toward their country and about what the Revolution had been fought for. The high school literature curriculum continued to have a predominantly British flavor throughout the last half of the nineteenth century and during the first half of the twentieth century; for example, George Tanner's 1907 survey for the English profession found that only nine of the 40 most frequently assigned plays, novels, and collections of poems and essays in grades 9–12 in 67 high schools in the Midwest were by American authors. Nevertheless, elementary school readers, reading programs, and social studies curricula (grades 1–8) typically featured American legends and folktales, stories and poems by distinguished American authors, biographies of important Americans, and selections on American history, as Charlotte Iiams (1980) and Diane Ravitch (1987) have noted. Other stories and poems, Iiams observed, expressed pride in this country's political values, principles, and achievements and offered models of civic behavior or good citizenship.

Overall, these shared reading experiences, especially in the elementary (or grammar) schools, helped to develop a civic identity in generations of students, thereby preparing them for responsible participation in a republican form of government at all levels. Despite its manifest flaws and failings, students could take pride in being citizens of the country in which they lived. And they could continue to do so as adults even while striving to remedy the social or political ills they perceived.

Concerns About Contemporary Literature Programs

Since the middle of the twentieth century, school literature programs have been changing rapidly, and today many scholars and educators (e.g., Mortimer Adler, 1982) believe they no longer offer all students a substantial common core of authors or works representing significant intellectual traditions and literary movements in this country's cultural and political history. Some evidence to support this belief may be found in *What Do Our 17-Year-Olds Know?* (Ravitch & Finn, 1987), a report of the results of the first national assessment of knowledge of history and literature. The average score on the literature assessment, developed and administered by the National Assessment of Educational Progress, was 52 percent. In other words, only a bare majority, on the average, could answer the questions correctly.

Unfortunately, there are no nationwide surveys that compare what individual English teachers teach in their own classrooms, what individual students read in their secondary school years, or what individual schools require all students to read—with a list of the most frequently mentioned works across classrooms and schools. However, there is some empirical evidence suggesting that one teacher's classroom literature program today may have little in common with another's. Recently, Sandra Stotsky and Philip Anderson (1990) conducted a survey for the New England Association of Teachers of English (NEATE) to compile a list of teacher-recommended readings for grades 7–12. English teachers who are members of NEATE and other professional organizations for English teachers in the six New England states were asked to recommend well-known and less well-known titles of literary works that they had successfully taught in their own classrooms. Stotsky and Anderson were surprised to find that the 132 members of NEATE who responded to the survey mentioned 720 unique titles; they had expected much less variation than that. Moreover, only 328 titles appeared at least twice, and no more than 12 titles were mentioned by 20 or more teachers. Although the findings of this one study cannot be generalized beyond New England or even to all English teachers in New England, this wide variation in individual profiles strongly hints at the possibility that students across our secondary schools may be experiencing an extraordinary diversity of readings in their literature courses, with very little material in common.

Some of this literary diversity undoubtedly reflects a lack of serious thought on the part of many educators about what a secondary school curriculum should offer in order to create the feeling of civic kinship necessary for motivating responsible civic participation in a country with many ethnic, racial, and religious groups. On the other hand, some of this diversity quite legitimately reflects the broadening of the range of interests, backgrounds, and abilities in high school students from the nineteenth century to the end of the twentieth.

Today, a responsible literature program must offer good literature that is accessible to students with poor reading skills, feature a large body of contemporary texts in addition to those that help students understand the cultural and political history of the country, and include examples of the best literature about the many ethnic and religious groups that inhabit our civic communities. Thus, simply reducing some of this literary diversity through a straightforward adoption of a core of literary works based primarily on their broad cultural and political significance would not address all the reasons why a common core has rapidly disappeared. However, even if it did, it is not clear that adopting a broad common core of literary works that included a substantial number of contemporary works would necessarily serve the civic purposes of the secondary schools. Much depends on what is taught, how it is taught, and the context in which it is taught.

This chapter has several purposes. We first discuss the possible effects of twentieth-century American literature on the development of the values that sustain responsible participation in a republican form of government, suggesting a number of analytical questions for teachers to explore in their own classrooms or with their colleagues. We then raise several ethical questions for them to consider about the literature, the pedagogical goals, and the learning strategies that may be used for classroom literary study today. We conclude by offering some practical strategies that teachers and their students might use to examine the possible civic and social effects of the literature they read.

TWENTIETH-CENTURY AMERICAN LITERATURE

Can Literary Works Have Anti-Civic Effects?

In his preface to *Jeffersonianism and the American Novel*, Howard Mumford Jones (1966) claims that the American novel in the twentieth century has seriously weakened if not caused the disappearance of the concept of the adult American as a "being capable of both rational and moral choice" (p. xi). And "upon this assumption," Jones proposes, "the republic rests." At the end of his first chapter, he urges readers to examine such questions as: "whether American novelists have been for or against the American state," "what picture they give the American of the American as citizen," and "whether they believe . . . in moral principle as the founding fathers did." Clearly, many of the culturally significant works of twentieth-century literature most frequently taught in the secondary school curriculum, such as Arthur Miller's *Death of a Salesman* and *The Crucible*, F. Scott Fitzgerald's *The Great Gatsby*, John Hersey's *Hiroshima*, and John Steinbeck's *The Grapes of Wrath*, offer an ambivalent if not unflattering picture of the values of American society and may not foster civic self-esteem. Jones's concerns raise questions about the effects of modern American literature as a whole not only on our students' personal values but also on their implicit judgments about the moral character of American society—judgments that are probably being shaped more by intellectual trends within our cultural tradition than by experience itself.

According to Ben Nelms (1989), editor of the *English Journal*, some contemporary English educators have already begun to raise questions about the effects of a small literary canon of contemporary works that they perceive to be in place in the secondary curriculum— a canon that includes such works as William Golding's *Lord of the Flies*, John Knowles's *A Separate Peace*, J. D. Salinger's *Catcher in the Rye*, S. E. Hinton's *The Outsiders*, Paul Zindel's *The Pigman*, and Robert Cormier's *The Chocolate War*. These critics, Nelms notes, suggest that these works tend "to focus on the experience of adolescent male protagonists who are loners, separated from the influence of family and adult mentors, to reify adolescence as a state rather than show the successful passage of the young into adulthood, to idealize adolescence and adolescent characters at the expense of adults, and to emphasize depressing, negative conditions—confusion, alienation of the young, instability, irresponsibility, loneliness, and moral ambivalence" (p. 13). In much of what they read, these critics imply, students may not find protagonists who have a sense of intellectual or social purpose, moral principles, or a feeling of roots in any community.

Their judgment is shared by Paula Burns (1985), a high school English teacher. In an essay published in the *English Journal*, she asks her colleagues for help in a "search for twentieth-century literary works that are not 'so depressing'—works generally accepted as 'good' literature that include at least one character of high moral standing" (pp. 76–77). John Cameron (1990), another high school English teacher, also argues that the "spirit of disillusionment, despair, and cynicism so often associated with the artistic achievements of our time receives a disproportionate amount of attention in our classroom" (p. 1). Cameron recently spent a year investigating how this pessimism can be effectively countered by twentieth-century artists "who offer a balanced understanding of the human heart and who renew our faith in the human spirit" (p. 1). One result of this search, an annotated reading list entitled "Reclaiming Our Humanity in Twentieth-Century Literature," appears as the appendix to this chapter. Cameron's list of 44 works, which includes both American and non-American works, complements the annotated list of 25 "positive" twentieth-century works that Geraldine Vale (1989), another high school English teacher, offers in the *English Journal* to add to the list of 18 works in Burns's article. Vale pleads for more suggestions "to make twentieth-century American literature a more positive experience for students as well as for their teachers" and notes that, with one exception, she has been unable to locate works written in the past decade for her list.

The "best" of children's literature in the late twentieth century has itself not been immune from some of the criticisms directed toward adolescent or adult works of fiction. John Dunlap (1989) discusses the dominance of "problem" books among the books receiving the Newbery Medal since 1960. In his judgment, among the 38 books to receive Newbery Medals from 1922, when the award was established, to 1959, only two could be defined as "problem" books. On the other hand, he believes that since 1960, 20 of the 30 books honored by the most prestigious children's book award could be judged as "problem" books. "The keynote in problem books," he proposes, "regardless of theme, seems to be a preoccupation with the self, so that feelings per se wind up taking center stage rather than modestly serving the storyline" (p. 20).

Is it possible that some of the self-centeredness or concern for self-advancement that many cultural critics perceive in students (or adults) today is a subliminal response to a cynical, alienating literature in which constructive goals, principled thinking, a sense of community, and a spirit of optimism are strikingly absent? This is one question that English teachers might well explore in their own classrooms. If the critics to whom Nelms refers are correct in their observations about the kinds of works students now tend to read in their school literature programs, students may well believe that the exercise of civic virtue is unworthy of their efforts or a waste of time.

Can Literary Works Have Anti-Social Effects?

Many contemporary works that focus especially on the early experiences of various social groups in this country understandably express hostility toward the majority of the people in this country. Laurence Yep's novel *Dragonwings*, written for middle school students, is one example.

A Newbery Honor Book for 1975, *Dragonwings* is about a person-able young Chinese boy who comes to America to live with his father in the Chinatown of San Francisco in the first decade of the twentieth century. The novel, which is narrated in the first person by the young boy, portrays two groups of people: the immigrant Chinese in China-town, and the "demons," "white demons," or "white demon-esses," which is how all Americans are consistently referred to in the novel. Aside from the Chinese boy's young American friend and her aunt, there are no positive portraits of Americans in this novel; in fact, no others emerge clearly as individual characters. The older Chinese characters are portrayed as seeing only hostility and preju-dice toward them from the "white demons." A deeply negative im-age of Americans is consistently conveyed, beginning with the open-ing paragraph of *Dragonwings*.

> Ever since I can remember, I had wanted to know about the Land of the Golden Mountain, but my mother had never wanted to talk about it. All I knew was that a few months before I was born, my father had left our home in the Middle Kingdom, or China, as the white demons call it, and traveled over the sea to work in the demon land. There was plenty of money to be made among the demons, but it was also danger-ous. My own grandfather had been lynched about thirty years before by a mob of white demons almost the moment he had set foot on their shores. (p. 1)

Even the Chinese boy's young American friend does not escape unflattering touches. After reporting her enjoyment of E. Nesbit's children's stories, the narrator goes on to reveal her real tastes in literature in the following way:

> *"I've got some of these, too,"* the demon girl pretended to say casually. She slipped some *dime novels* from behind her back. . . . There were *Ned Buntline* specials about the adventures of *Buffalo Bill* in the wild, wild West (to me it was east, though, since I judged things geographically in relation to the Middle Kingdom). There were others about *Jesse James* and how he tortured his robbery victims. But her pride and joy were the *Nick Carter* detective stories, with a dead body on almost every page, as she boasted. (p. 127)

While the "demon" girl has some positive traits, she may not be very appealing to many young female readers.

As Robert Scholes (1985) notes, criticism of a literary work re-

quires an examination of its assumptions and values. But in this
novel, readers are told why the author wrote the story. In a three-
page afterword, Yep writes: "It has been my aim to counter various
stereotypes as presented in the media. Dr. Fu Manchu and his yellow
hordes, Charlie Chan and his fortune-cookie wisdom, the laundry-
men and cooks of the movie and television Westerns, and the house-
boys of various comedies present an image of Chinese not as they
really are but as they exist in the mind of White America" (pp. 247–
248).

Given that this book was published in 1975, a reader might question whether the stereotypes that the writer believes exist in the
minds of most Americans really do exist today, at least to any significant extent, and whether they exist in particular in the minds of
the 10- , 11- , and 12-year-olds for whom this book was written.
Nevertheless, Yep has created a literary work expressing the truth as
he believes it, and no one would dispute that his novel may accurately depict a general social reality for the period in which the novel
is set. What is of concern are the effects of the author's own stereotypes on today's young readers.

One worries whether *Dragonwings* elicits hostility toward white
demons in Chinese-American children *today*. Further, does it elicit
hostility toward all white demons in other nonwhite children? And,
finally, does it also elicit hostility, shame, or guilt in children who are
designated as white and who accept this stereotype of themselves?
While we do not know, of course, we can only imagine what our
own responses to *Dragonwings* might be if we were impressionable
young readers. What effects does a work like *Dragonwings* have?
These are questions that English teachers might explore in their own
classrooms. They might also discuss with other colleagues how best
to handle works like these in the classroom.

Can a Selected Series of Literary Texts
Have Cumulative Negative Effects?

In all likelihood, most teachers at all educational levels do not
think about the possible rhetorical effects of an individual literary
work when selecting literature for their classroom programs. Most
teachers have probably used, and undoubtedly still use, aesthetic
criteria to guide their choice of works. At the elementary or middle
school level, they generally select books for whole-class instruction
that they think have literary quality and tell an interesting story,

especially if these books have received critical acclaim. For example, the following reviewers' comments are reprinted on the back cover or inside page of *Dragonwings*:

> "Yep's images and perspectives are breathtakingly original."—*Publishers Weekly*

> "If it were only a fantastic story of high adventure, *Dragonwings* would be a success, but as an exquisitely written poem of praise to the courage and industry of the Chinese-American people, it is a triumph."—*The New York Times*

> "A fine, sensitive novel written with grace."—*ALA Booklist*

Such comments would hardly lead any teacher to suspect the dark underside of this work. In fact, most teachers may be completely unaware of the possibility that literary works could have negative effects on their students' feelings toward white as well as nonwhite groups. Many scholars have explored racial and gender stereotypes in literary works, or the ways in which women or members of some racial groups are portrayed in literature, and the possible effects of these stereotypes on readers' perceptions of women or members of these groups. But none so far as we know have explored the stereotypes of whites in literature or the negative effects of these stereotypes on readers' images of whites.

However, far more serious than a teacher's lack of awareness of these possible effects of reading an individual work is a teacher's deliberate selection of a group of literary texts for classroom study in order to influence negatively students' feelings of self-worth as citizens of this country and their attitudes toward the majority of its inhabitants. One possible example of such a grouping appears in an article by Patricia Taylor (1988), a university teacher in California. For a suggested high school literature unit on the theme of the search for justice and dignity, Taylor explicitly groups *Death of a Salesman, I Know Why the Caged Bird Sings*, and *Farewell to Manzanar* in order to lead students to see this country as she apparently sees it—as materialistic, racially prejudiced, discriminating against women, and unjust. The main teaching goal she offers for *Death of a Salesman* is to "study the struggle of the individual to find personal dignity in a materialistic society" (p. 18). The main teaching goal for Maya Angelou's *I Know Why the Caged Bird Sings* (an autobiography describing a black woman's childhood and adolescence in a small town in Georgia) is to "see how the main character, through her struggle to mature as a black female, evolves into a person who has a strong feeling of self-worth" (p. 18). The main teaching goal for *Farewell to Manzanar* (a true story by Jeanne Wakatsuki Houston about the internment of Japanese-born immigrants and their American-born children in California while Japan and America were at war in the 1940s) is to "show how the members of the Wakatsuki family struggled to maintain dignity in an unjust society" (p. 18). The latter story, published in 1973, is narrated in the first person by the author, who was seven years old at the time the internment began.

The article offers few topics for classroom discussion or homework assignments focusing on the aesthetic elements in these three works, even though each is considered a literary work. Instead, most of the topics Taylor recommends for discussion or homework seem designed to stimulate students' own feelings of victimization by others, to foster their sense of ethnic separateness, to intensify their negative feelings toward their own government (and, by implication, their own society), and to engage them in political activities on behalf of public policies she apparently desires. For example, to prepare for reading *I Know Why the Caged Bird Sings*, Taylor suggests that students write in their journals about a time when they "felt discriminated against" (p. 18). To prepare for reading *Farewell to Manzanar*, Taylor suggests that students "interview parents or grandparents to determine their ancestry and report on any injustices perpetrated upon their ancestors" (p. 18). To help students while reading the book, she suggests that the teacher "invite a guest speaker who lived in an internment camp for a first-hand perspective" (p. 18). After they have finished reading the book, Taylor suggests as a follow-up activity that they "conduct a mock trial of our government's policy of internment during WW II and write persuasive letters to the legislators regarding reparations for those who were interned" (p. 18).

One wonders what the effects on students may be from this unit of study. The author of *I Know Why the Caged Bird Sings* frequently (and understandably) divides her world between blacks and whites, while the author of *Farewell to Manzanar* seems to divide her world as often between whites and nonwhites as between Caucasians and Orientals. Will hostile feelings toward white Americans be evoked in nonwhite students? Will hostile feelings toward Anglo-Americans specifically also be evoked in children of Middle Eastern or European ethnic groups? Children of Armenian-Americans, Irish-Americans, and many others will undoubtedly be able to add to the tales of discrimination against ancestors that nonwhite children will contribute. And in children of Anglo-Americans, or in all those who accept the stereotype of themselves as white Americans, will feelings of shame, guilt, or even national self-hatred be evoked? Are there serious cumulative effects on readers from a series of works selected to provide an unrelenting critique of this society, especially if they are not explicitly labeled "critical" or "protest" literature to indicate that they were selected for that purpose? These are questions English teachers might well explore with their colleagues before selecting a group of literary texts for classroom presentation.

Clearly, these are all works that individually merit a place in the curriculum if a teacher so chooses. Students should become familiar with the dark view of American society that Arthur Miller and many other writers share. They should also learn about the long history of prejudice against black Americans and Japanese immigrants in this country. And they should understand that Japanese immigrants were long denied the opportunity to become citizens. These are morally reprehensible aspects of this country's history whose details *I Know Why the Caged Bird Sings* and *Farewell to Manzanar* illuminate from the perspective of those who experienced them directly. What is of concern is a teacher's deliberate grouping of literary works to convey her point of view about her society (as expressed in her teaching goals), her attempt to arouse and manipulate students' feelings against their own government and the majority of the people in this country, and her use of literary study for predominantly rhetorical rather than aesthetic ends. A larger issue is her apparent assumption that teachers should use literary study primarily as a vehicle for imposing their value judgments about their fellow citizens on their students, for instigating political activity on behalf of a cause the teacher favors, and for fostering their students' ill-will toward their own civic communities.

Even when an English teacher appears to be offering a positive goal to justify the negative effects he or she hopes will be created by a particular selection of literary works, the issues remain the same. Jody Price's (1989) article, describing a two-semester course in American literature that she created and teaches at the college level, provides an informative case in point. Using the theme of the "American Dream," Price has grouped together a number of texts from the nineteenth and twentieth centuries to expose students to "those who are disempowered within society because of gender, race, sexual preference, or economic status" (p. 22) and to expose "American society and its ability to disempower groups of people so effectively" (p. 25). Her stated positive goal is to help students develop a "broader, more inclusive definition of the Dream" (p. 22). This goal seems to mean

helping students see *both* that not everyone wants money, possessions, and a social position, *and* that not all Americans have been
able to achieve the Dream, that is, money, possessions, and a social
position—a contradiction in meaning that the author never clarifies.
This teacher is quite explicit about what ideas she plans for her students to "discover" and end up with. "Although," she writes, "at
the beginning of the year, the students believe their interpretation of
American life is right and natural, they will discover that such security is only part of the power of the ideology" (p. 22).

For nineteenth-century works, Price teaches Mark Twain's *The
Adventures of Huckleberry Finn* because it offers a "redefinition of the
family" and calls for racial equality, Herman Melville's *Bartleby the
Scrivener* and Henry James's *Washington Square* because they reveal
"the spiritual sufferings of many who work in business or live in
wealth during this time, yet who find no contentment with their
lives," and Kate Chopin's *The Awakening* because it reveals "the quiet
oppression of the nineteenth-century woman" (p. 23). With this last
text alone, the author believes that she can call "into serious question" the "conventional American Dream" (p. 24).

For twentieth-century works, Price teaches John Steinbeck's *Of
Mice and Men*, Alice Walker's *The Color Purple*, Maya Angelou's *I
Know Why the Caged Bird Sings*, N. Scott Momaday's *House Made of
Dawn*, and Leslie Marmon Silko's *Ceremony* because they focus on
"nonwhite or non-middle-class lifestyles which exist within the present American social system" (p. 24) and because they "reveal characters who have been effectively disenfranchised from the system" (p.
23). Price's description of *Ceremony*, a novel published in 1977 and
set in the Pueblo Indian culture of New Mexico in the immediate
post-World War II years, suggests the scope of the negative effects
that this book might possibly create. She writes that its protagonist,
Tayo, a war veteran who has been a prisoner of the Japanese, struggles "to cure his mental illness, which is brought upon by his efforts
to be accepted within the white culture" (p. 24), and that his "mother's confusion over her identity and self-worth as a Native American
drive her to alcoholism, and what is worse, to white men" (p. 25).
One of the "most radical themes of the novel, for the students,"
she observes, "is the condemnation of Christianity as a destructive,
oppressive religion" (p. 25). In the end, the author sums up, Tayo,
after becoming alienated from both the Indian world and "white
ideology," regains "a spirituality more profound than any the white
world has offered" (p. 25).

Clearly, works of literary quality that focus on individuals or groups who have greatly suffered, and continue to suffer, from political policies and events that took place in the course of this country's history belong in the curriculum if a teacher so chooses. Nor can one quarrel with the goal of wanting to help students develop a "broader, more inclusive definition of the Dream" (p. 22), which includes the contemplative life and modest economic demands. And who could not want racial equality and greater tolerance of diverse ways of living that do not harm others? Perhaps this teacher's students do develop a greater tolerance of others. But one wonders what the other effects are of a course with such a vast dark underside, taught by a teacher who is emphatic about her belief that this country's social problems are unique. Could any student's civic self-esteem remain intact after a concentrated exposure to a seemingly dogmatically imposed point of view about works that have been selected not on the basis of aesthetic criteria but because they show few, if any, positive aspects of white middle-class American life? Moreover, if any of these works had any other meaning for her students, it is not clear that they would be able to defend or even express them. At the end of the second semester, the teacher requires her students to decide if their definition of the American Dream has been changed or broadened as a result of the course; she does not indicate whether and how their responses are graded.

Although many American writers have had an adversarial relationship to their society, shouldn't students be given a broader perspective on American literature? And is a teacher's goal to "expose American society and its ability to disempower groups of people so effectively" (p. 25) an appropriate pedagogical goal in any society, much less an appropriate pedagogical goal for a teacher of literature or for literary study? These are also questions that English teachers might explore with their colleagues.

How Negative Social Effects May Be Created

To understand one source of the negative social effects that may be created by many of these works, one needs to appreciate the enormous power of the natural but subconscious process of identification that occurs in the reading of narrative texts. The psychological process of identification with the narrator and/or major characters in a literary narrative is undoubtedly the most powerful mechanism set in motion by the act of reading literature. Gregory Clark's (1990) observations on this topic help us to understand why. Drawing extensively on the work of the literary critic Kenneth Burke, Clark notes that

> Narrative texts make particular values present in a voice that presents itself as representative of the community comprised by narrator and readers. [These texts] invite readers to identify themselves with that voice and . . . this identification constitutes a far more thorough transformation of the reader than merely rational persuasion. (p. 1)

In other words, Clark suggests, by inviting the reader's identification with sympathetic narrative voices that present the values the author believes should be shared (or wants shared) between author and reader, the author of a narrative text engages the reader's subconscious emotional collaboration in accepting these values and avoids the struggle for the reader's intellectual assent to them.

The process of identification, as complex as it is powerful, would appear to be different for white and nonwhite students in many contemporary works of literature. If students find wholesome or sympathetic characters to identify with primarily in stories about young people or adults who have suffered because of the behavior of white Americans, they may be likely to internalize and then generalize these young people's or adults' views of American society, especially if works are narrated in the first person and portray few decent or sympathetic white American characters. Nonwhite students may end up hostile to white Americans and the country they both inhabit, while white students may end up ashamed of being American citizens and feel guilty about being members of the demographic entity that is implicitly, if not explicitly, being charged with cruel, discriminatory, or insensitive practices.

The problem is compounded when students read stories like *Dragonwings* or *Ceremony*, in which most Americans are denied individuality and the complex mix of positive and negative traits that individuality typically reflects. In *Ceremony*, for example, the Indian characters are individualized and clearly identified according to group, such as Navaho, Pueblo, Hopi, and so on (they are never referred to as "Native Americans"), and the Mexicans and Japanese are identified as such, while all non-Indian Americans are stereotypically labeled "white" and do not appear as individual characters. In reading such works, students may not learn about the mix of virtues and vices that exists in most people, regardless of background. A profoundly negative stereotype of white Americans may be strengthened when students read contemporary works without individual white characters, set in periods of American history when prejudice was much more prevalent and blatant, as in *Dragonwings* or *Farewell to Manzanar*. The recent award-winning film, *Driving Miss Daisy*, which is set in earlier decades of this century and presents a mono-

lithically negative stereotype of white Christian Southerners, also illustrates this problem. A setting in the past may facilitate the internal-
ization of a consistently negative stereotype by young students
because they generally have a poor or relatively undeveloped intellectual sense for the passage of long periods of time, as well as a lack
of formal knowledge of the social and political changes that have oc-
curred since the time in which the story is set. A past that does
not look very different from the present is likely to be considered
contemporaneous with the present in the minds of young students.

Most English teachers enjoy reading new works of literature and
welcome new literary voices in the classroom. However, many of
these new voices are understandably hostile to groups they believe
have wronged them or their social group and manifest their anger in
a variety of ways. Teachers who ask their students to read these
works have a responsibility to help the students understand this
anger. At the same time, teachers are also responsible, professionally
and as individual citizens, for building a genuine sense of community, not just surface tolerance, in today's students. How they can do
both at the same time is perhaps the central dilemma they need to
explore.

ETHICAL ISSUES IN TEACHING LITERATURE

Although we believe that few English teachers at the secondary or
college level would subscribe to the teaching goals and learning strategies suggested in the two articles we have just described at length,
the fact that these articles were recently published in two of the most
widely read professional journals for English teachers suggests an
urgent need to examine in more detail the ethical issues embedded
in their pedagogical approaches to literary study. All teachers have a
professional obligation to think about the effects of their own and
other teachers' curricular goals, texts, and activities on their students
and on the civic communities they inhabit together. We raise these
issues as questions because our principal purpose is to initiate discussion of them, even though we suggest how we would answer them.

Asking Students to Draw Social Generalizations
from Selected Literary Works

Should students be asked to draw generalizations about a society
from a group of literary works selected by their teacher? There would
seem to be several ethical reasons why students should not be asked,

implicitly or explicitly, to draw blanket social generalizations from a group of literary works the teacher has selected. To understand these reasons, one must first remember the way in which teachers ordinarily select literary texts for study by a class. Teachers usually select a small group of works for study to illustrate a theme, an author's oeuvre, a historical period, or a literary movement that they wish to use as an organizing principle. This procedure is academically and ethically sound so long as the works do, in fact, illustrate the theme, the author, the period, or the movement the teacher has in mind. In this respect, Taylor's grouping is pedagogically responsible; the three works she recommends do reflect the theme of the search for justice and dignity. (In Price's article, however, none of the works illustrates the American Dream.) If the works selected by the teacher illustrate the organizing principle positively, or at least illustrate it *both* positively and negatively for contrast, as in the suggested unit on the American Dream on pages 198 and 199 in *Fostering the Reader's Response: Rethinking the Literature Curriculum, Grades 7–12* by Peter Smagorinsky and Steven Gevinson (1989), it is then, in general, appropriate for students to be asked to discuss the nature of the society portrayed in these works and to compare the various authors' perceptions of society, as revealed by the civic communities in their literary works, with the students' own perceptions of their society.

The first ethical issue concerns the way in which the learning process is framed by the teacher. Is it legitimate for a teacher to select a small group of literary works for study and then ask students to reason inductively to arrive at the very social generalizations that the teacher used for selecting the works? This procedure would appear to be a misuse of inductive learning; in such a framework, students can "discover" only what the instructor has arranged for them to discover about their society. No genuine open-ended learning can take place.

A second, related issue concerns the learning outcome formulated by the teacher. How legitimate are the generalizations students arrive at after studying a teacher-selected group of literary texts? They would not appear to have much validity since other works almost always exist as counter-evidence for these generalizations and could have been read instead of or, better yet, in addition to those that were read. For example, Price has chosen certain works because they lend themselves to the development of the generalization about "American society" that she wants her students to discover. She does not use works that do not lend themselves to this end. Thus, her students are being asked to draw conclusions from a systematically limited sample of a phenomenon.

If, for example, her students were to read Willa Cather's *My Antonia* or *O Pioneers*, or Louisa May Alcott's *Little Women* or *Jo's Boys*, in addition to Kate Chopin's *The Awakening*, and if they were to compare all these novels with, for example, Gustave Flaubert's *Madame Bovary*, Leo Tolstoy's *Anna Karenina*, Pearl Buck's *The Good Earth*, or Thomas Hardy's *Tess of the D'Urbervilles*, they could not reach the exact conclusion that she has sought to have them reach—that the nineteenth-century "oppression" of women in America was monolithic and unique. It also is unlikely that her students could reach the precise conclusions that she has sought to have them reach about the disenfranchisement of black Americans if they also read James Comer's *Maggie's American Dream*, a true story about a strong-minded black mother whose stress on hard work and the value of formal education contributed to her children's many academic and professional achievements despite the realities of racial discrimination. This work might offer valuable insights to white, black, and nonblack, nonwhite students alike.

Similarly, if students in a course based on Taylor's suggested unit of study were to read Monica Sone's autobiography, *Nisei Daughter*, published in 1953, in addition to *Farewell to Manzanar*, they would gain a broader perspective on how Japanese-American adults who as children experienced internship in California during World War II have reflected on and integrated this experience. And if students also read *Maggie's American Dream* or Charles Willie's *Five Black Scholars*, a book about the stages of development in the careers of five black American scholars and the factors that led to their achievement, they might develop a more balanced point of view about the possibilities for black Americans to achieve justice and dignity in a country in which prejudice exists. They might also see white Americans as individuals, rather than as stock characters in fairy tales symbolizing various evils or vices.

An academic issue that emerges from these ethical issues is the question about the extent to which works of fiction can be used as primary sources for drawing generalizations about a society. The works that students are asked to read for literary study are not a random sample, and certainly not a large enough random sample, of a large body of literature from which one might, like a social scientist, draw a valid, if tentative, conclusion about society. Nor are they even a representative sample. Works of literature cannot strictly be chosen as representative of a particular society in the same sense that researchers devise representative samples of a phenomenon. For a sample to be representative of a phenomenon, all distinguishing features of the phenomenon must be accounted for, but only to the extent that they reflect their true proportions in the whole phenomenon. A selection of literary works for classroom study can at best reflect only an individual instructor's beliefs and professional judgments.

Even if it were possible to select a random or a representative sample of literary works set in a particular society at a particular time, any conclusion students might draw could be *only* about what literary writers seem to have to say about their society, that is, their personal visions. And what literary writers say is not necessarily a realistic description of a society, especially since so many frequently live on its psychological edges. Unless one equates works of the imagination with ethnographic reports, thereby reducing the imagination to little more than a mirror of reality (no matter how many literary qualities an ethnographic report may have), even a large random sample from a corpus of literary works is unlikely to provide a completely realistic and accurate picture of a particular society at a particular time. Literary works express many different truths about a society, but no one single truth. Thus, the extent to which a work of the imagination can be used to derive a social generalization is inherently limited.

Unfortunately, these uses of literature are apparently not confined to the English class. A recent textbook focusing on the motives and experiences of American immigrants in the nineteenth and twentieth centuries (Glade & Giese, 1989), provides an example of these ethical issues in the secondary school social studies class. In one of the chapters, students are given different types of reading selections and asked to "try to decide whether [they] believe the immigrants were treated unfairly and, if so, who was responsible" (p. 14). One of the selections consists of excerpts from Anzia Yezierska's novel, *Bread Givers*, published in 1925. The excerpts depict a Russian-Jewish immigrant woman's experiences in New York City with her employer, her landlady, and her teacher at night school, all of whom behave cruelly or insensitively to her. The following passage, one of the excerpts published in this social studies text, depicts her experience with night school:

> Great dreams spurred my feet on my way to night school.
> "What do you want to learn?" asked the teacher at the desk.
> "I want to learn everything in the school from the beginning to the end."
> She raised the lids of her cold eyes and stared at me. "Perhaps you had better take one thing at a time," she said, indifferently. "There's a commercial course, manual training—"

"I want a quick education for a teacher," I cried.

A hard laugh was my answer. Then she showed me the lists of the different classes, and I came out of my high dreams by registering for English and arithmetic.

Then I began five nights a week in a crowded class of fifty, with a teacher so busy with her class that she had not time to notice me.

The other selections on the immigrant experience are similarly pitched. On the basis of these selections and the excerpts from the novel, there is only one conclusion the students can arrive at concerning fair treatment of immigrants.

In a later section on "evaluating sources," students are asked to think about whether "a novel is less reliable because the author may alter the 'facts' to make a point" (p. 25), the implication being that it is not. Clearly, no one would dispute that Yezierska's novel reflects her own vision of the immigrant experience and perhaps her personal experiences in detail; it is a valuable work for students today to read. What is at issue is the ethical nature of the invitation the editors of this textbook have extended to students in asking them to draw a conclusion about the immigrant experience from these and the other literary and nonliterary excerpts that the editors themselves have provided. The students have done no independent research to discover the range of materials available on the topic and what is in them.

Using Literary Study to Impose Social Views on Students

Should teachers use literary study deliberately as a means for imposing their social views on their students and for attempting to change students' cultural values? What is also of concern in Price's (1989) description of her pedagogical rationale is her view of her students' cultural values. She believes they have a view of life that is "narrow and exclusive" (p. 22); they seem, to her, to want nothing more than financial success, material possessions, and a conventional family. She thus strangely implies that most of those "who have been effectively disenfranchised from the system" (p. 23) do not necessarily want these things too. Yet, to mention only one contradictory point of view, this does not seem to be the judgment of the editor of *Issues & Views*, a newsletter "on issues affecting the black community." In an article in the Winter 1990 issue on why she believes so much of the black community has failed to advance in the past decade, Elizabeth Wright writes, "the key to escaping poverty lies in a commitment to business enterprise. . . . we failed again [in the 1980s] to make the vital connection between the possession of wealth and the ability to control what happens to our families and our communities" (p. 3). It is not clear why Price assumes her college students come to her course with no decent values and beliefs and why she thinks she has the right to impose her own social views on them and to try to change whatever values and beliefs they have. Such an assumption is contrary to the meaning of a liberal education and its goal of moral and intellectual autonomy.

Choosing Literature for Its Possible Rhetorical Effects

Two final ethical questions are perhaps of greatest concern. First, should literature be selected and taught, at the secondary school level especially, for its possible rhetorical effects, that is, chosen and used with chiefly nonaesthetic criteria in mind? This question involves what may be an implicit double standard. We suspect that most teachers would agree that it is morally reprehensible and intellectually irresponsible for teachers to use the study of literature to create blind, unthinking devotion to a civic community (and we believe it is). If so, then isn't it equally morally reprehensible for teachers to select literature or to use the study of literature for the purpose of fostering ethnic or religious animosity and of creating in their students ill-will toward their civic communities? We believe it is, especially in a republican form of government in which teachers have a responsibility to reduce ethnic and religious animosity, to create in their students a sense of responsibility for the common good, and to prepare them for responsible participation in community life. Thus, it would appear to be unethical for literature to be selected and taught chiefly for its negative effects, particularly when selecting literature on aesthetic grounds frequently results in works that are highly critical of society. Moreover, while teachers have a right to expose students to literary voices that may be filled with anger toward American society, do they have a right to exclude other equally worthy literary voices—voices that would broaden the range of perspectives that students are exposed to—on nonaesthetic grounds? The problem of internal censorship lies at the heart of this question.

The second ethical question concerns the responsibility of teachers of literature toward their own discipline. If teachers of literature do not teach literature for its aesthetic effects, nor engage students in appreciation of the writer's craft and the literary imagination, who else can or will?

Professional educational organizations have an obligation to discuss the ethical issues embedded in pedagogical goals, literary choices, and learning activities that seem to promote students' latent or active hostility to their civic communities and to other students or adults who happen to belong to any group whose individual members engaged in, or are perceived as having engaged in or benefited from, discriminatory practices in the past. Professional organizations may well need to formulate ethical guidelines to prevent students from being manipulated by those teachers who would attempt to use the study of literature (or history, current events, or science) to foster inter-ethnic animosity or national self-hatred, or whose courses of study seem to have that effect even when the ostensible pedagogical goals appear to be reasonable and worthy of a liberal education. A distinction would need to be made between the kind of socially conscious literature that depicts social flaws and points to specific social or political reforms, as did Harriet Beecher Stowe's or Upton Sinclair's works, and a kind of socially conscious literature that seems to have destructive force. Such works should be studied for what they do and how they do it, and may best be studied in the context of a broad range of perspectives. Moreover, as Vale (1989) points out, negative works can also be studied positively.

Professional educational organizations also need to help all teachers understand clearly the mechanism, and the power of the mechanism, by which some of these anti-civic and anti-social effects are created.

CURRICULAR IMPLICATIONS AND CONSIDERATIONS

The contemporary thrust in school literature programs is a positive one of including, from the primary grades on, works of literary quality about the many social groups in this country, in addition to works of intellectual and historical significance in general and works with particular reference to our own civic communities. From a humanistic perspective, such a curriculum is part of a liberal education. Moreover, many of the same works or authors should be offered to all students, regardless of race, religion, or ethnicity. Even if the works all students read have few negative effects, the end result of a literature program in which white students read works centering only on white adults or children, and nonwhite students read works centering only on nonwhite children or adults, is not a liberal education. Public schools should be liberal, not parochial, in their spirit and

content, and the minds of *all* students need to be intellectually broadened.

From a civic perspective, however, much depends on the works
that are chosen, how they are taught, and the context in which they
are taught. Curriculum developers, teachers, and students need to
be aware that artistic expression has rhetorical as well as aesthetic
effects on the reader, a topic that has been frequently addressed by
Kenneth Burke since he published *Counter-Statement* in 1931. They
also need to be aware that some of these nonaesthetic effects may
concern the reader's civic identity as well as his or her civic conscience; that these effects on the reader's civic identity may range
from highly positive to highly negative; that negative effects may or
may not be consciously intended by the artist; and that negative
effects may lead to different forms of anti-social and anti-civic behavior, depending on the student's social group.

Theoretically, all works of literary quality should be eligible for
consideration in the curriculum. As long as works are appropriate for
grade level and reading ability, English teachers have a professional
obligation to introduce students to culturally and politically significant works in the past and in the present, from this country and
from other cultures, and from the entire range of ethnic and religious
communities in this country, regardless of topic or treatment. Works
of literary quality expressing a harsh critique of society belong in the
curriculum. At the same time, however, teachers have an ethical
obligation to explore whether their literature programs inadvertently
foment ethnic and racial animosities, alienate students from this
country's political principles and processes, or prevent development
of the intellectual and moral values that motivate responsible participation in a republican form of government. We badly need both
informal and formal research in the classroom on these issues.

At the close of his preface, Howard Mumford Jones (1966) warns
that "modern teaching and modern criticism must find some way
simultaneously to protect the autonomy of art and to warn readers
that art may conceivably betray the political republic" (pp. xi–xii). "It
may betray the political republic," he goes on to say, "by naively
assuming that a primary duty of the political republic is to protect the
republic of letters but that it is no primary duty of the republic of
letters to protect the health and safety of the political republic" (p.
xii). Jones's fears about the subtle but powerful anti-civic effects of
imaginative literature were expressed almost 30 years ago. The complex problem into which he had such profound insight has only deep-
ened and broadened.

While civic communities in earlier twentieth-century literature might be seen as callously indifferent, as in *The Grapes of Wrath*, or small-minded, as in Sinclair Lewis's *Main Street*, they were not generally portrayed as malignant. The entrepreneur, the corporate world, or capitalism itself might be depicted as driven by unprincipled and insatiable greed, often in collusion with corrupt politicians, but the civic communities in which corporate enterprise was embedded did not themselves embody evil and could still be considered redeemable even if indifferent or unwilling to exert themselves on behalf of citizens needing help. Today, however, many works of literature seem to feature a variety of wholesome, sympathetic nonwhite adults or children who have suffered greatly not from community indifference but from conscious community will, as in *Farewell to Manzanar* or, as another example of a frequently assigned work in the middle grades, Eleanor Coerr's *Sadako and the Thousand Paper Cranes*, a biography about a 12-year-old Japanese girl dying of a leukemia she contracted as a result of the bombing of Hiroshima.

Jones's warning poses an extraordinary challenge to English teachers today. English educators need to continue to incorporate the best and most illuminating literature from all the ethnic and religious communities that inhabit this country, regardless of the author's point of view toward his or her civic community or the majority of its citizens. At the same time, teachers also need to help their students understand how the effects of free artistic expression may unintentionally subvert the very political principles and processes that protect this expression.

To accomplish these goals, English educators might wish to explore with their students not only the aesthetic effects of a literary work but also its civic and social effects. They might also wish to explore the assumptions and values embedded in the design of the literature programs that they have created or that have been created for them to teach, for above all else, English teachers need to make sure that their literature programs are designed to foster a love and understanding of literature as literature.

PRACTICAL APPLICATIONS

To help teachers explore both the civic and social effects that may be created by the works of literature in their school programs, we suggest two related learning strategies. The first is a set of questions with a civic focus that their students can discuss to become aware of a work's possible civic and social effects. We use the term works of literature broadly to include plays, poems, biographies, autobiographies, essays, letters, song lyrics, cartoons—indeed, anything expressing verbal thought and imagination.

Suggested Questions for Classroom Discussion

Although most of the following questions can be asked about any work to spark classroom discussion, teachers should select the questions they believe are most appropriate for the work under discussion. We have organized them into seven clusters corresponding in most cases to the literary elements students would usually discuss.

1. Civic and Non-Civic Communities in the Work
What civic and non-civic communities are in the work? (Civic communities may be local, regional, state, or national; non-civic communities are frequently ethnic, religious, or racial in nature, although there are other kinds of non-civic communities.)
What symbols, images, and/or metaphors are used to describe these communities? How do they convey meaning? What is their effect?
What ethical principles or values seem to be embedded in these communities?
Do any of the communities in the work exhibit a pathology? If so, how is the dysfunction manifested?
Does the work provide an overall negative, mixed, or positive view of these communities?
Would you like to live in any of these communities? Why or why not?

2. Characters in the Work
In which communities are the major characters?
What are the social attributes of the major and minor characters in the civic communities and in any non-civic communities in the work?
What beliefs or values do they have?
Are there sympathetic or wholesome characters in both the civic and non-civic communities? Are there unappealing characters in each? If not, why do you think that is the case?
Could the behavior of the unappealing people be more civic-minded or socially responsible? If so, how?

3. Interaction of the Characters with the Community

How would you describe the interaction between each community and the main characters?

Is the community supportive or nonsupportive of the major characters? What suggests your answer?

If there are dysfunctions in the civic or non-civic community, do they affect all characters? Which ones? How?

4. Author's Language

Does the author use stereotypes or labels to refer to people? If so, what are they?

Do these labels apply to people in both the civic and non-civic communities in the work, or in only one? If so, which one?

Why do you think the author uses these labels?

Would you want these labels applied to you? Why or why not?

5. Context for the Novel and for the Events in the Novel

When does the story in the novel take place?

If there are serious social or political problems in this novel, do you know if these problems existed in other countries at the time the events in the novel took place?

Do you know if they exist today, here or elsewhere? If so, do they exist to the same degree? If not, what has changed? Do you have evidence to support your statements?

6. Overall Rhetorical Effects of the Work

How does this work make you feel about the various peoples and faiths in this country?

How does this work make you feel about your own civic community (local, state, or national) after you finish reading it?

How does it make you feel about the other communities in the work (if they are present)?

Do you think the author wants you to feel that way? Why?

7. Students' Local Civic or Non-Civic Communities

Are the communities in the work similar to your own community? If so, in what ways?

How are they different?

Do you know people who act like the characters in the work?

Do you think the people in your community today are like the people in the work (if the story took place a long time ago)?

The Civic Spectrum

We suggest the second strategy for teachers who wish to examine the kind of balance they now have in their literature programs. We are not suggesting that literary works be chosen for the particular effects they may have, only that teachers and students should be aware of them and that teachers should consider whether they have subconsciously engaged in a form of internal literary censorship that excludes some kinds of works, especially humorous ones. The English and social studies teachers who have used this "civic spectrum" have told us that they found class discussion a stimulating experience.

All the questions in the clusters can be used by students as they attempt to locate a work on a civic spectrum—a dimension along which literary works may be placed with respect to the overall attitudes their authors display toward the civic communities in their work. These attitudes may be reflected not only in the description, values, and/or behavior of the characters, major or minor, but also in the description of the setting, in the events that take place in the work, and in stylistic aspects of the literary work. We have classified the overall judgment a reader might make about an author's attitudes toward the literary civic community in his or her work into five categories, or points, on the spectrum. We emphasize that the spectrum cannot itself determine how an author's attitudes are embedded in the characters, setting, plot, language, and tone of a work; the placement of a literary text on the civic spectrum can only reflect the reader's judgment of the author's overall attitudes toward the civic community in his or her text. The spectrum is like the scale used for a holistic assessment of writing. It is an instrument for comparing readers' judgments about authors' attitudes toward their literary civic communities. Just as many compositions in a holistic assessment of writing do not appear to fit the points on the scale cleanly, so too many literary works cannot be categorized cleanly. Nevertheless, students can discuss their reasons for their judgments and arrive at a consensus judgment. Figure 3.1 illustrates the range of points on the civic spectrum from its negative pole to its positive pole.

We label one set of attitudes that an author may display about the civic community in his or her literary work "civic negation or antagonism," a point of view that forms one end of the civic spectrum—its negative pole. Ralph Ellison's *The Invisible Man* might be a prose example of civic negation, as suggested by the powerful passage describing his grandfather's death ("agree 'em to death and

Figure 3.1   The Civic Spectrum

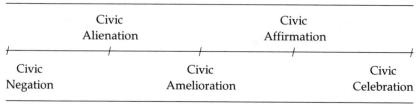

destruction"). Another kind of example of total civic negation might be Lou Reed's song "Hold On" in his album, *New York*. The song presents a view of the city as inexorably grim and victimizing of its citizens. The Statue of Liberty is called the Statue of Bigotry. The civic community seems to be pathological without qualification, with no hope of amelioration or escape by its citizens. Such a work may leave readers so overwhelmed by the total civic antagonism expressed in the piece that they feel paralyzed to do anything about it.

As we move across the civic spectrum, we use the phrase "civic alienation" or "civic dissaffection" to designate a second set of attitudes toward a civic community in a literary work. Works in this category exhibit pessimism, malaise, apathy, or extreme self-absorption, but not outright rejection of the civic community. One example might be Herman Melville's novella, *Bartleby the Scrivener*. In it, he shows the corruption of municipal government in nineteenth-century New York City and dramatizes civic alienation in both the employer as well as the scribe. The former is willing to sacrifice the good of the city for private gain; the latter is completely detached from the demands of the civic community itself. The civic community of the novella does not protect the common good, but functions according to self-interest alone. No opportunity for amelioration is presented in the literary text. But even though the work triggers a mood of cynicism, and its effect on the reader is quite negative, no hatred toward the civic community is evoked.

Moving toward the center point on the civic spectrum, we use the phrase "civic amelioration" to designate a third set of attitudes toward a civic community in literary work. Works in this category focus on this country's flaws and implicitly or explicitly urge a correction for a pathological condition in society or in some of its citizens. However, they express no rejection or hatred of the civic community as an entity. A well-known example is Upton Sinclair's *The Jungle*, a novel about the Lithuanian immigrants at the turn of the century who worked under nauseating conditions in the Chicago stockyards.

His novel is commonly acknowledged to have changed significantly the American meatpacking industry and caused the passage of the Pure Food and Drug Act. Other imaginative works of literature have also changed the ways in which people thought about social issues and social policies. Harriet Beecher Stowe's *Uncle Tom's Cabin*, for example, had a major impact on thinking about slavery in nineteenth-century America, while Anna Sewall's *Black Beauty*, a nineteenth-century British work, gave impetus to the formation of societies to prevent cruelty to animals and children.

We move past the center point of the civic spectrum toward its positive pole. We call a fourth set of attitudes toward a literary civic community "civic affirmation." Although works in this category show this country as an imperfect society with moral flaws, they emphasize its positive features. John Hersey's *A Bell for Adano*, a novel set in World War II in Adano, Italy, is one example of this category. His portrait of American society is strongly affirmative, even though the American community in the novel—primarily the American military—represents a spectrum of American society in which moral infractions are evident. In Major Joppolo, an Italian-American around whom the action occurs, the novelist presents American civic behavior at its best; Joppolo is a citizen with an abiding faith in the principles and values of American democracy and an unswerving commitment to its practices.

At the opposite end of the civic spectrum from civic negation or antagonism is a fifth set of attitudes that we call "civic celebration." A familiar example to most readers would be the short essay, "What Is an American?," from *Letters from an American Farmer*, written by J. Hector St. John de Crevecoeur and first published in 1782. The praise Crevecoeur expresses for this new nation is extravagant; this country gives the poor European immigrant "his land, bread, protection, and consequence." Another kind of example of civic celebration of the national community might be Katherine Lee Bates's poem, "America the Beautiful," an example of a lyric as unlike Lou Reed's "Hold On" as is possible. It praises the physical beauty and riches of this country and its heritage, and although its verses urge divine help in "mending" its flaws and in strengthening its self-control and dedication to law, it also invokes divine blessing on what she believes are its national values and purposes—brotherhood in freedom.

The questions we have suggested for discussing the civic community in an individual work and for locating a work on a civic spectrum can also be used for discussing the nature of the non-civic communities that frequently co-exist in these works. They can also be used for facilitating comparisons with the civic communities in cross-cultural works. By focusing students' attention on the nature of the civic communities that may exist in literary works—in essence, foregrounding their backgrounds—teachers may heighten students' awareness of the civic and social effects of a literary work and the ways in which literary authors may enhance or lessen their motivation to promote the common good.

REFERENCES

Adler, M. (1982). *The paideia proposal: An educational manifesto*. New York: Macmillan.

Burke, K. (1931). *Counter-statement*. New York: Harcourt, Brace.

Burns, P. (1985). Desperate in Peoria. *English Journal, 74*, 76–77.

Cameron, J. (1990, November). *Shafts of sunlight: Reclaiming our humanity in twentieth-century literature*. Paper presented at the National Conference of Teachers of English, Atlanta.

Clark, G. (1990, March). *The epideictic function of narrative*. Abstract of paper presented at the Conference on College Composition and Communication, Chicago.

Dunlap, J. (1989, December). Kiddie litter. *American Spectator*, pp. 19–21.

Glade, M. E., & Giese, J. R. (Adapters). (1989). *Immigration: Pluralism and national identity*. Boulder, CO: Social Science Education Consortium.

Iiams, C. (1980). *Civic attitudes reflected in selected basal readers for grades one through six used in the United States from 1900–1970*. Unpublished dissertation, University of Idaho, Caldwell.

Jones, H. M. (1966). *Jeffersonianism and the American novel*. New York: Teachers College Press.

Nelms, B. (1989). Holden's reading. EJ Forum. *English Journal, 78*, 13.

Price, J. (1989). Teaching the American dream. *The Leaflet, 88*, 22–26.

Ravitch, D. (1987). Tot sociology, or what happened to history in the grade schools. *The American Scholar, 56*, 343–354.

Ravitch, D., & Finn, C. (1987). *What do our 17-year-olds know?* New York: Harper & Row.

Scholes, R. (1985). *Textual power: Literacy theory and the teaching of English*. New Haven: Yale University Press.

Smagorinsky, P., & Gevinson, S. (1989). *Fostering the reader's response: Rethinking the literature curriculum, grades 7–12*. Palo Alto, CA: Dale Seymour Publications.

Stotsky, S., Anderson, P., with Beierl, D. (1990). *Variety and individualism in the English class: Teacher-recommemded lists of reading for grades 7–12*. Pull-out section. *The Leaflet, 89*, 1–11.

Tanner, G. (1907). Report of the committee appointed by the English Conference to inquire into the teaching of English in the high schools of the Middle West. *The School Review, 15*, 37–45.

Taylor, P. (1988). None of us is smarter than all of us: The reform in California's curriculum. *English Journal, 77,* 14–19.

Vale, G. (1989). Mollified in Madison: Optimism in contemporary American literature. *English Journal, 78,* 19–24.

Windhover, R. (1979). Literature in the nineteenth century. *English Journal, 69,* 28–33.

Wright, E. (1990). Still no economic path in sight: Doing our famous re-run of the 1960s. *Issues & Views, 6,* 1, 3, 5, 6, 8, 10, 12.

FICTION AND NONFICTION WORKS CITED

Alcott, Louisa May. (1868/1947). *Little women.* New York: Grosset & Dunlap.

Alcott, Louisa May. (1886/1933). *Jo's boys.* Boston: Little Brown.

Angelou, Maya. (1969). *I know why the caged bird sings.* New York: Random House.

Bates, Katherine Lee. (1978). ''America the Beautiful.'' In N. Sullivan (Ed.), *The treasury of American poetry: A collection of the finest by America's poets* (pp. 299–300). Garden City, NY: Doubleday. (Original work published 1893)

Buck, Pearl. (1932). *The good earth.* New York: Grosset & Dunlap.

Cather, Willa. (1913). *O Pioneers.* Boston: Houghton Mifflin.

Cather, Willa. (1918). *My Antonia.* Boston: Houghton Mifflin.

Chopin, Kate. (1899/1981). *The awakening and selected stories.* New York: Modern Library.

Coerr, Eleanor. (1977). *Sadako and the thousand paper cranes.* New York: Putnam.

Comer, James. (1988). *Maggie's American dream: The life and times of a black family.* New York: New American Library.

Cormier, Robert. (1974). *The chocolate war.* New York: Pantheon.

de Crevecoeur, J. Hector St. John. (1782/1926). *Letters from an American farmer.* New York: J. M. Dent.

Ellison, Ralph. (1952). *The invisible man.* New York: Vintage Books.

Fitzgerald, F. Scott. (1925). *The great Gatsby.* New York: Scribners.

Flaubert, Gustave. (1881/1957). *Madame Bovary.* (Lowell Bair, Trans.). New York: Bantam Books.

Golding, William. (1954). *Lord of the flies.* New York: Coward McCann.

Hardy, Thomas. (1891/1980). *Tess of the D'Urbervilles.* New York: Zodiac Press.

Hersey, John. (1944). *A bell for Adano.* New York: Sun Dial Press.

Hersey, John. (1946). *Hiroshima.* New York: Knopf.

Hinton, S. E. (1967). *The outsiders.* Boston: Little Brown.

Houston, Jeanne Wakatsuki. (1973). *Farewell to Manzanar.* Boston: Houghton Mifflin.

James, Henry. (1881/1950). *Washington Square.* New York: Doric Books.

Knowles, John. (1959). *A separate peace.* New York: Bantam.

Lewis, Sinclair. (1920). *Main Street*. New York: Harcourt Brace.

Melville, Herman. (1853/1949). *Bartleby the scrivener*. In Jay Leyda (Ed.), *The complete short stories of Herman Melville*. New York: Random House.

Miller, Arthur. (1949/1989). *Death of a salesman*. Atlantic Highlands, NJ: Humanities Press International.

Miller, Arthur. (1953/1989). *The crucible*. Atlantic Highlands, NJ: Humanities Press International.

Momaday, N. Scott. (1968). *House made of dawn*. New York: Harper & Row.

Reed, Lou. (1988). "Hold On." In the album *New York*. Metal Machine Music.

Salinger, J. D. (1951). *Catcher in the rye*. Boston: Little Brown.

Sewall, Anna. (1877/1983). *Black Beauty: The autobiography of a horse*. New York: Rand McNally.

Sinclair, Upton. (1906/1981). *The jungle*. New York: Bantam.

Silko, Leslie Marmon. (1977). *Ceremony*. New York: Viking Press.

Sone, Monica. (1953). *Nisei daughter*. Boston: Little Brown.

Steinbeck, John. (1937). *Of mice and men*. New York: Modern Library.

Steinbeck, John. (1939). *The grapes of wrath*. New York: Viking Press.

Stowe, Harriet Beecher. (1852). *Uncle Tom's cabin*. Boston: Jewett & Co.

Tolstoy, Leo. (1873/1963). *Anna Karenina*. New York: Dell.

Twain, Mark. (1884/1967). *The adventures of Huckleberry Finn*. New York: St. Martin's Press.

Walker, Alice. (1982). *The color purple*. New York: Harcourt Brace.

Willie, Charles V. (1986). *Five black scholars: An analysis of family life, education, and career*. Lanham, MD: Abt.

Yep, Laurence. (1975). *Dragonwings*. New York: Harper & Row.

Yezierska, Anzia. (1925). *Bread givers*. New York: George Braziller.

Zindel, Paul. (1968). *The pigman*. New York: Harper & Row.

Reclaiming Our Humanity in Twentieth-Century Literature

JOHN W. CAMERON

Having taught twentieth-century literature to secondary students for more than 30 years, I am convinced that the spirit of disillusionment and despair so often associated with the artistic achievements of our time receives a disproportionate amount of attention in the classroom. To counter this cynicism and pessimism, I recently spent a year as a National Endowment for the Humanities/*Reader's Digest* Teacher-Scholar in search of works by artists who offer a balanced understanding of the human heart and who renew our faith in the human spirit. The topic of my research was "Reclaiming Our Humanity in Twentieth-Century Literature, Music, and Art." This annotated reading list is one of the results. It introduces to fellow teachers and their students some writers who have written joyfully and honestly of our dignity and potential.

The Family as Unifying Force

Allende, Isabel (1986). *House of the Spirits*. New York: Bantam.
> The struggle and survival that are such a vital part of the lives of three valiant women in this family saga of four generations provide the peace and reconciliation that emerge finally from the bloody and tragic events of this political novel.

Busch, Frederick (1981). *Rounds*. New York: Ballantine.
> There is much grief in this story of lives shattered by death; however, Busch ultimately celebrates the dignity of the family and demonstrates convincingly that love lost can be regained. Here is the Job story for our times; we are inspirited by these characters' responses to life.

Courtenay, Bryce (1990). *The Power of One*. New York: Ballantine.
> South Africa during and after World War II serves as the testing ground for Peekay, who is determined to become boxing champion of the world. This highly readable novel illustrates "the power to believe in yourself . . . and then daring your courage to follow your thoughts." (For a comparison, read Lynn Freed's *Home Ground*, which presents the problem of growing up in South Africa with a female hero.)

Cunningham, Laura (1989). *Sleeping Arrangements: A Memoir.*. New York: Alfred A. Knopf.

Here is a very special and unconventional look at family life. Eight-year-old Lily Shaine is raised by her two bachelor uncles in the AnaMor Towers, which is set on "a baseball fault zone" near Yankee Stadium. (A marvelous companion to E. L. Doctorow's *World's Fair*)

Doctorow, E. L. (1986). *World's Fair* (a novel-memoir). New York: Ballantine-Fawcett Crest Book.

The sights, smells, sounds of a Bronx neighborhood and the rituals of family life are captured through the eyes of Edgar Altschuler during the first nine years of his life. The most effective section is the last 100 pages when the narrator pays two visits to the World's Fair of 1939 and meshes the fears of annihilation brought on by the beginnings of World War II with the hope for the future represented by the fair itself.

Hoffman, Alice (1989). *At Risk*. New York: Berkeley.

The sense of everyday life is captured so well in this novel that has the AIDS issue in the forefront. The effects on a family and community when 11-year-old Amanda Farrell contracts AIDS reminds us how it is possible for ordinary people to be ennobled by suffering.

Jackson, Shirley (1948/1989). *Life Among the Savages*. Chicago: Academy Chicago.

Jackson deserves recognition beyond "The Lottery," and this book of family life is a constant reminder of her skills as a writer in a much lighter and more loving vein.

Kauffman, Janet (1987). *Collaborators*. New York: Penguin.

The title characters here are mother and daughter, two of the most exceptional and yet ordinary characters you are likely to encounter in literature. Kauffman retells "the age-old tale of how one generation replaces another . . . and thus makes it possible for us . . . to endure."

Kingsolver, Barbara (1988). *The Bean Trees*. New York: Harper and Row.

The problems of a search for self, of single parenthood, and of commitment to a political cause are handled with both humor and wisdom in this novel of the adventures of Taylor Green.

Shange, Ntozake (1987). *Betsey Brown*. New York: St. Martin's Press.

The black community of St. Louis in 1959, the year of school integration, is the background to the adolescent awakening of Betsey Brown. The loving family life presented here helps us understand why, in spite of personal and social obstacles, the young hero has a marvelous sense of confidence assuring her that she "was surely going to have her way."

Welty, Eudora (1970/1978). *Losing Battles*. New York: Random House-Vintage Books.

This sprawling novel is not particularly easy reading, but it is the best antidote to *Long Day's Journey into Night*. The human comedy of family life bursts forth on every page, and we are given little time to catch our breath before Welty presents us with another tall tale or an insight into the solidity of family life. This novel is wonderful proof of Welty's observation on her purpose as a writer: "It does lie in my nature to praise and celebrate things."

Coming to Awareness Is Coming Alive

Baker, Russell (1984). *Growing Up*. New York: New American Library.

Baker treats us to a nostalgic look at growing up in an America that has disappeared. This autobiography is more than a sentimental journey. The depiction of the strong bonds between mother and son— and the eventual breaking of this tie—becomes the reader's experience as well.

Hurston, Zora Neale (1937/1978). *Their Eyes Were Watching God*. Urbana: University of Illinois Press.

Hurston celebrates the life of a black woman who struggles long to discover her real self and how to live for that self and how to find a love that does not suffocate that self. Hurston writes prose that is celebratory of the ordinary things that make up our world.

MacNeil, Robert (1989). *Wordstruck*. New York: Penguin.

As the title suggests, MacNeil's memoir of youth concentrates on his growing fascination with words and the glories of the English language as he encountered them in his experiences growing up in Halifax, Nova Scotia. We need to be reminded and reassured that words do indeed deserve our attention because of their wonderful powers to fascinate, enthrall, and empower.

McClanahan, Ed (1984). *The Natural Man*. New York: Penguin.

There are so many coming-of-age stories that some of the best are likely to be lost: Here is my nomination for one that deserves attention. The humor here is downright earthy and life-affirming in the adventures of Harry Eastep from Needmore, Kentucky, and his friendship with "natural man" Monk McHorning, a six-foot-five, 238-pound, 15-year-old orphan.

Paulsen, Gary (1989). *The Winter Room*. New York: Watts.

This novel could be read as early as the fifth grade as well as appeal to adults. Paulsen's prose presents us with a kaleidoscope of the senses as they are experienced by an 11-year-old boy. This novel deserves to be read aloud.

Percy, Walker (1961/1988). *The Moviegoer*. New York: Ballantine-Ivy Books.

A young "successful" man realizes that his present life is without a base, and in the course of this short novel we see his groping to a genuine moral engagement as he breaks out of the "everydayness" of his life. Percy is a strong believer in "a divinity that shapes our ends."

Love Triumphant!

Burns, Olive Ann (1986). *Cold Sassy Tree*. New York: Dell.
>   Thankfully, Burns is not afraid to write about those old-fashioned virtues that make people caring and decent human beings: "I wanted to express the lyric wonder and electric yearning between two people in love." She succeeds, and her novel has the same appeal to me that Harper Lee's *To Kill a Mockingbird* evoked many years ago.

Carr, J. L. (1984). *A Month in the Country*. Chicago: Academy Chicago.
>   Dr. Johnson's definition of a novel as " . . . a small tale, generally of love . . . " is an apposite description of this wonderfully serene story of renewal, rejuvenation, and redemption. By story's end, a shell-shocked veteran of World War I finds the pulse of living beating strongly within him once again.

Garcia-Marquez, Gabriel (1989). *Love in the Time of Cholera*. New York: Penguin.
>   There is no such thing as unrequited love in this story of Florentino's half-century patient wait for Fermina's acceptance of his marriage proposal. We witness love in all its guises—young, old, conjugal, romantic, carnal. When we finish, we know the falsity of the old adage, "There is no greater glory than to die for love." We ask ourselves, "How many other novels of our time end on such a joyous note?"

Price, Reynolds (1963). *A Long and Happy Life*. New York: Avon-Bard Books.
>   There is more than a touch of irony in this title, but the love story of Wesley Beavers and Rosacoke Mustian delineates the search for love and the compromises that must be made by lovers. There is kindness, gentleness, and innocence in these portraits of North Carolina country people. The opening paragraph and the closing pages at the Delight Baptist Church Christmas Pageant are reason enough to understand why Price is a writer who never lets us forget the joy and renewal that can be present in our lives.

Stegner, Wallace (1988). *Crossing to Safety*. New York: Penguin.
>   In his examination of the lives of two couples, Stegner writes knowingly of strong friendships and enduring marital love. In these very ordinary lives, Stegner invests significance in what it really means to live life with purpose so that survival is made "a grace rather than a grim necessity." (Harriet Doerr's *Stones for Ibarra* handles the same themes with equal sensitivity.)

Let Us Now Praise (Extra)Ordinary Men and Women

Bambara, Toni Cade (1981). *Salt Eaters*. New York: Random House.
>   This novel asks much of its readers with its mosaic technique of relating the story of a despondent woman who is restored to life by her acceptance of risk, commitment, and solidarity. ("Are you sure you want to be well? . . . wholeness is not trifling matter. A lot of weight when you're well.")

Berry, Wendell (1975). *The Memory of Old Jack*. HBJ-Harvest Book.

All of Berry's fiction, poetry, and essays celebrate the rural way of life. We are present in the mind during the final day of life of this 92-year-old Kentucky farmer as he remembers his "faithfulness to his place" and his imminent kinship with the land. His own fulfillment as a human being shines through in the final pages before his death.

Brown, Rita Mae (1977/1988). *Rubyfruit Jungle*. New York: Bantam.

Being an outsider—female, gay, illegitimate, poor—does not stop Molly Bolt from making her way with defiance, intelligence, and good humor in this world. There are matchless evocations of childhood in this gutsy novel.

Cheng, Nien (1988). *Life and Death in Shanghai*. New York: Penguin.

Here is a moving testament to the strength and endurance of the human spirit in Cheng's account of her years of solitary confinement and torture during the Cultural Revolution.

Gaines, Ernest J. (1982). *The Autobiography of Miss Jane Pittman*. New York: Bantam.

Through his creation of the life of one remarkable black woman, Gaines has written the autobiography of a whole people, those who struggle against fate and hold on to their dignity and self-esteem. (Readers might wish to compare Miss Jane Pittman with Lucy Marsden in Alan Gurganus' *Oldest Living Confederate Widow Tells All* and, of course, the actual voice of Nat Shaw in *All God's Dangers*.)

Gardner, Herb (1988). *I'm Not Rappaport*. New York: Grove Press–An Evergreen Book.

Playwright tips his hat to lovable eccentrics and old age and reminds us once again—as he did in *A Thousand Clowns*—that we must not give up on this broken planet of ours.

Least Heat Moon, William (1984). *Blue Highways*. New York: Ballantine-Fawcett Crest Book.

I find this "travel book" much richer than Steinbeck's *Travels with Charley*. There are so many voices to listen to on the backroads of America, and the author is adept at finding people "who worry less about making a living than making a life." To know the importance of our own lives is undoubtedly what we want more than anything else.

Terkel, Studs (1975). *Working*. New York: Avon.

In its own way this book allows us to hear America singing—and the refrains are not always joyful. Terkel's honesty can only be applauded as he lets his workers/talkers reveal their despair and joy, their frustrations and aspirations about the work they do all day, almost every day of their lives.

The Magic in Ordinary Life

Beagle, Peter (1976/1988). *A Fine and Private Place*. New York: Ballantine.

Written when Beagle was 21 years old, this fantasy (grounded in reality) asks its readers to see life with a renewed sense of wonder—to see the magic in being human. Although the novel's setting is a cemetery, Beagle makes clear that his concern is not with life after death but the death-in-life.

Helprin, Mark (1984). *Winter's Tale*. New York: Pocket Books.

This mixture of fantasy and realism goes on too long for my liking. However, Helprin deserves to be known to serious readers of literature because of his visionary and poetic powers. This novel calls on its characters to "celebrate selfless love, devotion to beauty, desire to explore, and acceptance of responsibility." There are many wonderful set-pieces that could stand alone and be shared with others.

Keillor, Garrison (1989). *We Are Still Married: Stories and Letters*. New York: Penguin.

Often in less than a page or two, Keillor manages to elevate the ordinary lives of men, women, and children so that we are genuinely moved by their actions. "The Meaning of Life" is a particular favorite: "Gentleness is everywhere in daily life, a sign that faith rules through ordinary things." The title of Keillor's first collection sums up the theme of all his work: HAPPY TO BE HERE.

Kinsella, W. P. (1983). *Shoeless Joe*. New York: Ballantine.

The film *Field of Dreams* has already shown the appeal of this novel. Kinsella unashamedly celebrates the imagination most of us fail to use and reminds us that living and loving and striving after dreams are indeed worthy goals. (I have not met anyone who liked the film better than the novel.)

Wilder, Thornton (1973/1988). *Theophilus North*. New York: Carrol & Graf.

One fine summer in Newport, Theophilus North weaves his life-affirming magic on a number of denizens who have accepted too many of society's anesthetizing temptations and who need the help of such a magician. Wilder is having fun here, and so can the reader.

Willard, Nancy (1985/1989). *Things Invisible to See*. New York: Bantam.

There are so many classifications for this amazing story—a love story, a baseball yarn, a story of family life. But most of all, it is the story of things invisible to see: "a network of beings which are a part of life, though they pass among the living for the most part unrecognized." Willard allows her readers to see that so much of everyday life is filled with magic.

Discovering Our Relationship with All Things

Dillard, Annie (1974/1988). *Pilgrim at Tinker Creek*. New York: Harper & Row.

There is poetry and passion in Dillard's meditations on self, nature, and God—and their kinship. Dillard always begins with immediate experience ("I am no scientist. I explore the neighborhood.") and then soars as she reminds us of the free gifts that the universe gives us daily.

Erlich, Gretel (1986). *The Solace of Open Spaces*. New York: Penguin.

This book contains 12 ruminations on Erlich's personal attachment to the "planet of Wyoming." She lets us see vividly the beauty of this world along with the harshness of solitary living that can diminish rather than bolster the human spirit. Although there is seriousness in her observations, she offers somber truths with humor: "We fill up space as if it were a pie shell, with things whose opacity further obstructs our ability to see what is already there."

A Conspiracy of Goodness: Solidarity of Spirit

Beauchemin, Yves (1988). *The Alley Cat*. New York: Holt.
This French-Canadian novel celebrates the struggle between good and evil on a grand and comic scale. The passion and humor of this story make us root loudly for the young hero and his accomplices in this tale of temptation and redemption.
Camus, Albert (1942/1972). *The Plague*. New York: Random House-Vintage Books.
This novel takes on a new significance for its readers in our AIDS-haunted times. Published soon after World War II, this novel vividly reminds us that "the first thing is not to despair." We must fight it as a condition of life. Together we must confront the plague—whatever it might be—with all our human resources.
Kenneally, Thomas (1983). *Schindler's List*. New York: Penguin.
The Holocaust has become the principal metaphor for the evil of our century, and Kenneally makes its evil all too palpable here. But he also shows us a man who saved the lives of 1300 Jews because of his profound moral passion. One book reviewer described this book as "the remarkable story of a man who saved lives when every sinew of civilization was devoted to destroying them." (Pierre Sauvage's film *Weapons of the Spirit* recounts the protection of 5000 Jews by 5000 Christians during Nazi-occupied France—a fitting companion to the novel.)
Lapierre, Dominique (1986). *The City of Joy*. New York: Warner Books.
This widely popular work makes concrete the belief that from human misery (the slums of Calcutta) can emerge joy and restorative powers. The story is peopled with those whose selfless actions have already earned them the title of saint (Mother Teresa) and those whose generosity of spirit comes naturally out of their love for their fellow beings.

Speaking Hopefully of Our Future

Moyers, Bill (1989). *A World of Ideas*. New York: Doubleday.
This work comprises interviews with 42 extraordinary men and women whose keen insights into our minds and hearts should make us generally hopeful about the future. Especially stimulating for me are the ideas expressed by William Gaylin, Vartan Gregorian, Sarah Lawrence Lightfoot, and Leon Kass.

Vittachi, Anuradha (1989). *Earth Conference One: Sharing a Vision for Our Planet*. Boston: New Science Library/Shambhala.

The threat of our planet's extinction was the topic of this 1988 conference in England, bringing together political, scientific, and religious leaders from around the world. In spite of all the articulated fears about the future of our planet, the message that emerges is that we can learn "again to be part of the Earth and not separate from it."

4 On Developing Independent Thinking and Responsible Writing

What We Can Learn from Studies of the Research Process

SANDRA STOTSKY

Although writing has traditionally been viewed by educators as a means for expressing the imagination and for communicating ideas, in recent years many educators have come to see writing as possibly the foremost tool for promoting thinking and learning. Current research in the field of writing provides some support for this hypothesis, as William McGinley and Robert Tierney (1989) note in a review of this research. However, they also observe that, for the most part, this research shows only how thinking has been influenced by the specific "types" and "sequences" of writing activities that students have been directed to engage in by researchers. McGinley and Tierney argue that researchers should focus much more on the ways in which critical thinking processes are stimulated when students can determine their own types and sequences of reading and writing activities, especially for complex, open-ended assignments. They believe that self-directed reading and writing activities, because they are apt to entail an examination of "multiple perspectives," or different ways of viewing a subject, may foster critical thinking more fully and effectively than teacher- or researcher-directed reading and writing activities. Their argument underscores the need for teachers and researchers to pay greater attention than they have to the thinking processes involved in the research assignment, probably the most important vehicle teachers at all educational levels have for fostering independent thinking and responsible writing—those critical habits of the mind that contribute to the ability to promote the common good.

THE VALUES OF THE RESEARCH PAPER

Beyond its perceived institutional function of preparing students for academic research and writing in other disciplines, what intellectual values do English teachers attach to the research paper? In general, they seem to view it as a means to develop students' thinking and to help them learn how to satisfy their intellectual curiosity on their own. This view is as prevalent at the college level as in the secondary school. For example, Thomas Trzyna (1983), a college teacher, sees the development of students' critical thinking skills as the teacher's primary objective for the research paper. Jean Johnson (1987), the author of a handbook on the research process for college students, explains that in writing a research paper students learn how to conduct a "deliberate, directed search" beyond their own experience for something they want to know. The research assignment, she elaborates, gives them the opportunity to explore the ideas and experiences of others and to make discoveries about these ideas and experiences.

Similarly, Richard Corbin and Jonathan Corbin (1978), the authors of a guide for high school English teachers, propose that the research assignment helps students learn

1. How to explore and become more knowledgeable about a subject of concern to them, whether it is related to their plans for the future or to some present hobby or other personal interest
2. How to select and use the standard tools of research
3. How to carry to its conclusion a process of critical and logical thinking
4. How to organize and report the ideas and information collected on a subject in the standard form expected in business and college writing

Lee Allen and Bethany Nichols (1985), the authors of a guide for the research process in English classes, grades 6–12, also see the purpose of the research assignment as helping students to learn something they did not know before and to demonstrate that they have thought about it. For Allen and Nichols, the research project is an opportunity for students to acquire

a number of important life skills, including the ability to formulate hypotheses, to use a variety of research techniques to gather information, to use the resources of a library, to organize and synthesize information, to draw reasonable inferences and conclusions, and to present the results of an investigation effectively and interestingly, both orally and in writing. (p. 1)

Discussing the research assignment from a somewhat different perspective, Moffett and Wagner (1976) claim that the most crucial skill developed in the composition of informative articles is "explaining one's material" (p. 362).

The intellectual values these teachers mention range from broad thinking processes to a number of more specific ones. Clearly, as students learn how to satisfy their curiosity about a topic of their own choosing without reliance on a teacher, they must of necessity engage in a variety of thinking processes in order to locate, evaluate, organize, and present relevant ideas and information. But the research-based writing assignment can also help develop critical ethical values—values that are embedded in the process of carrying out and reporting research, values that students cannot learn as easily from other kinds of writing assignments. For example, students can learn as part of doing research and writing research papers that responsible writers seek information on all points of view about a question, evaluate the quality of the information that is gathered, support their generalizations with reasonable evidence, and present the results of their research clearly. Indeed, as students learn how to do research and to write research papers, they can develop much of the moral reasoning that should characterize public as well as academic discourse.

Yet the research assignment is not viewed favorably by many English educators; they feel it poses too many problems to be a meaningful writing assignment and ends up as a poor or negative learning experience for most students. For example, in a survey of composition instructors at their own university, Robert Schwegler and Linda Shamoon (1982) found that many of their colleagues believe students are "overwhelmed by what they find in outside sources and are incapable of weaving the information they have gathered into an argument that presents and defends their point of view" (p. 817). In a survey of 397 schools across the country, James Ford and Dennis Perry (1982) found college instructors frequently commenting on their students' inability to use a library well. Some college students themselves, as Jennie Nelson and John Hayes (1988) comment in a study of the research process at the college level, regard a research assignment as little more than an exercise in gathering and assembling chunks of material from library references and citing these chunks in academically acceptable ways. Thus, it is not surprising that many college English educators, according to Ford and Perry's nationwide survey and to Schwegler and Shamoon's survey of their own colleagues, have recommended abandoning the research paper altogether, not only in freshman composition courses but even throughout the entire undergraduate program.

In addition, some high school teachers consider the research paper an unjustifiable burden on all but the most capable college-bound students. Those teachers feel it is not worth the time and effort it takes to teach the research paper to students who may never complete high school or go on to postsecondary education. A few even claim that research papers that require students to examine sources other than works of literature as the primary documents are not the proper domain or responsibility of the English teacher. Nonetheless, to judge by the curriculum in most elementary and secondary schools and by the number of college composition programs in which the research paper is taught, most English educators must believe that the research assignment has enough intellectual benefit to warrant a place in the curriculum at all educational levels and for all students, despite the many problems students encounter with it.

THE PURPOSE OF THIS CHAPTER

In light of the intellectual and moral values the research assignment can embody, McGinley and Tierney (1989) are right to call for more research on the ways in which complex, self-directed writing and reading assignments stimulate critical thinking processes. And in light of all the concerns teachers have about the research paper, we also need more research on how teaching and learning with respect to the research paper can be improved. But before more research is carried out, it would be useful for both teachers and academic researchers to be aware of the findings and limitations of existing empirical studies in this area so that future research can be as pedagogically informative as possible. Remarkably, there seem to be only a few studies that touch on what students do as they go about selecting and narrowing a topic, locating sources, sifting through these sources, and developing, however tentatively, a central research question or thesis statement. However, there is much that we can learn from these few studies, especially with respect to the intellectual significance of when and how a thesis or controlling idea is formulated. Before we examine these studies in detail, we turn first to a closely related body of research on report writing. Its limitations will suggest why we have so few studies of the research process and its role in the development of independent thinking and responsible writing.

REPORT WRITING BASED ON GIVEN SOURCES AND TOPICS

Perhaps the best-known studies addressing report writing are the two by the National Assessment of Educational Progress (Applebee, Langer, & Mullis, 1986; Applebee, Langer, Mullis, & Jenkins, 1990). Report writing, subsumed under informative writing in these two studies, was assessed by two types of tasks. Students in grades 4, 8, and 11 were asked to write one report based on information drawn from their own experience and several other reports based on given information. The latter tasks required students to summarize a science experiment depicted in a brief series of pictures showing different stages of a plant's growth, to describe a surrealistic painting, to write a newspaper article about a haunted house based on provided notes, and to explain to a business firm that an item ordered had not been received and to propose a course of action to the firm. (Another kind of informative writing assessed in these two studies was analytical writing; students in both studies were given informational material on "food on the frontier" and were asked to explain why modern-day food differs from frontier food. In the 1986 study, they were also given a second analytical writing task: to tell what their favorite type of music was and why.)

While all these types of tasks yield useful information on the development of some writing skills, they are not necessarily informative with respect to all the kinds of thinking and writing a research report entails. First, report writing based on personal information—on what the writer already knows—does not entail research at all; it requires reflection and recall. On the other hand, report writing, or even analytical writing, based on information (and a topic) provided by someone else does not tap what may be the four most crucial tasks in an open-ended research assignment—selecting a topic of interest, generating questions to pursue about the topic, locating seemingly relevant information, and then generating a working hypothesis, controlling idea, or point of view to govern the rest of the search and the final organization of the information. The authors of the 1990 study state that the tasks they have given students "reflect the diversity of purposes for which informative writing is undertaken" (p. 11). Yet, ironically, the tasks do not address the purpose of their own informative writing—to report on the development, synthesis, and significance of created, not given, information.

Nor do we really learn, from the self-reported data presented in another part of these studies, how frequently students are assigned research papers. The researchers collapsed all the types of writing students reported doing in school into two broad categories called imaginative writing and informative and persuasive writing, the latter category comprising essays, book reports, other reports, and letters (1986, pp. 76–77; 1990, p. 70). Because report writing in these assessments of student writing includes writing based on personal information, it is not possible to determine, from the statistics provided by the researchers for other reports, to what extent students even do research reports.

The way in which report writing was assessed and reported on in these studies raises several questions. First, is it useful for researchers to include in the same category reports based on personal information (what someone did or knows) and other kinds of reports? Second, is it useful to include journalistic accounts of an event with others kinds of reports? In his discussion of the research paper, Trzyna (1983) recommends making a distinction between inquiry, debate, and "mere reporting." Finally, and perhaps most important, how much do we really learn about the ability to write a research report when the information and the topic or research question are given to the students as part of the writing task? Clearly, the methodology used in assessing ability in report writing in these studies severely limits what we can learn about the skills involved in writing a research paper under natural conditions.

Regrettably, the NAEP studies are not the only ones to examine in this manner the thinking involved in academic writing. In a number of other studies on reading or writing in the past decade, researchers have assigned students writing tasks requiring a synthesis of given information for a given topic. The study by Margaret Kantz (1989) and the one by Nancy Spivey and James King (1989) are two examples. In the Kantz study, a small group of college undergraduates was asked to use the best ideas from research-given source materials "to explain to a group of engineering students how to write creatively" (p. 1). In the Spivey and King study, students in grades 6, 8, and 10 were asked to write a report "to inform people about Texas rodeos" using researcher-given source materials.

Robert Tierney and Timothy Shanahan (1991) refer to a number of other, similar studies in a section labeled "How Reading and Writing Contribute to Learning New Ideas'' in a comprehensive review of research on reading/writing relationships. As informative as the studies by David Hayes (1987), Kathleen Copeland (1987), Ann Penrose (1988), William McGinley (1988), John Ackerman (1989), and Stuart Greene (1989) may be about some of the thinking processes involved in academic writing, they give us little, if any, information about the thinking processes involved in the research process; the students in their studies were given the general topic and/or the sources to use for their writing activities. What these studies have inadvertently bypassed is how the selection of information from sources and the actual writing of a report are affected when students have the responsibility for choosing their own topic, locating possibly relevant information, and then generating their own controlling idea. Because they have controlled the topic, the sources of information, or both in their investigations of the thinking processes stimulated by academic writing, researchers have been unable to learn about the initial and fundamental stages in the research process. Moreover, their studies have possibly given teachers a misleading model of the nature of the research process.

Although the NAEP studies and the Spivey and King (1989) study described earlier provide no direct information about the research process, they do provide evidence on the significance of another major component of the research process—the ability to read. In these studies, and in earlier research by Spivey (1984), Kennedy (1985), and others, the researchers found that better readers tended to be better writers, whether of syntheses, essays, or other forms of writing. Apparently, the ability to evaluate, integrate, and organize information in a coherent way is strongly related to reading ability. It is reasonable to assume that poor readers are hampered at least as much during the research process as in a synthesis task or in composing an essay in response to given source material.

RESEARCH ON THE RESEARCH PROCESS

A Study of "Retrieval Skills" in Middle Grade Students

A possibly unique study focusing on "retrieval skills" of fourth- and eighth-grade students suggests how much students may vary in the quality of their research questions and working hypotheses (which in turn may affect the material that is selected for inclusion in a report). Although Akira Kobasigawa's (1983) research did not examine report writing itself, her study is informative because it examined thinking processes that are an essential part of the research process.

For part of her study, Kobasigawa asked 20 students in each grade to generate research questions for a possible report on China after listening to a short informational selection about that country. Among other things, she found that only one of the fourth-grade students generated an open-ended question, in contrast to 15 of the eighth-grade students. In another part of her study, the students were asked how they would proceed, using several books on the subject, to locate information on why China cannot produce enough food; they were also asked to formulate a tentative hypothesis to help guide their search (the researcher asked them to guess why China cannot produce enough food). Again, there were significant developmental differences between the two groups, as well as variation within each group, in the number of topic, or key, words students could generate to locate relevant information on the question and in their ability to construct an adequate hypothesis. In still another part of her study, students were asked to judge the suitability of given information as answers to specific questions. Again, Kobasigawa found significant developmental trends in what the two groups of students judged to be suitable or irrelevant, as well as variation within each group.

It is evident that the differences in the kinds and range of questions students ask about a subject of interest cannot help but affect what information they end up with. It is also more than likely that the working hypothesis a student constructs is influenced by the quantity and quality of the information gathered in an initial search (and by the way in which the student goes about evaluating and organizing initial notes). When students undertake research on a topic of their own choice, they may well discard some of the information they gather after sifting through it to form a controlling idea. Although we do not know exactly how the writing of a report is influenced by variations in the way in which students go about the various phases of the search process, the results of Kobasigawa's study give us reason to believe that report writing when the subject of research is self-selected and the search process completely self-directed may be different from report writing in response to given information and a given question. In all probability, the range in achievement may be extraordinarily broad; some students may compose better reports, and others much worse reports.

A Study of the Research Process in High School Students

Even the point at which students work out a tentative controlling idea or working hypothesis may influence how the material is organized and the ease of writing the first draft of the report. An intensive case study of how 26 Advanced Placement high school English students went about using library sources and writing two term papers each brings this issue, as well as several others, to the fore. As one of her findings, Carol Kuhlthau (1983) was able to identify six fairly distinct phases in the search process. In the first phase, which she labels Task Initiation, students sought possible topics for their research by talking with others and browsing through the library. In the second phase, labeled Topic Selection, students decided on a topic, usually after a preliminary search of library sources or after discussion with their friends, their teacher, or a librarian. In the third phase, labeled Pre-focus Exploration, students located information, took some notes, and surveyed a wide range of material in order to find a focus (or controlling idea) for their research. In the fourth phase, called Focus Formulation, students formed a focus around which to center their information gathering. To do this, they read their notes for ideas and used their notes in various ways to come up with one focus. In the fifth phase, labeled Information Collection, students systematically gathered information to "define, extend, and support their focus" (p. 245). At this point in the research process, students searched library sources comprehensively and took detailed notes. In the sixth phase, called Search Closure, students used various criteria to determine that their search was complete and organized their notes. They also rechecked sources and confirmed the information they had gathered. In a small follow-up case study of a few of the students four years later, Kuhlthau (1988) confirmed her six-phase model of the search process, although she found that these phases were far more interactive later than they had been in the high school years.

In her 1983 study, Kuhlthau found that, for most students, all six phases were completed before drafting began and, for the most part, the students considered the writing of the research paper a separate process following the search process. As Kuhlthau's fourth phase suggests, she also found that most students formulated the focus, or controlling idea, for their research after an initial open-ended exploration of their topic but well before drafting began. Further, she found that the few students who failed to find a controlling idea during the search process and attempted to find one during the drafting process reported difficulties in writing their papers. As a result, Kuhlthau suggests that the fourth phase may be the most important phase with respect to the later writing of a report. However, Kuhlthau gathered no data on the grades the students received for their papers. Thus, we do not know from her study how a student's formulation of or failure to formulate a controlling idea before drafting is related to the quality of the final draft as judged by the teacher.

Studies of the Research Process in College Students

A study of the research process in college undergraduate and graduate students also focused on the way in which students searched for information and organized their work in preparation for writing a research paper. In the first of the two studies they report, Nelson and Hayes (1988) gave eight college freshmen and eight upperclassmen and graduate students a specific topic on which to gather information and compared the way in which they planned and searched for their information. The researchers report that most, if not all, of the older students used what the researchers call issue-oriented strategies to locate information, while the freshmen generally used content-oriented or fact-amassing strategies. Nelson and Hayes attribute the differences in the strategies used by these two age groups to differences in the way in which the students defined their role as writers in this particular context. However, it is not clear that the differences in role definition by the two age groups were the cause of the differences in the strategies they used. Nor is it clear that the differences in the strategies used can be attributed to developmental differences in research skills, a question that their second study (described later) helps to clarify. The results of the first study may in fact be misleading—for reasons that, again, relate to the writing task constructed by the researchers.

Unlike the students in the Kuhlthau study, the students in the first Nelson and Hayes study did not actually write a research paper. The researchers asked them only to do their research in five days and to explain how they went about doing it. The students were also given a highly specific topic to explore ("to research and write on some aspect of the relationship between the U.S. and Chile during the overthrow of President Allende in the early 70's", p. 2), a topic about which older, politically sophisticated students might already have an opinion. In fact, that does seem to be the case. Nelson and Hayes do not describe any freshman as knowing anything about the topic in advance of his or her library search. (In some respects, therefore, a content-oriented search made sense for these students.) On the other hand, the researchers describe most of the older students as knowledgeable about the topic before planning their library search; one graduate student, they report, apparently formulated his hypothesis before he ever got to the library. The limitations of a five-day study and the political sophistication of the older students may easily have affected the extent and open-endedness of their search process. That is, given the time limits imposed by the researchers, the knowledge the older students already had on a frequently discussed political topic may have enabled them to formulate a controlling idea quickly without having to gather and sift through a lot of informational material. Thus, the differences between the two groups may be a function more of political sophistication than of the writer's perception of his or her role in a specific writing situation or of developed skill with the research process.

The limitations of this study are instructive in several respects. First, they reinforce the point that researchers' methodology should not reflect a misleading model of how academic research usually originates or is carried out. Second, they suggest that if researchers use topics that have sharply defined public opinions attached to them, as is likely with contemporary social and political issues, they may obtain misleading information about the nature of a normal search process. Finally, they inadvertently raise the possibility that, even for a real assignment, students may formulate a hypothesis prematurely—that is, before they have engaged in genuine inquiry—and turn the research paper into a sterile academic exercise, "proving" what they already believe. Clearly, students who prematurely formulate a controlling idea are likely to zero in directly on the information that fits with their controlling idea and give only a passing nod to opposing ideas. As a result, they may be able to compose very quickly. They may also find the experience of doing research and writing a paper personally satisfying. But from a pedagogical perspective, the premature formulation of a hypothesis for a research paper is even more intellectually unsatisfactory than the delayed formulation of a hypothesis (which may result chiefly in a disorganized first draft). Students who do not undertake an initial open-ended exploration of a topic bypass the intellectually crucial process of sifting through unorganized and frequently conflicting ideas. They not only fail to learn how to tolerate this (more often than not) torturous process, but they also miss the opportunity this process offers for sparking unexpected insights about the structure of the phenomenon under examination. More often than not, this agonizing process turns out, eventually, to be a major source of the intellectual stimulation and gratification from academic research.

In the second case study described in their 1988 report, Nelson and Hayes examined the way in which eight college undergraduates (five freshmen, two juniors, and one senior) carried out and actually wrote research papers in the context of courses in which they were enrolled (such as history of drama, beginning physics, and literature), from the time the assignment was given by the instructor until the instructor graded the final paper. Although the students used various strategies in researching and writing their papers, the researchers explicitly note no differences in the strategies the students used that could be related to age or to prior knowledge or interests. However, to judge from the examples given, the students' topics in these real courses were not politically controversial issues with polarized public opinions already attached to them. Thus, the results of this study seem to strengthen the possibility that political sophistication might have helped account for the reported differences in the strategies used by the students in their first case study—and that age differences did not.

On the other hand, the researchers also report some clear differences—between two groups of two students each—in their willingness to invest time and intellectual effort in the research process and in their satisfaction with the assignment as a learning experience. For one of these groups, the researchers believe that the way in which the research assignment was shaped by the students' instructors and the instructors' interaction with them during the research and writing process did make a difference in whether the students spent time thinking about the topic, gathering information, and revising ideas.

Unfortunately, despite their stated interest in the development of a thesis, Nelson and Hayes report very little about how and when students formulated their thesis or controlling idea. In fact, they mention thesis formulation in connection with only two of the students in the study. Interestingly, the experiences of these two students are compatible with Kuhlthau's findings. One student, who is described as making her research assignment a productive learning experience, appears to have developed a working thesis before she began drafting, even though she revised her thesis in successive drafts. The researchers describe another student as receiving his first draft back from his instructor with an indication that it was unsatisfactory because he had not yet developed a thesis. However, this is as much as we learn about thesis formulation in this study, possibly in part because there seems to be a confusion in terminology. The term *topic*, as it is used in this study, seems to signify both the subject of a student's research as well as the controlling idea for a paper, a confounding of two very distinct conceptual entities.

THE FIT WITH PEDAGOGICAL AND THEORETICAL MODELS

These empirical studies on the research process may be few in number (and it should be noted that neither Kuhlthau nor Nelson and Hayes could find prior studies on the research process per se, according to their reviews of the literature). But they clearly raise the possibility that the quality of the first draft, of the final draft, and of the entire intellectual experience itself (independent of the grade a student might receive) may be significantly related to the point at which a focus, working hypothesis, or controlling idea is formulated. Of interest, therefore, is how these empirical findings mesh with current pedagogical and theoretical thinking about when and how a focus, thesis statement, or controlling idea is formulated. We look first at pedagogical thinking.

Pedagogical Models

Kuhlthau found that students who had worked out their focus before drafting had more successful writing experiences than those who attempted to find their focus in their drafts, a finding that was corroborated to some extent by data reported by Nelson and Hayes. This finding supports the advice that current composition textbooks at the high school and college level tend to offer students. Most suggest that students formulate a tentative thesis at some point before they begin drafting. For example, in her handbook for college students, Johnson (1987) suggests that a focus may come before initial exploration of sources, or that it may be revised or fully formulated after gathering all information. But she discusses all these variations before discussing drafting, implying that drafting follows the formulation of a controlling idea.

However, this finding seems to be at variance with pedagogical advice urging the value of a discovery draft—a first rough but full draft of one's ideas and information for the purpose of discovering one's focus. Clearly, a discovery draft may be successful in helping writers find their point of view for experience-based writing and for very short research reports. But Kuhlthau's finding calls into question extending the notion of a discovery draft from writing based on re-called experience to writing based on researched ideas and information, especially for older, more mature writers.

Theoretical Thinking

Kuhlthau's identification of six phases for the search process, all of which involve various kinds of reading and writing activities, and each of which may influence the other phases in the search process, also calls into question the conceptualization of the planning process as a mental phenomenon in cognitive process theories of composing (see Stotsky, 1990, for a detailed discussion of this issue). Finding a focus, or controlling idea, may well depend on how much information is gathered in an initial search process and how students organize and evaluate their initial notes. Categorizing, organizing, recategorizing, and reorganizing may be the most significant generative activities in the search process, utterly dependent on a dynamic interaction between thinking and writing. The act of "discovery" may well take place—at least initially—during the search process rather than during the composing process for most academic research and writing, with important revision or even complete refocusing still possible (and frequently occurring) during drafting. McGinley (1988) also found in his research that insights could result from self-directed reading and writing activities during the pre-drafting, or planning, process.

By raising the possibility that the search process may be distinguishable from the composing process, Kuhlthau's study also casts doubt on the validity of existing models for the composing process. The implication is that they are applicable to all forms of academic writing, including the research paper, yet they do not seem to provide a conceptual framework for exploring the search process independently from the composing process. Nor do these models provide a conceptual framework for analyzing whether the point at which a controlling idea is formulated is related to the quality of the exploratory reading, thinking, and information gathered for a chosen subject or to the coherence of the final text. If the planning process in models based on a cognitive process theory of composing is conceptualized chiefly as a mental phenomenon, as it now appears to be, to subsume the entire search process under it may be detrimental to an understanding of the nature of the search process. Its complexities may elude investigation when the search process is examined as if it were synonymous with the planning process for short, impromptu essays. Indeed, a model of the search process that includes both reading and writing processes within it may be far more fruitful—and sensible—for studies of the research process and the writing of a research paper than a model of the composing process that attempts to include the entire research process within it. Moreover, it may be more pedagogically useful to view drafting as a tentative culmination of the research process (with further development of thinking taking place through revision of drafts) than to view the entire research process as preparation for the writing of a research paper. In an academic context, the research process may well deserve weight at least equal to, if not more than, the composing process, especially in studies where data are created on the basis of a carefully thought out conceptual design and methodology.

RECOMMENDATIONS FOR FUTURE RESEARCH

Clearly, further investigation is needed to help us understand the complexities of the research process. At present, we have too few studies on which to base any firm generalizations about the research process. However, because the few studies that have been carried out inadvertently raise such a variety of issues and concerns, the following guidelines are recommended if the results of further studies on the research process are to help teachers of academic writing in their efforts to stimulate the growth of independent thinking and responsible writing through research papers.

1. Research on report writing or other kinds of academic writing requiring researched information should be based on student-selected topics and student-gathered information if we are to gain a valid picture of all the thinking processes entailed by academic writing. At present, I would put in the category of student-selected topics not only those chosen completely freely but also topics selected by students from a long, varied list supplied by the instructor or chosen in consultation with an instructor.

2. The results of studies in which students pursue a topic of their own choice (and must consequently locate the sources for their information) should be interpreted differently from the results of studies in which students are assigned the topic for research, provided with the sources of information, or severely limited in other ways in the search process or the writing process.

3. Conceptual distinctions should initially be made among (a) the subject of the research, (b) the focus, thesis, working hypothesis,

or controlling idea for the research, (c) the search process, and (d) the composing process. The usefulness of these distinctions should then be explored.

4. Research on the research process should relate observations and findings to an evaluation of the quality of the final report; the criteria used for the evaluation should be clearly spelled out. Clearly, the grade a research paper receives is not the only criterion for determining the developmental value of the thinking processes entailed by the research assignment. But the professional judgment a teacher makes about the quality of a student's effort to express clear, sound, and substantive thinking on a self-chosen topic of interest is a major index of that student's intellectual and moral growth.

5. Studies of the research process should include a measure of reading ability, for college students as well as for younger students.

6. Data from both case studies and experimental studies should be reported systematically and in a meaningful way. Without all the data from a study aggregated and displayed in some form, readers cannot judge for themselves whether a researcher's interpretations or conclusions are valid.

7. Sex differences should be investigated with respect to the research process, as such differences have been apparent in writing assessments for many years. In the NAEP assessments, for example, females wrote significantly better than males at all three grade levels assessed (grades 4, 8, and 11). Many other studies have also shown females to be better writers than males, regardless of grade level. On the other hand, as Donald Graves (1973) found in his dissertation research with second graders, the boys tended to like informational writing, while the girls tended to like personal and imaginative writing. The research paper may be more appealing to male students, something we especially need to know in order to help low-achieving male students.

8. A model of the composing process that attempts to include the composing of a research paper should be based on observations of, and data from, students engaged in the research process for the paper. Data from students composing spontaneous essays or other kinds of writing may be highly misleading when offered as a model.

9. Last but not least, academic researchers should direct some of their attention to helping teachers find solutions for the problems that teachers themselves perceive with respect to the research paper. Articles in professional journals by teachers or other educators on the research paper suggest a wide range of reasons for the failure of the research assignment to lead to satisfactory academic and moral

learning for all students. All of these problems merit examination.

In the final section of this chapter, I discuss the problems that I have been able to cull or infer from published articles on the research paper.

TEACHERS' PERSPECTIVES ON THE RESEARCH PAPER

In recent years, academic researchers and classroom practitioners have begun to evolve various modes of collaboration to try to eliminate the sharp dichotomy between research and practice that has frequently resulted from their independent efforts. This section represents an effort to blend teachers' insights into the nature of their pedagogical problems concerning the research paper with a few of their own suggested solutions and my speculations about sources or solutions for these problems. I do not critique teachers' perceptions of the problems their students encounter with the research paper, but simply report them; the problems they note are the problems they have observed first-hand. It is difficult to determine how widespread a problem is without large-scale formal research, but teachers' reported perceptions at the least suggest the kinds of problems that may well be widespread. I have also made no grade-level distinctions among these problems. While most of the articles I note were written by high school or college teachers, the problems almost all have their roots in the upper elementary grades, when the research paper starts becoming a frequent, or at the least, annual assignment.

Should different approaches to research be sequenced in the secondary school? The research guide created by Allen and Nichols (1985) for the Needham, Massachusetts, public schools suggests a specific sequence of types of research for students in English classes, grades 6–12. For grades 6, 7, and 8, the authors emphasize active research in which students learn techniques of observation and interrogation through interviews and survey/questionnaires. In grades 9 and 10, Allen and Nichols recommend that students gather information through reading both primary and secondary source materials. By the end of grade 11, they believe students should show mastery of these various techniques for investigation and, in grade 12, should choose their own methods of investigation.

The specific sequence recommended by Allen and Nichols for teaching various methodologies for research in the secondary school may not be desired by all educators. But the concept and content of a sequence might well be explored by groups of teachers and researchers. The unsystematic and uncoordinated way in which the research paper is integrated into most school curricula might well be remedied by a systematic and multidisciplinary approach spanning grades 6–12 and including coordination with the school's librarians.

How can teachers encourage open-ended and nonpolarized thinking during the search process? In a discussion of the problems she has identified in student research papers, Anne Coon (1989) notes that college students "often [hold] strict black/white opinions on complex questions" (p. 86). Schwegler and Shamoon (1982) also report that students view the research paper as a "close-ended," "skills-oriented" exercise in "information-gathering, not an act of discovery" (pp. 819–820). While developmental factors cannot be ruled out, several pedagogical sources at earlier grade levels may account for this problem at the college level.

The frequent assignment of the position paper on current social or political issues in English and social studies classes at the secondary level may be one major source of the polarized thinking Coon notes. For example, Adele Mazurek-Suslick and Audrey Wells (1989) provide an illustrative list of controversial propositions their high school seniors have developed for a unit in argumentation; almost all are polarized positions (e.g., "Bilingual education should be abolished"), and they are apparently formulated before the students undertake their research. Needless to say, open-ended inquiry is almost completely precluded if students take a position on an issue before going to the library—although it is possible for students to change their positions after gathering information. If students begin with a clear-cut point of view, they are unlikely to be motivated to sift carefully through alternative points of view in order to address opposing arguments. A paper on a visibly polarized public issue may also discourage nonpolarized thinking. And even if students do their research before formulating a position on an issue, whether or not it is a polarized public issue, the format of a position paper may automatically restrict their thinking to a pro or con stance. Students may be more likely to engage in nonpolarized thinking and an open-ended search process when they are encouraged to investigate subjects that do not have clear or polarized public positions already attached to them and when they are not required to prepare their papers as position papers.

Moreover, the customary format for classroom debate may also hinder students from coming up with a nonpolarized understanding of an issue. Chapter 7 by Richard A. Katula addresses this point and offers teachers practical suggestions for reducing polarized thinking in classroom discussions.

Finally, teachers or composition textbooks sometimes encourage students to formulate a thesis before they have spent sufficient time in an open-ended investigation of a possible topic. For example, Ford and Perry (1982) quote one teacher in their survey who believes that the research process consists of "forming a thesis and discovering sufficient evidence to support it, marshalling and organizing that evidence so as to argue persuasively to a clearly identified audience, and marshalling a tone appropriate to the subject and the audience" (p. 830). Clearly, an early formulation of a controlling idea may curtail exploration of diverse sources, thus diminishing the quality of the learning experience. A thesis statement for a research paper should result from thinking about information gathered from an initial search and should not be imposed on the whole search process.

If close-ended and polarized thinking is indeed a prevalent problem at the college level, teachers might well consider reducing the number of position papers they assign at the high school and even at the undergraduate level. They might also consider stressing the writing of question-driven research papers throughout most of the secondary school years and delay the writing of a thesis-controlled research paper until the final year of high school. For a description of how this idea has been embedded in an interdisciplinary curriculum sequence for a high school's English and social studies courses, see Henry Kiernan (1990).

How can students learn to begin the search process with productive self-generated questions? Bruce Peterson and Jill Burkland (1986) remark on how many college students are unable to formulate researchable questions or hypotheses. Similarly, Margaret Queenan (1986) notes how few high school students are able to ask themselves the kind of questions that help them get to the significance of their material. David Wray (1985) also observes that many middle grade students seem to think their primary goal is to amass information on the subject they have chosen, not on what they want to know about that subject. In other words, students are apt to be subject-driven, not question-driven.

Teachers probably need to give students many opportunities to generate and evaluate their own questions on a variety of topics in whole-class or small-group sessions from the upper elementary grades on. In an article (Stotsky, 1986), I describe a whole-class approach to developing students' ability to generate their own questions. Kathy Coffey (1989) describes an unusual whole-class activity in which each student is responsible for offering every classmate a question to pursue on the classmate's chosen research topic before the research is undertaken. Although Coffey sees peer-generated questions as a strategy for giving each student in a class a sense of a real, interested audience for his or her eventual paper, it is clear that these questions clearly serve a needed directive function as well.

How can students learn to find sources for research papers both within and beyond libraries? As both James Ford (1986) and Thomas Trzyna (1986) suggest, many students seem to think that the library is the primary, if not only, source of information for a research report. In their articles, they suggest how college students can learn about the variety of sources available for research papers both within and outside libraries. At all educational levels, local community-based projects offer students many opportunities for learning about sources of information beyond the library. John Mahoney (1981), in a comprehensive description of a community history project undertaken by several classes of junior high school students in an Ohio township, offers many helpful guidelines for locating sources inside and outside the library for community-based research projects.

What are the ethical responsibilities entailed in doing and reporting research? Probably the most notorious ethical issue raised by teachers at all levels is plagiarism, the failure to attribute borrowed ideas or copied or paraphrased materials to their authors. Alice Drum (1986) is one of many college instructors who have commented on this problem (e.g., see the references in the study of plagiarism reported by Barry Kroll, 1988). Drum also points out that one reason the research paper is taught is to help students learn to handle reference material with integrity. However, there are many other serious ethical responsibilities that developing academic writers need to learn to observe. Chapter 5 in this book illustrates and discusses these responsibilities, many of which are located in the search process itself.

How can teachers encourage a sense of audience for the research paper? Many teachers feel that the lack of a genuine audience for a research report is one of its critical deficiencies as a piece of writing, accounting for serious problems with tone and coherence. Yet, teachers often assign a research paper in a way that they are the only possible audience for it; at least Schwegler and Shamoon (1982) report that many students perceive this to be the case (p. 819). Both James Strickland (1986) and Richard Bullock (1985) note this problem at the college level, suggesting ways in which the student's peers, or other readers beyond the classroom, can serve as real or potential audiences for the research paper. In the secondary school, a student's research report can be written with a variety of possible audiences in mind: members of the class, another class, younger students in the school, patrons of their local library, or a municipality's historical society.

How can teachers discourage unthinking syntheses of copied materials? A primary problem at all educational levels, as has often been noted (e.g., Queenan, 1986; Wray, 1985), is the tendency for students to copy large amounts of information from reference materials and to present the information without much thought about its meaning as well as its relationship to a particular central issue, question, or controlling idea. Fact-amassing is an egregious problem in the elementary school, but it is by no means limited to that level. And, as Wray points out, some students may simply amass facts for a research report because they believe that is what their teachers want them to do.

To cope with this problem, teachers can ask students to talk with each other in small-group discussions about the material they have gathered on their research topic and then answer each other's questions about their own information. These small-group discussions can make students verbalize researched material in their own words and help them understand what they are writing about. Teachers can also encourage students to use a variety of formats for reporting their research. Students cannot simply stitch copied material together if they use such genres as diary entries, posters, letters, editorials, or historical fiction for reporting research, or if they write narratives of the search process itself, along the lines suggested by Ken Macrorie (1980). Marilyn Lutzker (1989), a college librarian, offers college teachers a number of imaginative alternatives to the traditional research paper, while I (Stotsky, 1984) do so for middle-grade teachers in English or social studies classes. Teachers can also assign many short research assignments rather than one long one per year.

How might teachers phase in the conventions of documentation from the middle school through the high school? According to Marlene Shanks (1988), a high school teacher, and the information Schwegler and Shamoon obtained from their survey of their colleagues at the college level, many students feel that their teachers are more concerned about the conventions of documentation and the format of a research report than the process of research itself. An excessive emphasis on the conventions (or skills) of documentation may go hand in hand with an underemphasis on the search process itself.

To address this problem, middle school teachers might phase in some documentation skills more gradually and omit some altogether. Middle school students probably need only write the identifying information for the references they have used on a provided form that asks them to indicate author, title, publisher or journal, place of publication, year of publication, and the pages they have used. In the last two years of high school, students can learn how to construct citations within a text, footnotes, and the other, more technical aspects of documentation.

What should teachers use as primary criteria for evaluating a research report? Teachers need to think carefully about what they value most in a research paper: authority of information, quality of reasoning, or expressions of personal involvement? And should all three be equally weighted? Unquestionably, all three are desired qualities in a research paper; however, the first two are the major purposes for teaching the research paper, and teachers should probably be less concerned about the presence or absence of "voice" or the manifestation of personal involvement. A student who has written a research paper with much enthusiasm and feeling but with poor information and many gaps in logical (or moral) reasoning has not learned the essential components for a report of research. This does not mean that students should not have a personal interest in the subject of their research; they should if they have chosen the topic themselves. As Donald Graves (1983) notes, lack of real interest in a topic often shows up in student writing in a "lack of voice" or a lack of personal involvement in the subject. Sandra Mitchell (1989) suggests that this may be the case for a required literary research paper, even when students can choose their own specific topic. But personal interest does not have to manifest itself in expressions conveying personal involvement. A research paper written with substance and logic, even though its style is matter-of-fact and dull, is a worthy piece of writing.

CONCLUDING REMARKS

Despite the paucity of research evidence to inform decision making, teachers and curriculum developers need to try to make the research paper a more intellectually and morally stimulating learning experience than it now is. Teachers and curriculum developers may wish to explore more than the questions above. But these questions seem to be significant and could profitably be explored by researchers as well as by teachers. Data from descriptive research would be useful for many of these questions. But many important issues involved in the research process may be better explored experimentally or through theory-based longitudinal case studies. While it is helpful for teachers to know what students at different grade levels actually do, they would benefit even more from information on how they might make the assignment of a research paper a more significant learning experience for all their students. They particularly need to focus on the research process. As can be seen, many of the problems that can be discerned in the pedagogical literature center on the generative phases of the research process.

Teachers also need to be mindful of Richard Larson's (1982) comments about the research paper as a ''non-form'' of writing in college writing courses. Larson argues that there is no generic entity that can be labeled a research paper, and that a research paper has whatever form is required by the discipline in which it is written. What students need to learn, he suggests, is how to incorporate references to sources of information beyond their experience into any writing they do when these references could support the assertion and development of their ideas.

Larson's observations deserve much consideration today. Currently, many English educators are encouraging extended discussion of social and political issues in English classes. If English teachers choose to use much of the class time they would otherwise spend on teaching composition or literary study for discussing broad contemporary social and political issues, then these discussions should be accompanied by self-directed reading and writing activities in which students learn how to support their thinking with references to multiple perspectives in sources of information beyond their experience. Clearly, social and political issues can be discussed in English classes as well as in social studies classes, so long as such discussions are enriched by open-ended inquiry, independent reading and thinking, and responsible writing.

However, English teachers should consider whether the time

they might spend helping students learn how to do research on broad contemporary issues would be better spent helping students learn how to engage in research on the local community, its government, and its history. Given the extremely limited time most teachers seem to have for teaching students how to locate information both inside and outside libraries and how to use primary as well as secondary sources of information, research on the local community might be a far more valuable learning experience for all students than research on broad social issues, which is apt to lead to almost total reliance on secondary sources of information.

First, as Henry Kiernan (1990) and Susan Duncan La Peer (1990) both observe in discussing ways in which interdisciplinary teams of teachers can foster research on the local community, such a context is apt to stimulate original research. There is usually little information available on most local communities in encyclopedias or other standard references, and students are therefore compelled to learn to use primary sources of information, such as minutes of meetings of local citizen groups. Second, research on the local community may provide useful information to their peers, to the local historical society, and to contemporary public bodies or officials. Third, while students are likely to need to refer to some written materials, whether of primary or secondary nature, research in the local community almost always requires use of local informants, a source of information that is accessible to students with low reading ability. They need not be deprived of the opportunity for learning how to do research and to engage in critical thinking simply because most written materials may be beyond their comprehension. Last but not least, as La Peer found in her project, research on the local community can develop students' sense of shared membership in the local community and help them see a variety of ways in which they can actively contribute to its well-being.

REFERENCES

Ackerman, J. (1989). *Reading and writing in the academy*. Unpublished doctoral dissertation, Carnegie Mellon University, Pittsburg, PA.

Allen, L., & Nichols, B. (1985). *The research process: English department, grades 6–12*. Needham Public Schools, Needham, Massachusetts.

Applebee, A., Langer, J., & Mullis, I. (1986). *The writing report card: Writing achievement in American schools* (National Assessment of Educational Progress, Report No. 1, 15–W–02). Princeton, NJ: Educational Testing Service.

Applebee, A., Langer, J., Mullis, I., & Jenkins, L. (1990). *The writing report card, 1984–88: Findings from the nation's report card* (National Assessment of Educational Progress, Report No. 19-W-01). Princeton, NJ: Educational Testing Service.

Bullock, R. (1985). Athens/arts: Involving students in research on their community. *College Composition and Communication, 36*, 237–238.

Coffey, K. (1989). Playing the accordion and framing the research question. *English Journal, 78*, 45.

Coon, A. (1989). Using ethical questions to develop autonomy in student researchers. *College Composition and Communication, 40*, 85–89.

Copeland, K. (1987). *Writing as a means to learn from prose.* Unpublished doctoral dissertation, University of Texas at Austin.

Corbin, R., & Corbin, J. (1978). *Research papers: A guided writing experience for senior high school students.* New York State English Council. (Available from the National Council of Teachers of English, Urbana, Illinois)

Drum, A. (1986). Responding to plagiarism. *College Composition and Communication, 37*, 241–243.

Ford, J. (1986). The research loop: Helping students find periodical sources. *College Composition and Communication, 37*, 223–227.

Ford, J., & Perry, D. (1982). Research paper instruction in the undergraduate writing program. *College English, 44*, 825–831.

Graves, D. (1973). *Children's writing: Research directions and hypotheses based upon an examination of the writing processes of seven-year-old children.* Unpublished dissertation, State University of New York at Buffalo.

Graves, D. (1983). *Writing: Teachers and children at work.* Portsmouth, NH: Heinemann Educational Books.

Greene, S. (1989). *Intertextuality and moves to authority in writing from sources.* Paper presented at the National Reading Conference, Austin, TX.

Hayes, D. (1987). The potential for directing study in combined reading and writing activity. *Journal of Reading Behavior, 19*, 333–352.

Johnson, J. (1987). *The Bedford guide to the research process.* New York: St. Martin's Press.

Kantz, M. (1989). Written rhetorical syntheses: Processes and products (Technical Report No. 17). Berkeley and Pittsburgh: Center for the Study of Writing, University of California, Berkeley, and Carnegie Mellon University.

Kennedy, M. (1985). The composing processes of college students writing from sources. *Written Communication, 2*, 434–456.

Kiernan, H. (1990). Freedom of expression: Civic literacy and civic identity. *English Journal, 79*, 41–44.

Kobasigawa, A. (1983). Children's retrieval skills for school learning. *The Alberta Journal of Educational Research, 29*, 259–271.

Kroll, B. (1988). How college freshmen view plagiarism. *Written Communication, 5*, 203–221.

Kuhlthau, C. C. (1983). *The library research process: Case studies and interventions with high school seniors in Advanced Placement English classes using Kelly's theory of constructs.* Unpublished dissertation, Rutgers University, New Brunswick, NJ.

Kuhlthau, C. C. (1988). Longitudinal case studies of the information search process of users in libraries. *Library Information Science Research, 10,* 257–304.

La Peer, S. D. (1990). Mock town meeting: An interdisciplinary project to prepare students for informed participation in local government. *The Civic Perspective, 3* (3), 10–12.

Larson, R. (1982). The "research paper" in the writing course: A non-form of writing. *College English, 44,* 811–816.

Lutzker, M. (1989). *Research projects for college students: What to write across the curriculum.* New York: Greenwood Press.

Macrorie, K. (1980). *Searching writing: A contextbook.* Rochelle Park, NJ: Hayden.

Mahoney, J. (1981). *Local history: A guide to research and writing.* Washington, DC: National Education Association.

Mazurek-Suslick, A., & Wells, A. (1989, Fall). The inside-out classroom: An interdisciplinary approach to senior year. *Illinois English Bulletin,* pp. 58–67.

McGinley, W. (1988). *The role of reading and writing in the acquisition of knowledge: A study of college students' reading and writing engagements in the development of a persuasive argument.* Unpublished doctoral thesis, University of Illinois at Urbana-Champaign.

McGinley, W., & Tierney, R. (1989). Traversing the topical landscape: Reading and writing as ways of knowing. *Written Communication, 6,* 243–269.

Mitchell, S. (1989). *Before* the search: Genuine communication and literary research. *English Journal, 78,* 46–49.

Moffett, J., & Wagner, B. J. (1976). *Student-centered language arts and reading, K–13* (2nd ed.). Boston: Houghton Mifflin.

Nelson, J., & Hayes, J. (1988). How the writing context shapes college students' strategies for writing from sources (Technical Report No. 16). Berkeley and Pittsburgh: Center for the Study of Writing, University of California, Berkeley, and Carnegie Mellon University.

Penrose, A. (1988). *Examining the role of writing in learning factual versus abstract material.* Paper presented at the American Educational Research Association, New Orleans, LA.

Peterson, B., & Burkland, J. (1986). Investigative reading and writing: Responding to reading with research. *College Composition and Communication, 37,* 236–241.

Queenan, M. (1986). Finding the grain in the marble. *Language Arts, 63,* 666–673.

Schwegler, R., & Shamoon, L. (1982). The aims and process of the research paper. *College English, 44,* 817–824.

Shanks, M. (1988). The research paper: Two more alternatives. *English Journal, 77,* 81–82.

Spivey, N. (1984). *Discourse synthesis: Constructing texts in reading and writing.* Newark, DE: International Reading Association.

Spivey, N., & King, J. (1989). Readers as writers: Composing from sources. *Reading Research Quarterly, 24,* 7–26.

Stotsky, S. (1984). Imagination, writing, and the integration of knowledge in the middle grades. *Journal of Teaching Writing, 3,* 157–190.

Stotsky, S. (1986). Asking questions about ideas: A critical component in critical thinking. *The Leaflet, 85,* 39–47.

Stotsky, S. (1990). On planning and writing plans—Or beware of borrowed theories! *College Composition and Communication, 41,* 37–57.

Strickland, J. (1986). The research sequence: What to do before the term paper. *College Composition and Communication, 37,* 233–236.

Tierney, R., & Shanahan, T. (1991). Research on the reading–writing relationship: Interactions, transactions, and outcomes. In R. Barr, M. Kamil, P. Mosenthal, & P. D. Pearson (Eds.), *Handbook of reading research* (Vol. II, pp. 246–280). New York: Longman.

Trzyna, T. (1983). Approaches to research writing: A review of handbooks with some suggestions. *College Composition and Communication, 34,* 202–207.

Trzyna, T. (1986). Research outside the library: Learning a field. *College Composition and Communication, 37,* 217–223.

Wray, D. (1985). *Teaching information skills through project work.* Kent, England: Hodder & Stoughton, in association with the United Kingdom Reading Association.

Part II

WRITING and SPEAKING:
The Expression
of a Civic Ethic

5 Teaching Academic Writing as Moral and Civic Thinking

SANDRA STOTSKY

Teaching has never been a value-free activity. It proceeds in part from the belief that individual development should have intellectual direction; teachers are expected to develop their students' ability to think critically. In contrast to indoctrination, as Israel Scheffler (1976) observes in an essay on philosophical models of teaching, "teaching respects the student's intellectual integrity and capacity for independent judgment" (p. 120). That is, it is concerned with students' growth in independent critical thinking. But teachers are expected to stimulate more than their students' growth toward intellectual autonomy. Teaching also proceeds on the belief that individual development should have moral direction. Teachers are expected to develop—and evaluate—their students' moral thinking, not only for the students' sake, but also for the sake of their disciplines and the civic communities that support their work and their schools. Both independent and moral thinking are fundamental to scholarship and the meaning of citizenship in a republican form of government.

THE NEGLECT OF ETHICAL CONCERNS IN TEACHING WRITING

Accounts of Moral Education in the Schools

How do teachers and schools influence students' moral development? In an illuminating account of the history of moral education at Harvard University, President Derek Bok (1988) mentions several ways in which ethics may presently be taught at the university level. Universities, he suggests, may well "affect the moral development of their students by the ways in which they administer their rules of conduct, by the standard they achieve in dealing with ethical issues confronting the institution, by the manner in which they counsel their students and coach their athletic teams" (p. 44). The curriculum itself, he goes on to note, "undoubtedly helps in many ways to develop ethical awareness and moral reasoning" (p. 44). The study of literature, he points out, "can awaken one's conscience by making more vivid the predicament of others," and "studying the social sciences can help students to understand the causes and effects of various policies and practices and thus appreciate their moral significance more precisely" (p. 44). Bok concludes that "almost any well-taught course can strengthen the capacity to think more carefully about intellectual problems, including ethical issues" (p. 44). But, surprisingly, he fails to note that the very instrument that scholars use to contribute to the development of knowledge—their academic writing—should itself be a model of ethical reasoning and may be their primary means for cultivating moral thinking in their students.

The literature on moral education also seems to see the context for moral education almost exclusively in discussions of the moral issues embedded in the students' academic subject matter, in the functioning of public institutions, or in contemporary life. One example is Richard Paul's (1988) essay entitled "Ethics Without Indoctrination." Like Bok, Paul believes that teachers can foster moral reasoning in students by engaging them in critical thinking about the moral principles involved in resolving contemporary social problems, the moral issues that arise in the lives of the characters in the literary works they read, the moral implications of applied scientific findings, and the moral significance of specific historical events. Clearly, such discussions contribute to an understanding of moral principles. But he, too, fails to note that moral reasoning may also be encouraged in the course of a student's development as an academic writer, regardless of discipline and current events.

Textbooks and Articles on Composition Teaching

In some respects, it is not surprising that the teaching of academic writing has been overlooked, by those interested in moral education, as a means for developing moral thinking. The topic is discussed only briefly in composition textbooks at all educational levels. In composition and grammar texts for high school students, allusions to the moral obligations of the academic writer appear primarily in discussions of plagiarism or adequacy of references in chapters dealing with the library paper. Occasionally one finds a brief discussion of the "fallacies"—lapses in logical and moral reasoning such as plagiarism, begging the question, or setting up "strawmen"—although distinctions are rarely made between logical and moral fallacies. A lengthier discussion of the fallacies is apt to appear in college composition textbooks, although there, too, distinctions between logical and moral fallacies are rarely if ever made.

Except for the issue of plagiarism, the ethical values embedded in the process of academic research and writing have received little attention from either secondary school or college teachers of composition, to judge from the abstracts of articles on ethical concerns by writing instructors that one may find in the Educational Resources Information Center (ERIC) for the past 20 years. A pedagogically oriented essay by Alice Drum (1986) exemplifies concern for the widespread problem of plagiarism at the college level. In her essay, Drum notes how inadequately college composition textbooks address the problem of plagiarism. Eugene Garver's (1985) and David Harrington's (1981) essays are among the few with a broad view of ethical issues. Garver argues philosophically for an equation between teaching writing and teaching virtue. In a more pedagogically oriented essay, Harrington suggests that standards of ethics should be taught explicitly in composition classes, particularly with respect to the judgments students must make about whether they have adequate evidence to support generalizations. Harrington believes that the "best lessons in ethical writing are to be found in the processes used in academic scholarship, in the processes used by researchers in all fields of inquiry, in their objective search for truth" (p. 13).

It is also rare to find a discussion in other disciplines of the ethical responsibilities students have as academic writers. In an essay on student writing in a college level course in political science, Marianne Mahoney (1979) uses an explicit civic framework for commenting on her students' deficiencies as writers. Mahoney stresses that student writers should see themselves and their teachers as members of a civic community. According to her, this perception might make the students feel obligated to express their ideas coherently and to support their ideas with adequate evidence in order to facilitate communication in their community. Mahoney's point of view is refreshing but unusual.

Scholarship in Rhetoric and Composition

Nor is there much indication in current scholarship in rhetoric and composition that both moral and logical kinds of reasoning are necessary for academic research and writing. According to Richard Young (1987), most of the writing on the subject of ethics in rhetoric appears not in the field of rhetoric and composition but in the field of speech communication, where, not surprisingly, it seems to arise in connection with the strategies speakers use in public argument to win assent to their positions. Nevertheless, even there, Sheryl Friedley (1982) notes, most textbooks on the coaching of contest speakers offer qualitative, not ethical, criteria for addressing questions about the use of evidence. When the subject of ethics is dealt with in the field of rhetoric and composition, it arises for the most part in connection with discussions of persuasion or public argument, as, for example, in James Kinneavy's (1980) *Theory of Discourse*. Harrington's (1979) essay, "Encouraging Honest Inquiry in Student Writing," is again one of the few exceptions. In this essay, Harrington argues for a need to encourage students to make a "serious attempt to get at the heart of a problem, to look at the many sides of a question, to take into account conflicting data, to consider the relative merits of alternative hypotheses, to concede weaknesses, if any, as well as claiming strengths in one's conclusions, and to admit that what one is proving is 'probability' rather than 'absolute truth'" (p. 182). It is important to note that Harrington locates most of his ethical concerns in the discovery process, or invention, the first step in classical rhetoric, rather than in the final stages of presenting an argument.

Writing Research and Theory

Although there is a growing literature on the influence of writing on thinking and learning, writing researchers, too, have so far not addressed the ethical issues entailed by academic research and writing. William McGinley and Robert Tierney (1989) offer a useful synthesis and review of this literature in a recent article. They note that, for the most part, this literature shows the influence on thinking of only the specific types and sequences of writing activities that students have been directed to engage in by researchers. McGinley and Tierney argue that researchers should focus much more on ways in which critical thinking processes are stimulated when students can determine their own reading and writing activities, especially for complex, open-ended assignments. But they do not mention specifically the moral thinking these assignments entail as an integral part of learning to write in any discipline.

In theories about the composing process, we also find an absence of thinking about the moral dimensions of the composing process. In the past two decades, much research and thinking in the field of composition teaching have been stimulated by two somewhat different theories of writing. One theory, based on certain views about the nature of creativity, sees the act of writing as a continuous process of making meaning. The other theory, based on work in cognitive psychology, sees the act of writing as a process of decision making and problem solving. Although proponents of both theories have in recent years been exploring the influence of the social context for writing on the act of composing, none, to my knowledge, has as yet explicitly addressed the role of moral reasoning in composing academic texts, regardless of discipline.

To some extent, the lack of attention to broad ethical concerns in theories about the composing process and in the teaching of academic writing may reflect the fact that a writer's relationship to his or her readers has been viewed, in theory and in practice, almost wholly in terms of the writer's awareness, or lack of awareness, of the readers' characteristics, attitudes, beliefs, and needs. Thus, the focus of both scholarly inquiry and teaching has tended to be on issues of audience analysis—what the writer's readers need, not what the writer owes the readers independent of their needs. As a corollary to this perspective, a writer's failure to observe desirable standards of clarity, coherence, or courtesy, as in egocentric writing or writer-based prose, has been treated in recent years almost wholly as a cognitive, not moral, phenomenon. Moreover, while proponents of the writing process have rightfully insisted on a writer's need for "ownership" of a piece of writing vis-à-vis choosing topics or having latitude in responding to comments and/or criticism by teachers or peers—the writer's rights, if you will—they, too, have said little if anything about a writer's responsibilities to his or her readers as the counterpart to the author's rights.

Knowing effective *and* responsible ways to investigate and write about a subject in which one is interested is fundamental to both academic writing and participation in a republican form of government. As students learn how to become academic writers, they are expected to develop the moral reasoning that should characterize public discourse as much as it should characterize academic discourse. The qualities we value in academic discourse are similar to many of the qualities we value in public discourse in the larger, civic communities that support the work of scholars, their students, and their schools. Indeed, it is possible that learning to understand and observe the obligations embedded in academic writing may play a more important role in the development of a student's moral character as a citizen than discussions of the moral meaning of historical events, contemporary public issues, fictional dilemmas, or applied science and technology.

The Purpose and Approach of this Chapter

The immediate purpose of this chapter is to elaborate on the different kinds of responsibilities teachers of academic writing should cultivate in their students as academic writers—responsibilities that are necessary for both scholarship and citizenship in a republican form of government. Its larger purpose is to make more visible a topic that needs far more exploration than it has received and to offer an empirically derived framework for examining the subject. This chapter should be seen as an initial attempt to build on Harrington's pioneering essays. I do not claim to offer an all-inclusive discussion of the possible responsibilities an academic writer might have. The topic needs much fuller exploration than is possible here. Nor do I discuss the topic of plagiarism and its complexities; these are elaborated on in recent writing on the topic (e.g., see Barry Kroll's 1988 research on the subject and his bibliography).

I have grouped in four categories the varied responsibilities that I believe developing academic writers must learn: in the first, I place those responsibilities relating to the nature and purpose of academic language; in the second, those relating to other writers; in the third, those relating to the integrity of the subject of their research; and in the fourth, those relating to the integrity of their readers. All these responsibilities are owed a writer's readers, but their division into these specific categories may help student writers better grasp their varied thrust. Some of the various obligations I discuss may be found scattered throughout a variety of texts and essays in the field of rhetoric and composition. Others reflect my own insights into the moral constraints I have found myself consciously trying to observe in my own academic writing, as well as what I have found others observing, or failing to observe, in theirs—constraints that may need much explicit attention today if the examples of irresponsible writing I offer (which I came across without much looking) are symptomatic of widespread problems.

As much as possible, I offer examples from contemporary published academic writing or curriculum materials to illustrate a writer's observance, or lack thereof, of a particular ethical responsibility. Some of these curriculum materials may have passed through the hands of numerous editors in the course of their development over several years, and thus authorial responsibility may be unclear. Nevertheless, when academic scholars, or others, allow their names to be used as authors of instructional material (and collect royalties), I believe they can be held responsible as writers.

The examples I offer will undoubtedly suggest that some responsibilities are more serious than others. And, indeed, a failure to observe some of these responsibilities can be considered more clearly a violation of ethical standards than an act of simple thoughtlessness. A thoughtless writer may be deficient in moral thinking, but he or she is not necessarily an immoral writer. Nevertheless, as important as the distinction may be, it is not an easy one to establish, especially without clear evidence of a writer's intentions. Moreover, it may not be wise, as Harrington notes, to consider a student writer's failure to exhibit a particular responsibility as necessarily an immoral act; it is better, he suggests, to assume a lack of knowledge rather than dishonesty or laziness behind a student's failure to write responsibly. For these reasons, I have chosen to make no distinction between an act of thoughtlessness and an act of immoral thinking. I believe that all the obligations discussed can be placed under the general rubric of a writer's responsibilities as a member of an academic and civic community, regardless of the degree of seriousness of the lapse or the factors that may account for a failure to fulfill an obligation.

RESPECT FOR THE PURPOSES OF ACADEMIC LANGUAGE

The Obligation to Define Key Terms

One of the most important obligations developing writers have concerning the purpose of academic language is to provide definitions of key terms or to clarify their exact meanings in other ways. This is one of the obligations William McCleary (1986) especially emphasizes. In order to share ideas and information with readers across time and space for the purpose of developing knowledge, an academic writer's key words must have as precise a meaning as possible. The major reason for the word coining that is particularly characteristic of the sciences is the need for unambiguous meanings for key concepts. Sometimes this need can be met only by creating a new word. But usually writers can use existing words. Frequently, the word a writer wants, or needs, to use has a vague meaning, or multiple meanings. The following passage is an example of how a writer has clarified the meaning of a word that may have vague or differing associations for different readers. The writer suggests the different contexts in which his key word can be used, describes what he believes are its salient characteristics, and shows how it differs from a related entity.

The term *mentor* has been used sporadically in higher education for years but first caught my ear when used formally by Empire State College, one of the nation's first colleges created exclusively for older students. Although mentors obviously continue to serve young people, the term has since come into much wider use as a neologism meaning "teacher of adults." Mentors generally have a wider role than conventional faculty advisers. They may or may not teach classes, but they are inevitably engaged in one-to-one instruction and are consequently more concerned than regular teachers with the individual learning needs and styles of their students. (Daloz, 1986, p. 20)

Sometimes a word or phrase that a writer wants to use is reasonably new to a particular area of academic inquiry. The following passage is part of a paragraph that illustrates how a writer has comprehensively defined an existing term for use in a new context. The writer suggests what the term refers to, what functions this entity serves, what elements it consists of, how it manifests itself, how it differs from possibly similar or related entities, and, later in the paragraph, what it may be associated with.

As the term is used here, *pre-text* refers to a writer's tentative linguistic representation of intended meaning, a "trial locution" that is produced in the mind, stored in the writer's memory, and sometimes manipulated mentally prior to being transcribed as written text. As mentally generated and stored "trial locutions," pre-texts have both a semantic and a syntactic component, and they may take the form of phrases, dependent clauses, sentences, or sentence sequences. Pre-texts differ, therefore, from all nonlinguistic representations of intended meaning such as nonverbal images and feelings. . . . Pre-texts also differ from the more abstract plans writers generate. (Witte, 1987, p. 387)

Regardless of how familiar an academic writer believes the meaning of a key concept to be, the writer is obligated to offer a definition and/or examples in order to ensure, to the extent possible, that the intended meaning is the meaning readers will infer. An academic writer is also obligated to indicate when the meaning of a previously defined term is being altered, as frequently happens in the course of an extended investigation into a particular phenomenon, or when a word with an already familiar meaning is being used in a different sense. The failure to define key terms, or to make their meanings reasonably clear through examples, has personal and communal consequences. It can prevent writers from detecting problems with the meaning of material in their own writing or in the writing of others. It also leads to confusion for others who may wish to build on the writer's ideas. (See Stotsky, 1990, for an expanded discussion of these problems.)

The Obligation to Write Clearly

Developing academic writers have an obligation to avoid excessive use of abstract and multisyllabic words, so that they can convey their meaning clearly and allow readers reasonable access to it. A fine line always exists between language that is unnecessarily abstruse and language that cannot be simplified without sacrificing the real complexity of the subject. But all academic writers are obligated to strive for intelligibility and lucidity. The following passages, on closely related topics, provide an informative contrast that illustrates the significance of this responsibility.

> General systems theory, an idea originally constructed by naturalists as a way of comprehending growth and change in nature, brings fruitful explanatory power to the study of human beings as well. Rather than resting simply on the most obviously "changing" objects in a field of possibilities, the eye of the general systems theorist looks at the *relationships* among those objects; it seeks the invisible threads of influence within which any action inevitably occurs. Systems theory thus allows us to see not only how individuals behave but how individuals and environments interact. It reminds us that we must look to complex sets of "contingencies" that affect the developing person in a variety of ways. (Daloz, 1986, p. 187)

> If a radical theory of literacy is to encompass human agency and critique as part of the narrative of liberation, it must reject the reductionist pedagogical practice of limiting critique to the analyses of cultural products such as texts, books, films, and other commodities. Theories of literacy tied to this form of ideology critique obscure the *relational* nature of how meaning is produced, i.e., the intersection of subjectivities, objects, and social practices within specific relations of power. As such, criticism as a central dimension of this view of literacy exists at the expense of developing an adequate theory of how meaning, experience, and power are inscribed as part of a theory of human agency. (Giroux, 1987, p. 11)

Although both writers are describing the nature of a theory they wish to use or to clarify, and therefore need to use a number of abstract concepts, in the first passage most of the main verbs are monosyllabic and simple in meaning (e.g., *brings, looks, seeks*). Even some of the nouns are monosyllabic or simple in meaning (*eye, idea, sets, study, thread*). In contrast, in the second passage almost every meaning-bearing adjective, verb, or noun is multisyllabic and abstract. Not only can a reader get lost in a thicket of abstractions, even the writer can. By the time the writer has moved from a "radical theory of literacy" in the first sentence to a "theory of human agency" three sentences later, he has seemingly moved from declaring that the first theory needs to encompass the second to declaring that the second needs to encompass the first.

The language of the first passage respects a reader's efforts to comprehend a high level of abstraction—general systems theory—by providing explanatory paraphrases (e.g., "relationships" becomes "invisible threads of influence" and then "how individuals and environments interact"). The reader unfamiliar with this theory can nevertheless finish reading the passage with some confidence that this theory is about human behavior and the various interactions with the environment that influence it. On the other hand, the effect of the second passage is to leave the reader wondering whether the writer is unwilling to spend time revising his writing or really does not know what he means. Whichever it is, the writer—and his editors—have not respected the purpose of academic language or the reader's time.

RESPECT FOR OTHER WRITERS

The Obligation to Consider Other Writers as Sincere as Oneself

Developing academic writers need to assume that other writers are as sincere about their ideas as they themselves are about their own ideas. By imputing base motives to other writers, they belittle themselves and invite the charge of sanctimoniousness. The following passage offers one example. Here the writer supports and elaborates on an unacceptable imputation by another academic writer about the motives of academic researchers in general. In the process of agreeing with the other writer and expanding on his observation, she displays two more lapses in responsible writing. She makes blanket generalizations about researchers and offers no evidence at all to support her generalizations.

> Bolster reminds us that researchers are striving for recognition from their peers and superiors. In fact, they may not necessarily be trying to improve the profession of teaching. The primary goal of the teacher is to find something that works well with a particular group of students

within a context. The researcher, however, is looking for a general principle that applies in all situations. . . . Researchers focus on small parts
and are therefore reductionist in their thinking. Teachers focus on whole
classes functioning within school environments and are inclusive in
their attempts to manage the many decisions necessary to successful
teaching. Basically, teachers see teaching as a process, something that is
done in the classroom with people and situations; researchers see teaching as an achievement resulting in a product, usually a test score.
(Grindstaff, 1987, p. 48)

The effect of such a passage is to reduce the reader's respect for
both the writer cited in the passage and the writer of the passage.
Not only should developing academic writers avoid impugning the
motives of other writers, they should also avoid making blanket generalizations about any phenomenon, as there are always exceptions
to even strong regularities. Moreover, writers must always provide
both adequate and sufficient evidence to support any generalization
they offer. Otherwise, they will appear to be simply voicing personal
prejudices rather than offering conclusions based on extensive and
impartial research.

Developing writers also need to learn that an insulting caricature
of someone they disapprove of reflects poorly on themselves, not on
the person caricatured. Readers do not look kindly on those who
assume that only their own position is motivated by a concern for the
welfare of their field or their society, or that they alone know what is
best for their academic disciplines or their civic communities. The
following passage suggests the folly both of impugning another writer's motive and of making a blanket generalization, as the writer of
the above passage did. This writer, an academic researcher, clearly
indicates his concern for students.

Educational research is no mere spectator sport, no mere intellectual
game, no mere path to academic tenure and higher pay, not just a way
to make a good living and even to become a big shot. It has moral
obligations. The society that supports us cries out for better education
for its children and youth—especially the poor ones, those at risk, those
whose potential for a happy and productive life is all too often going
desperately unrealized.

So even as we debate whether any objectivity at all is possible,
whether ''technical'' research is merely trivial, whether your paradigm
or mine should get more money, I feel that I should remember that the
payoff inheres in what happens to the children, the students. That is
our end concern. (Gage, 1989, p. 10)

The Obligation to Consider Other Writers as Intellectual Equals

Developing writers need to respect the work of other writers as they would want others to respect their own work. They should not assume they are superior to other writers, thereby inviting the charge of elitism. A writer's attempts to belittle the intelligence and behavior of other writers are likely only to make a reader think poorly of the writer, not of those being demeaned. The following passage, which opens a long article on the subject of beginning reading, offers an example of this phenomenon. Here the writer conveys a conceited view of her own perspective on the subject and tries to dismiss the work of others by the use of a loaded label.

> My writing of this article was provoked by Marie Carbo's critique of Jeanne Chall's research and by Chall's rebuttal, for I find myself disagreeing with both of them and disturbed that the complex subject of children's early literacy development has been reduced in their debate to a battle over "methods." When viewed against the broader context of the past 20 years of research into the ways in which young children learn to read and write, the "Great Debate" can be seen as little more than a trivial argument over an issue that has no scientific relevance. Thus, I would urge both researchers and educators to look beyond this petty squabble. I am firmly convinced that if we can ignore such reductionist disagreements about currently dominant methodologies, we will be able to concentrate on building theoretically grounded explanations of reading and writing that will eventually enable us to develop a unified theory of literacy learning and instructional practices. (Taylor, 1989, p. 185)

In this passage, the writer has seemingly assumed that the reader will agree with her demeaning characterization of the thinking and ideas of the other two writers. In fact, the open-minded reader is likely to be so offended by the writer's dogmatically delivered expressions of condescension (e.g., that the preceding two articles are a "petty squabble," that a "broader" context seemingly unknown to the other two writers exists, that a long-acknowledged work of scholarship is a "trivial" argument with "no scientific relevance," and that these two articles can be seen as "reductionist disagreements") that the rest of the article is more likely to be ignored than read and taken seriously. The serious lapses in moral reasoning displayed in this passage call into question not only the professional judgment of the writer but also that of the editorial staff of the journal that published it.

On the other hand, the following introductory paragraph for an academic essay illustrates how disagreement with another writer can be stated not only with courtesy and clarity but also with a concise indication of the writers' common ground before the point of departure is introduced.

> In "A new verdict on juror willingness," Professor John P. Richert last month challenged our view that unwilling jurors are a myth and that juror attitudes are not significantly influenced by the size of fees they receive. His opposing arguments stress three major themes. First, he questions whether the Juror Exit Questionnaire we used really determines juror willingness. Second, he offers data that seem to contradict our major findings. Finally, he questions the traditional notion that jury duty is an inherent obligation of citizenship, irrespective of the conditions under which jurors are expected to serve.
>
> Though we accept the validity of Richert's data and we endorse his conclusion that the courts have a "moral obligation to improve the conditions of service," our stress is sufficiently different to represent a divergent view based on the same statistical picture. Therefore, we will contrast his themes with our own, adding information that we think is relevant to the argument. (Pabst, Munsterman, & Mount, 1977, p. 38)

The writers of the above passage do not summarily dismiss or demean oppositional views. The challenging views of a critic are impartially and unemotionally presented. It is clear that the authors respect the ideas of the person with whom they are arguing because they are responding to them seriously—without arrogance. After reading the introduction to this essay, readers have good reason to believe they will obtain a deeper understanding of the subject by reading the rest of the piece.

The Obligation to Present Another Writer's Views Fairly and Not to Misrepresent Them

Developing academic writers need to learn that when they want to criticize arguments made by other academic writers, they must first present the central views of the other writers—and present them fairly—before offering their criticism. They are responsible for giving their readers a clear indication, however brief, of the other writers' arguments and for not misrepresenting or ignoring the other authors' central views. They must be careful not to criticize minor points in another writer's argument without indicating first what the major thrust of the other writer's argument is. That is, when criticizing minor points, they must be careful not to appear to be claiming that what they are criticizing is the central point the other writer has made. Above all, they must be careful not to criticize something they claim or imply the writer has said when he or she has not actually said it. If they misrepresent another writer's views, or ignore the other writer's central points, they will make a reader wonder either whether they have indeed understood the other writer or whether they are deliberately setting up a "strawman" in order to knock it down.

The following passages illustrate one writer's misrepresentation of the ideas of another writer. In the article in which they appear, the writer notes that the "dominant trends" in United States and world history courses are still "the teaching of history as a chronological survey that glorifies the nation's past, texts written to avoid social controversy, and requirements to memorize vast amounts of material" (p. 85). Yet, his article focuses on the efforts by many educational and academic historians—in particular, Diane Ravitch—to revive the teaching of history in the nation's schools and implies that they wish to reinstate these trends.

> The guru of the revival of history is Diane Ravitch, an educational historian at Columbia University. Ravitch . . . and others are calling for the return to a tradition of old, teaching more history in a traditional manner. (Evans, 1989, p. 85)

Ravitch (1989) replies to this point in an article in the same issue of the journal in which Evans' article appears.

> Mr. Evans does not understand my views on history teaching. I am not a defender of the "traditional" method of teaching history. I think that history as it is presently taught is deadly boring: Most history instruction today consists of teachers lecturing and students reading a textbook. I have repeatedly criticized the quality of today's textbooks, for their avoidance of controversy, their superficiality, and their leaden, impersonal tone. . . . I have advocated the use of good literature in the history classroom, such as biographies and well-written historical stories. I also believe that students can learn a good deal about another time and place by reading its religious literature, its poetry, and its novels and by learning about its heroes, its architecture, sports, foods, occupations, technology, etc. This kind of empathetic examination of how people lived their lives should proceed not just through books, but through simulations, debates, role-playing, dramatics, computer games, videodiscs, field trips, movies, and anything else that teachers can find or

devise to get their students to understand that the past was a different world. . . . (p. 90)

Although it is not at all clear how Evans can accuse Ravitch and others of wanting to revive the traditional teaching of history when, according to his own report, the traditional teaching of history continues to this day, it is clear that Ravitch's own ideas about the way in which history should be taught are not what Evans implies they are.

The Obligation to Attribute Ideas Only to Their Authors and Not to Attribute Meaning Without Clear Evidence

To attribute another writer's ideas to that writer has been a traditional responsibility of the academic writer. It is equally incumbent upon an academic writer to make sure that ideas are not attributed, explicitly or implicitly, to the wrong author. This can happen especially when ideas or information from several different sources are juxtaposed or conjoined. Developing writers need to learn that when they integrate information and ideas from different sources, they must be careful not only to make it precisely clear what was said or found by whom, but also not to imply that a writer said or found something he or she actually did not say or find. The following passage illustrates not only an implied attribution of a remark that is improper but also several other lapses in moral reasoning flowing from the initial lapse.

> When the neo-conservative National Association of Scholars reacts to the emergence of ethnic and women's studies by declaring that "the barbarians are in our midst," we recognize the hysterical rhetoric of an empire in decline. Allan Bloom's characterization of Afro-American studies as "the Little Black Empire" plays on similar buzzwords, simultaneously denigrating the value and inflating the threat of the barbarians by projecting imperial ambitions onto them. (Mitchell, 1989, p. B3)

In this passage, the writer has taken a phrase about "barbarians," which he has attributed to the National Association of Scholars in the first sentence, and conjoined it in the second sentence with a reference to a comment he attributes to Allan Bloom about Afro-American studies as "the Little Black Empire." Even though the phrase about the "barbarians" was not Bloom's, by conjoining these key words or phrases, the writer has made Bloom appear to have

equated Afro-Americans with barbarians. In itself, this is a serious
lapse in responsible writing. It is even more serious because it leaves
the reader with the implication that Bloom is racist, a charge that
would need to be proven even if it were academically relevant. What
makes this remarkable example of irresponsible writing completely
offensive is the possibility that the writer's association of "barbarians" with the phrase about "the Little Black Empire" is in fact an
indication of his own view of African-Americans, since the phrase
about "barbarians" was not Bloom's. Although the writer's wording
would seem at first to impute racist views to another writer, a closer
analysis raises the possibility that these views are in actuality the
writer's.

RESPECT FOR THE INTEGRITY OF THE SUBJECT

The Obligation to Gather All Relevant Information on a Topic

Developing academic writers need to learn that they are responsible for carrying out a thorough search for all possibly relevant information on a topic they have selected for research. Sometimes this
responsibility results in what is called a review of the literature, which
precedes the carrying out of a more focused investigation or experiment. If writers fail to do a thorough search and examine only a
portion of the available information on a subject, they may not become aware of their subject's complexities. They may also miss information that is crucial for understanding their topic or for guiding
further investigation in a fruitful manner. Such a situation may lead
to a misinterpretation of the meaning of the information they do find
or to a poorly conceptualized piece of research. A good understanding of a topic requires sifting through all the information that can be
located on the topic. Thus, student writers owe it to the integrity of
their subject to locate and examine all the information and ideas that
appear to bear on it in some way.

The Obligation to Evaluate the Relevance and Quality
of Gathered Information

Not only are developing academic writers responsible for carrying out a thorough search for all possibly relevant information, they
are also responsible for evaluating the relevance and quality of the
information. Students should consider whether the information ap-

pears to bear directly on a seemingly important aspect of the topic. If it does, they then need to consider how. In addition, students should note how recent the information is and whether it has been superseded by more up-to-date information. Students also need to judge how much they can rely on their sources for providing complete, objective, and accurate information. Unfortunately, there are no completely satisfactory criteria they can use, as the notion of objectivity itself has become relativized by many scholars, and it is no longer clear that any one type of source is necessarily more reliable than others. Newspapers and other media often fail to give complete and accurate information about a subject; public officials may provide only partial information (orally or in writing) for a variety of reasons; and some scholars today may offer readers only "positioned objective knowledge," that is, "partial and self-limited" knowledge (Clifford, 1988, p. A8). Students need to try to determine whether the provider of the information seems to have financial or ideological interests that might render the information less complete or accurate than it otherwise might be.

One of the best criteria for judging the quality of a source is to note whether it discusses seriously all plausible alternative interpretations to the one it proposes as the best interpretation and whether it acknowledges the weaknesses or qualifications in the interpretation it offers. Another useful criterion for evaluating the quality of information or ideas on a particular subject is to compare a variety of sources from different points in time as well as from different contemporary perspectives to note points of convergence or difference on specific issues; it is worth keeping in mind that older sources are not necessarily less reliable than contemporary sources. A useful criterion for deciding whether to examine a specific source in depth is the author's academic or experiential qualifications for addressing the topic, or the credentials and breadth of perspective of the editorial advisory board. This applies particularly to material dealing with controversial public issues.

An example of curricular material that could be rejected as a reliable source of information simply on the basis of the lack of qualifications of its editorial advisory board is the curriculum guide produced by WETA (1989), the public broadcasting station in Washington, DC, to accompany *Arab and Jew: Wounded Spirits in a Promised Land*, a PBS film based on David Shipler's book by the same name. The guide, free copies of which were sent directly to social studies departments in 40,000 public and private schools across the country (thus bypassing school committee, faculty, and/or parent subcommittees on curriculum), lists as members of its editorial advisory board the following: Hisham Shirabi, Director of the Arab-American Cultural Foundation; Marshall Meyer, a congregational rabbi; Gail Pressberg, Executive Director of the Foundation for Middle East Peace; Ron Young, Middle East Representative of the American Friends Service Committee; Billie Johnson, a classroom teacher; Mounir Farah, chairman of a high school social studies department; Robert Gardner, co-producer of the film; and David Shipler, a journalist. The board contains not one recognized scholar on the Middle East—Palestinian, Islamic, Judaic, or Israeli, a fact a student could determine by noting the professional positions of each member or by showing the list of names to any scholar connected with a department of Middle East studies.

On the other hand, the intellectual breadth and credentials of the editorial advisory board responsible for *Building a History Curriculum: Guidelines for Teaching History in Schools* (Bradley Commission on History in Schools, 1988) would give a writer confidence that its information or ideas are of high quality. The scholars on its advisory board are: Kenneth Jackson, Columbia University; Charlotte Crabtree, University of California, Los Angeles; Gordon Craig, Stanford University; Robert Ferrell, Indiana University; Hazel Whitman Hertzberg, Teachers College, Columbia University; Nathan Huggins, Harvard University; Michael Kammen, Cornell University; William Leuchtenburg, University of North Carolina; Leon Litwack, University of California, Berkeley; William McNeill, University of Chicago; Diane Ravitch, Teachers College, Columbia University; and C. Vann Woodward, Yale University. In addition, it includes classroom teachers in a variety of public and private schools around the country.

The Obligation to Address All Relevant Information

Significant ideas or controversial issues are usually complex, and writers who do a thorough search for relevant information will usually find some information that turns out to be contradictory to, or incompatible with, whatever controlling idea they eventually formulate. Developing academic writers need to learn that they are responsible for addressing all relevant information in their writing in an adequate manner, that is, for dealing with complexity in a way that is reasonable for their age and ability. Responsible writers not only acknowledge all relevant information judged to be of quality and/ or useful to their discussion, they also indicate how contradictory information or information that does not fit in with their controlling idea can be accounted for and why they have come to the particular interpretation or conclusion that they have. They do not engage in reductive or simplistic thinking. Nor do they offer their readers an oversimplified understanding of the topic or offend readers' integrity by appearing to "load the dice" in favor of the particular interpretation or conclusion they have come to.

Many examples of irresponsible writing with respect to this obligation are provided in Andre Ryerson's (1989) review of 28 current textbooks and teacher's guides on China, ranging from five of the most popular elementary texts to three recent global studies texts and five of the most popular secondary world history texts. According to Ryerson, a chief purpose of these texts (with six exceptions) seems to be to show the present Chinese government in as positive a light as possible, despite its nondemocratic nature—in part, as some of the texts themselves suggest, "as an antidote to students' tendencies to ethnocentrism" (p. 12) regarding their own form of government. Most materials, Ryerson notes, "avoid those questions that pertain to issues of democratic government, democratic values, and human rights" (p. 12). Ryerson further notes that several even urge students to compare the American Bill of Rights with the rights afforded the Chinese under their constitution, leading our students to believe that the two countries hardly differ in the realm of rights. According to Ryerson, few provide contradictory information to allow students to judge whether the Chinese government is good for its people. For example, he points out, only two texts inform students that the people of China do not enjoy freedom of movement. And on the topic of human rights, he adds, only three of the 28 texts "so much as glide over the subject," even though the bulletins of Amnesty International have made it clear that "China to this day has among the worst human rights abuses in the world" (p. 50).

If writers discuss only the information that supports the interpretation they offer, the reader is denied the right to judge the validity of their interpretation. The reader is also denied the opportunity to learn about all the relevant information on the topic and to gain a more complete picture.

The Obligation to Account for All Significant Components in an Analogy

Academic writers often make analogies between the phenomenon they are examining and another better-known and easier-to-understand phenomenon in order to help their readers better grasp the phenomenon they seek to explain. For an analogy that illuminates an interpretation or explanation of a phenomenon to be valid, it must be based on a high degree of similarity in the functions or characteristics of the major components of the two phenomena being compared. It is thus the responsibility of academic writers to make sure they have identified all significant components so that the analogy they offer is valid. If a writer gathers or offers only limited information about the two phenomena, he or she may not construct a valid analogy, and readers will be misled about the nature of the phenomenon the writer seeks to explain.

The PBS guide written to accompany *Arab and Jew: Wounded Spirits in a Promised Land* offers an example of an analogy that is invalid because all elements in the two phenomena being compared have not been identified, nor are they similar. The controlling idea for the guide is that the major source of the conflict between Jews and Arabs in Israel is the "prejudice" the former have toward the latter. To help students understand the dynamics of this psychological relationship, the guide asks them to analogize the "patterns of prejudice and discrimination between Jews and Arabs" in Israel to the relationships between "blacks and whites in the United States" (p. 16). However, the guide discusses the Jewish population of Israel only in terms of its European origins (p. 12). While it mentions that 60 percent of Israeli Jews are Sephardim (p. 12), it does not explain that these Israelis are refugees (or children of refugees) from Arab or Moslem countries in the Middle East and North Africa (see, for example, Martin Gilbert's *The Jews of Arab Lands: Their History in Maps,* 1975). Nor does it point out that the large number of Ethiopian Jews who are in Israel are black. Nor does it mention the cooperation between the Nazis and Palestinian Arabs before and during World War II, the role of the then Grand Mufti of Jerusalem in the formulation of the "final solution," and his kinship to Yassir Arafat (see, for example, Chapter 6, "The Nazis and the Palestine Question," in Bernard Lewis's *Semites and Anti-Semites,* 1986; Chapter 2, "The Arabs and Nazi Anti-Semites," in Dafna Alon's *Arab Racialism,* 1969). All of these facts are relevant to an understanding of the psychological relationship between Arab and Jew in Israel, but have no counterpart in an analysis of the psychological relationship between blacks and whites in this country. The guide's suggested analogy is thus not based on the comparability of all significant elements in the two phenomena being compared and reflects an abysmal lack of respect for the complexity and integrity of the topic.

The Obligation to Present Facts Accurately

The integrity of any topic a writer chooses to write about depends at its most basic level on the accuracy of the facts the writer offers. Developing academic writers must learn the importance of copying information accurately, rechecking original sources at least once if not several times, and even checking the same facts in several sources to make sure that one source is itself not in error. If they are creating facts, such as the data obtained from surveys, interviews, or experiments, they must be just as scrupulous about reporting what they obtained, without altering it unintentionally (or intentionally). Accurate factual data are part of the foundation of any substantive piece of academic writing. Not only do they frequently help the reader grasp the writer's larger, more abstract propositions, but small facts are sometimes the only elements in a piece of writing that a reader remembers clearly after time has elapsed.

For all these reasons, facts offered in curriculum materials need to be checked out carefully. Sometimes, of course, errors creep into a manuscript unintentionally as typographical mistakes during the revising process and may not be discovered before publication. Once such errors are discovered, acknowledgment by the author, or notices of errata by an editor, are in order, especially if an error has significant misleading implications.

An example of inaccurate factual material with serious misleading implications is the information about our national budget appearing in *Choices: A Unit on Conflict and Nuclear War*, curriculum materials for junior high school students prepared by the Union of Concerned Scientists in conjunction with the National Education Association and the Massachusetts Teachers Association. Linda Chavez (1983) notes that a worksheet called ''The Proposed 1987 National Budget'' on p. 59 of the guide claims that nearly half (9/20ths) of the ''national'' budget (based on actual fiscal year 1983 federal budget figures) goes to defense. As she points out, this fact is inaccurate and highly misleading. ''The actual percentage of the federal budget spent on defense is about 29 percent (Congressional Budget Office, U.S. House of Representatives). . . . Nowhere does the guide distinguish between federal, state, and local taxes or provision of services. Rather, the guide disingenuously leads students to believe that nearly one in every two tax dollars will be spent on weapons'' (p. 21).

Accurate facts are not only critical building blocks in academic writing, they are also clues to the degree of care a writer takes with his or her writing and the degree of pride the writer has about his or her work. Factual errors, especially those that are used to make or imply important points, as in the above example, create a lack of confidence on the part of a reader and tend to reduce his or her respect for the entire piece of writing, especially scientific writing. Ultimately, errors of fact prevent the development of academic knowledge in a field. As Jacob Bronowski (1968) notes, "facts are the empirical stuff and bottom of our knowledge, from which our work begins and to which it constantly returns to be tested; and if we cannot rely on one another's testimony in this, then we have no common ground to build on" (p. 72).

The Obligation to Create Unambiguous Texts with No Erroneous Implications

Developing academic writers have an obligation to write unambiguous statements that do not contain false or unwarranted implications. Preciseness and clarity are prized qualities of academic writing, and the presence of ambiguous statements seriously affects the academic reader's ability to understand and benefit from the writer's text. The following passage illustrates a significant lack of responsibility with respect to this concern. The passage was created by an academic researcher as a methodological instrument to explore how well both more and less skilled fifth-grade students could use a synopsis of social studies material on "Life in the New England Colonies" as a preview in order to learn its content. Yet, one statement in particular in the first passage is highly misleading and may leave readers with extremely inaccurate knowledge of the past.

> People who settled in the New England colonies helped to form the states we call Connecticut, Massachusetts, New Hampshire, and Rhode Island. Many of the people farmed. Their animals grazed together on land called a *commons*. Farming was a difficult life, especially since the settlers still needed to import goods that they could not grow or make themselves. Since they could not grow or make everything they needed, some people became merchants. Merchants traded goods made in New England with Europe and also imported goods.
>
> Since the people lived near the sea, it was natural to earn a living from the ocean. Some people fished, others hunted whales, while still others built ships from the forests that grew in New England. Wood from the forests was used to make furniture, tools, plates, and spoons, as well as ships. These goods were traded or exported to other lands.
>
> Ships returning from Europe imported flour, meat, clothing, and

tools. People as well as goods were brought to New England by these ships. Some of the people could earn their passage across the ocean by working four to seven years. Black people kidnapped in Africa did not have the opportunity to earn their passage. They were sold into slavery. (McCormick, 1989, p. 235)

Because this researcher-created synopsis focuses on the people of New England, the ships they built, the goods they made, and the goods and people their ships brought back to this country, the final two sentences in the third paragraph seem to imply that New England shippers also brought back black people that they had kidnapped in Africa. The writer should have made it clear that while many of these black people were kidnapped in raids, usually by other black people, many others (probably most) were captured in frequent wars among African kingdoms and sold into slavery to Arab slave traders and to ship captains from various European countries as well as from British colonies (see, for example, Jonathan Derrick's *Africa's Slaves Today*, 1975). All the relevant details of a complex subject need to be mentioned to make sure that the text is not misleading or inaccurate.

This is not the only misleading material in this "research" instrument. The text on "Life in the New England Colonies" that the students are asked to read after reading this synopsis contains the following paragraph:

A few Europeans were kidnapped and brought to the colonies. But most came by choice. However, black people from Africa had no choice. Beginning in the 1600s merchant ships carried black Africans. Some black people became indentured servants, but most became slaves. (McCormick, 1989, p. 237)

The text itself implies that New England merchant ships kidnapped Europeans as well; it does not mention that the colonists in New England came primarily from England, or that the merchant ships they came on in the 1600s (slave or not slave) were mainly British ships. In addition, the text continues to imply that all black people in Africa who became slaves were kidnapped, seemingly by New England ship captains and their crews. Any normal fifth grader reading these passages may well wonder how the hundreds of thousands of Africans brought over to this country as slaves could have all been kidnapped by ship captains and their crews. These ambiguous and misleading statements result not only in irresponsible texts but also in a flawed instrument for assessing reading comprehension, whose deficiencies should have been pointed out by the editors of the journal that published the article. We have learned from research on reading comprehension too much about the comprehension problems associated with poorly written texts in social studies or science for researchers to commit these errors in the texts they create for their own research. The writer of this text should have been particularly scrupulous about avoiding ambiguity in her writing because her intended readers were only fifth graders.

The Obligation to Illustrate a Phenomenon with Representative Examples

When illustrating a particular phenomenon, academic writers must try to select those examples that could be considered typical of the phenomenon—examples that reflect its central tendency or tendencies. Atypical examples, or examples that infrequently occur, can prevent the reader from developing an understanding of the essential nature of the phenomenon, especially if no typical examples are also offered. A case in point is the exhibit at the National Museum of American History in Washington, D.C., entitled After the Revolution: Every Day Life in America, 1780–1800 (the exhibit closed in July, 1990 for renovation but is scheduled to be reopened in January, 1991). To illustrate life during the early years of the Republic, curator Barbara Clark Smith has chosen to highlight the life of three very different families: a farm family in Delaware with four slaves, a Virginia plantation family with many slaves, and a merchant's family in Longmeadow, Massachusetts with two "servants for life"—permanently indentured white servants. Numerous scripts on the wall and in display cases offer information about their daily life.

However, not one of these families represents the typical, or average, American family in those years. Just as visitors are about to complete their tour of the series of rooms in this extensive exhibit area, a script on the wall informs the reader that most Americans in those years were farmers, and that most white farmers owned their own land and did their own work. It is a script that might easily be overlooked as there is no exhibit to which it is attached and which might call attention to it. Thus, although the scripts for this exhibit do not claim that the families whose lives are featured in the exhibit are representative of American families in this period of American history, visitors to this exhibit might easily believe that most Americans in the early years of the Republic had servants, if not slaves, to do most of their work.

The Obligation to Provide Correct Examples for Generalizations

Developing academic writers are as responsible for providing correct examples of generalizations as they are for providing the examples themselves. It is an axiom of academic writing that examples must be offered to support or illustrate abstract statements, especially those that are critical points for the argument advanced in an essay or textbook. It is no less a principle of responsible writing that the examples should be true illustrations of the proposition. If such examples cannot be found for a generalization, it may be that the generalization is flawed or false. The following passage from an introductory economics textbook for high school students shows a remarkable lapse in responsible writing with respect to this obligation.

> Either democracy or totalitarianism as a political system can exist with either private or collective ownership. The Fascists in Italy and the Nazis in Germany allowed private ownership of even the basic industries, but there was little freedom, even for the owners of business. Democracy can be practiced in nations, such as our own, that rely primarily on the market mechanism for the allocation of resources, or in nations that have a great deal of central planning, such as Sweden. (Gordon & Dawson, 1987, p. 63)

Although the senior author of the textbook is an academic economist, and this assertion is a very important point in this chapter, the use of Sweden as a democratic country illustrating large-scale collective ownership or central planning (the textbook equated the two in an earlier paragraph) is completely wrong. As Lester Thurow (1990) notes in one of his monthly columns in the *Boston Globe*, ''the Swedes have never had much government ownership of the means of production'' (p. 28). In actuality, Sweden has a capitalistic economic system with extremely high rates of taxation on private property to support its social policies. Thurow goes on to note that Sweden's ''system now seems at the breaking point'' because it cannot solve the ''free rider problem'' (p. 28).

The Obligation to Create Consistent Categories for Classifying Information

Developing academic writers are responsible for creating categories for classifying data or other information about a phenomenon that reflect the application of the same organizing principle. By deriving categories consistently from the same organizing principle, the writer can construct a unified intellectual structure for analyzing a phenomenon that may shed light on the entire phenomenon. The consistent use of the same intellectual principles in classifying components of a particular phenomenon frequently illuminates significant similarities and differences among the components and may call attention to real or seeming exceptions (much like Linnaeus' "Paradoxa") that can serve as the point of departure for further inquiry. The consistent use of the same organizing principles for presenting information about a particular phenomenon also facilitates the comprehension and integration of knowledge by the reader. When a writer derives categories from different organizing principles, both the writer and the reader are unlikely to gain a clear understanding of the subject.

A good example of the intellectual confusion writers cause by inconsistently deriving categories for classifying and presenting information can be found in the unit titles for a world geography text for grades 7 to 10 (Hunkins & Armstrong, 1987). After two introductory units on the foundations of geography and geographic patterns, units 3 through 9 deal with major geographic areas, for the most part different continents. However, while Unit 3 is titled *Anglo-America* and Unit 4, *Latin America*, suggesting language as a unifying principle, Unit 5 is titled *Europe*; Unit 6, *North Africa* and *Southwest Asia*; Unit 7, *Sub-Saharan Africa*; Unit 8, *Asia*; and Unit 9, *Oceania*. Language turns out not to be the organizing principle at all; for the most part, the traditional names of continents are used. Chapter titles in each unit also reflect inconsistently derived categories. The two chapters in Unit 3 are "The United States" and "Canada," suggesting individual countries as the internal organizing principle of a unit. However, in Unit 5 (Europe), map directions are used for three of the four chapter titles ("Northwest Europe," "Mediterranean Europe," and "Eastern Europe"); only the fourth chapter title singles out a country ("The Soviet Union"). In Units 6, 7, and 8, no individual countries are specified at all, only map directions (e.g., "North Africa," "Southwest Asia," "East Africa," "South Asia," "East Asia," "Southeast Asia," etc.). In Unit 9, individual chapters focus partially on political entities (Australia and New Zealand in one, and the Pacific Islands in another).

Since neither language, names of continents, or map directions serve consistently to organize units or chapters, a reader may end up with an inaccurate, incomplete, or disconnected grasp of world geography. Clearly, a reader can gain no consistent picture of language relationships across the world. For example, there is no Anglo-Europe, Anglo-Africa, Anglo-Oceania, or Anglo-Asia to correspond with Anglo-America. A reader cannot tell from the table of contents that Australia and New Zealand, mentioned in Unit 9 under Oceania, are as much "Anglo" as the United States, part of Canada, and England, or that English is either the official national language or one official national language in India, Kenya, Zimbabwe, Uganda, Nigeria, Ghana, Botswana, and other countries in the British Commonwealth. Further, the classification of North America as "Anglo-America" obscures Canada as a bilingual and bicultural country. A reader may also be misled about the differences and similarities between peoples and cultures in Europe and Asia and the boundaries between Europe and Asia. Siberia is studied as part of the Soviet Union, not as Northern Asia, thus de-emphasizing the similarities between the peoples of Siberia and the rest of Asia, and the differences between them and the Russians and other European peoples in the European half of the Soviet Union. The singling out of the Soviet Union as one of the four chapters on Europe also confounds the boundaries between Europe and Asia, as it seems to imply that the parts of the Soviet Union east of the Ural Mountains are part of Europe. Finally (and mysteriously), the reader cannot learn that the Alps are in Central Europe, or what countries are in Central Europe, since it is missing altogether. Writers who use inconsistent organizing principles not only do an injustice to the integrity of their subject, they do a disservice to their readers, especially young readers.

The Obligation to Create Coherent Texts

Developing academic writers are also responsible for creating coherent texts for their readers. A coherent text is one in which all major ideas are presented in a way that shows clearly and logically how they are related to each other and to the purpose of the text. Otherwise the coherence of the text and the integrity of the topic are damaged. The following passage is an example of an incoherent text. It appears as one of the beginning pages in a history of the city of Boston, written especially for third graders in the Boston public schools. The page is entitled "Boston Beginnings—Puritans." It is as incoherent for older readers as it is for younger readers.

> Ten years after the Pilgrims landed another group came to Massachusetts. They were called Puritans. The Puritans were given permission by the government of England to set up a colony. They came to the new land to worship the way they wanted and to have a better life. They sometimes called their new land "New England."
> The Puritans decided to put their colony on the Shawmut penin-

sula. This area is now called Boston. It is named after a town in England. The Puritans' leader was John Winthrop.

Other Puritans came from England to "New England." They built small towns called Roxbury and Dorchester. They farmed and raised cattle.

In the ten years after the Puritans came, thousands of people came to Boston. Black people were brought from Africa. Many stayed in Boston. They were slaves. They worked on the land and in the fishing boats. Black people have been a part of Boston almost as long as white people. (Davis, 1986, p. 35)

This page, the only page on the Puritans in this social studies text, contains 18 sentences. Yet, the last five, almost one-third of the 18 sentences, are not about the Puritans at all, creating a serious lack of coherence. Moreover, the entire last paragraph is so cryptic that it will confuse, rather than inform, the reader. Who were the thousands who came after the Puritans? All black people? If they were not all black, how many were? Were the others Puritans or non-Puritans? Who brought the black people to New England—Puritans or the others, if there were others? Developing academic writers need to learn the importance of presenting all relevant information an intelligent reader might need to know, in order to preserve the integrity of their topic and to prevent the reader from obtaining an oversimplified and possibly inaccurate understanding of the topic. No reader— particularly a third grader—is served by incoherent and therefore incomprehensible texts.

RESPECT FOR THE INTEGRITY OF THE READER

The Obligation to Assume an Open-Minded Reader

The chief purpose of academic discourse, unlike other kinds of discourse, is not to give aesthetic pleasure, to mystify, or to ridicule. Its purpose is to communicate the fruits of inquiry for inspection and judgment by others in a spirit that reflects the necessarily tentative nature of any academic offering. If developing academic writers fail to respect the purpose of academic inquiry and assume a particular point of view on the part of the reader—especially one that may not in fact exist—they may alienate the reader and preclude communication. They are therefore responsible for learning how to communicate the results of inquiry in a tone or voice that conveys respect for the nature of the academic enterprise. In essence, students need to learn the courtesy required for placing their ideas before an unknown reader for a judgment of their worth.

Perhaps the best way to illustrate the tone appropriate for academic discourse is to contrast two passages, one in which the voice of the writer suggests the tentative nature of academic inquiry, the other offering opinionated assertions in a voice that is morally offensive to an academic reader. Both are the opening paragraphs of the articles from which they have been taken.

> Over the last ten years, research on writing has focused less on the form of the final written documents than on the activities that create them. Researchers have recently begun to extend their analysis of composing activities by looking at the writing processes of writers in the workplace. . . . These studies suggest that the composing of writers at work is affected by a strong awareness of the previous knowledge and beliefs of those they write for. They have thus extended our understanding of composing because, with a few exceptions, previous research had concentrated on student writers whose awareness of audience and context was, at best, limited. (Winsor, 1989, p. 270)

> "The barbarians are in our midst," intoned Alan C. Kors, a University of Pennsylvania historian, at a recent meeting in New York City of 300 conservative professors who have formed something called the National Association of Scholars. Speaker after speaker, including former United Nations Representative Jeane J. Kirkpatrick and Boston University's President John Silber, rose to shudder in public about the "politicizing" of the universities. (Parini, 1988, p. B1)

The tone of the first passage is modest and courteous; what we hear is the voice of the scholar. Major assertions are qualified (e.g., "research . . . has focused less on . . . than on . . . ," "studies suggest," "with a few exceptions," "at best"); the reader is treated as a formal and serious audience, waiting for new and potentially useful information; and a clear context for the study to be described (the work of other scholars or researchers) is provided.

In contrast, the tone of the second passage reeks with sarcasm ("intoned" and "shudder in public"). The writer, a professor of English, is commenting critically on those he describes as "academic conservatives," placing them, for the most part, in the "generation of scholars who attended graduate school in the 1950s" (Parini, 1988, p. B1). He seems to assume that the reader already agrees with his point of view that one can be sarcastic about anything labeled "conservative." The passage thus conveys a lack of respect for its readers, who are placed in the uncomfortable position of seeming to share the author's derisive view of some of his professional colleagues. He has, in effect, co-opted their judgment in advance.

The Obligation to Use Affectively Balanced Terms

Academic writers frequently devise or select terms as labels to organize large bodies of ideas or information. They may use these terms as the names for procedures, strategies, or categories of data. Often writers devise terms to set up an organizational framework for comparing and opposing large bodies of ideas and information to each other. Terms clearly need to make sense for the information and ideas they organize, which is an intellectual issue. They also need to be affectively balanced so that one term does not appear to have either a negative or a positive connotation in relation to the others. Even if writers try to promote the virtues of the ideas or information covered by one of the terms and to point out the weaknesses in the other, they are nevertheless responsible for not using "loaded" terms that subconsciously predispose the reader for or against a particular category.

A large number of affectively unbalanced sets of terms have been used in recent years in the field of education: such sets as process/product, process/skills, expressive/transactional, qualitative/quantitative, student-centered/subject-centered, self-sponsored/school-sponsored, personal/impersonal, and whole language skills/content skills. Almost all have been proposed by writers seeking to promote what is covered by the first term in each set. Sets of affectively unbalanced terms that seem to make one phenomenon look good, or another bad, abound in other fields (e.g., historically aware readers/historically naive readers). The ideas a writer is trying to promote should be able to stand on their merits, while the ideas the writer is trying to discredit should fall on their lack of merit, not on the basis of a pejorative label.

The Obligation Not to Make Racist Remarks

An obligation that looms large in both academic and public discourse today is the responsibility to avoid racist remarks—the gratuitous use of racial or ethnic labels in a negative context when they have no direct or obvious relevance to the subject matter at hand. An example of such a gratuitous remark can be found in the following passage, which appeared in the *Chronicle of Higher Education* in the article by Parini (1988) on "neoconservatives."

These Cold War ideologues have been joined, just to muddy the waters, by a few younger academic bureaucrats on the make as well as by some neoconservative Jewish intellectuals. They all enjoy raving about the shutdown of the so-called American mind. (Parini, 1988, p. B1)

Whether or not the term "neoconservative Jewish intellectuals" is intended to refer especially to Allan Bloom, the author of *The Closing of the American Mind*, the ethnic/religious/racial identity of whatever individuals the writer has in mind is irrelevant to a discussion of the battle between so-called conservatives and so-called radicals in the academic world. Are there no "neoconservative" Christian or atheistic intellectuals, no "neoconservative" Italian or Irish intellectuals, or no "neoconservative" black intellectuals allied with the so-called "Cold War ideologues"? Why is the Jewishness of "neoconservative intellectuals" important to note in an article that describes no other group of scholars in racial, ethnic, or religious terms? The writer has violated his readers' integrity by assuming that they do not object to the gratuitous identification of a particular ethnic/racial/religious group in a way that is reminiscent of the perpetrators of the most virulent form of racism this century has seen. Needless to say, the editors of the *Chronicle* were also irresponsible in not asking the writer to eliminate an irrelevant label that not only violates the integrity of many, if not most, of their readers but also raises doubts about his own integrity.

The Obligation Not to Stereotype Readers—Or Other Writers

The academic writer must avoid violating the integrity of any potential reader by predetermining or making assumptions about the content of their thinking, that is, stereotyping them. Readers can be stereotyped directly, or indirectly by the labeling of other writers. The following paragraph shows an inordinate number of lapses in moral thinking in an essay critiquing E. D. Hirsch's *Dictionary*.

Those seemingly disjointed quotations are not atypical: the mindset of a comfortable white gerontocracy can be traced throughout the *Dictionary*, from the "rule of lasting significance" to the made-up example-sentences in Hirsch's section "Idioms" to the Commonwealth-ignoring provincialism of treating "Literature in English" as only British and American to the choice of a grammatical vocabulary including "only the most widely shared, and hence most traditional, terms" (p. 140). Colonel Blimp has not achieved Nirvana but has suffered a cisatlantic reincarnation.

The superficiality consequent on the middle-class Anglo mindset manifests itself already in the table of "Contents"; "World Literature, Philosophy, and Religion" in 30 pages, "World Politics" in 18 ("American Politics" gets 27), and the elderly Virginian's view of "Literature in English" in just 19. (Sledd & Sledd, 1989, p. 386)

This passage is filled with both age-ist and racist stereotyping (e.g., the limitations the authors note in the *Dictionary* are not "atypical," they can be traced to the "mindset of a comfortable white gerontocracy," they are part of a "middle-class Anglo mindset," or belong to an "elderly Virginian's view" of literature). Readers who are also elderly, middle class, "Anglo," and Virginians have good reason to be offended by stereotypes that seem to deny them their own individual judgment and differences. Such stereotyping also conveys the notion that the content and quality of a writer's (or reader's) thinking is nothing more than a reflection of his or her physical, genealogical, and contextual characteristics. It thereby denies both personal responsibility for the quality and content of one's thinking, and the capacity of writers, reviewers, and readers with differing personal and contextual traits to understand each other's "mindsets" and to engage in rational discourse together. The passage also displays another lapse in moral thinking; the authors insult another academic writer, metaphorically calling Hirsch a reincarnation of "Colonel Blimp." Thus, they doubly violate the integrity of the open-minded reader.

It would not be surprising if a great deal of irresponsible writing about a particular writer's work might have the opposite effect on open-minded readers than the irresponsible writers intended. That is, it might generate sympathy and a more uncritical acceptance than would otherwise be accorded to the work. Hirsch's work has generated so much irresponsible academic writing that an open-minded reader might be tempted to conclude that his ideas are so sound that they cannot be responsibly criticized at all. However, this is not the case. The following passage, which criticizes Hirsch's first list of words, raises some of the same points that authors of the previous passage are attempting to raise, but does so, for the most part, in a responsible manner.

Hirsch does tell us something of how he arrived at his list of "What Literate Americans Know." The method might be loosely characterized as scientific. He got together with two colleagues from his fine university, an historian and a physicist. Each . . . [here follows a long quotation from *Cultural Literacy*].

When they finished the first version of their list, they "submitted

it to more than a hundred consultants outside the academic world."
This was an acid test, apparently; the three were heartened to discover
"a strong consensus about the significant elements in our core literate
vocabulary." In view of the importance of this test, it is disturbing that
Hirsch does not reveal the criteria for selecting these consultants,
though they are said to have comprised "educated Americans of different ages, sexes, races, and ethnic origins." The group was apparently
not stratified for class or region, we do not know how "educated" was
defined, and we do not know what other efforts were made that would
allow us to conclude that this group could represent what should be
held up as America's common background knowledge. Without knowing this, how are we to be persuaded that this is the list that we are to
install?

Professor Hirsch and his two colleagues are employing the same
methods, it seems, in producing their next work—a dictionary of the
associations literate Americans make with each of the items in his index.
(Warnock, 1987, p. 488)

The author of this passage critiques in detail the methodology
Hirsch employed in his research without mentioning his genealogy,
age, or physical characteristics. Nor does he attribute Hirsch's ideas
to his physical, genealogical, or contextual characteristics. Questions
about various influences on background knowledge are raised but in
reference to Hirsch's methodology, not his person. And Hirsch himself is referred to courteously. Only a slight touch of sarcasm ("This
was an acid test, apparently; the three were heartened to discover
. . . ") mars this passage. Whether or not a reader finally accepts the
validity of the author's criticism, the reader interested in the topic is
likely to read it and consider its points seriously because the author
has made the writer's ideas and methodology, not his person, the
focus of the review. And by not attributing the writer's ideas to his
various characteristics, the author also has not insulted or stereotyped any possible reader by implication, thus respecting the individuality and integrity of all possible readers.

CONCLUDING REMARKS

In his discussion of three models of teaching, Israel Scheffler (1976)
notes that the insight, or cognitive, model does not make "adequate
room for principled deliberation in the characterization of knowing"
(p. 128). Nor does the "impression" model—a model focusing simply
on the passing on of accumulated knowledge. "In contrast to the

insight model," Scheffler states, "the rule model clearly emphasizes the role of principles in the exercise of cognitive judgment" (p. 130). Ultimately, he adds, the rule model itself must be "embodied in *multiple evolving traditions* in which the basic condition holds that issues are resolved by reference to *reasons* themselves defined by *principles* purporting to be impartial and universal" (p. 132).

Clearly, the three models Scheffler describes all have a role to play in the way in which teachers carry out their responsibilities with respect to their students' development as academic writers. Although the insight, or cognitive, model should continue to exercise a healthy influence on how teachers in all disciplines view their responsibilities toward their students as developing academic writers, teachers need to place at least as great an emphasis on the role of principles in determining how one comes to know what one believes one knows.

In this chapter, I have discussed some of the many ethical principles that developing academic writers need to learn to observe. Stress by teachers of academic writing on these responsibilities may especially help student writers avoid a common problem with much academic writing—misinterpretation of the topic under investigation. Misinterpretation occurs for various reasons, but can easily occur when writers base their interpretations or conclusions on insufficient, inadequate, or erroneous information. Older students especially must be encouraged to feel they are responsible for gathering and evaluating all the possibly relevant information they can find on a topic and for wrestling with complexity, if they are to learn what academic writing is and to appreciate it. However, to avoid misinterpretation, writers need to observe more than the responsibilities this chapter has outlined. They need to understand the complete intellectual and/or historical context for their topics. They also need to examine enough instances of a phenomenon in which they are interested before making a generalization, at the same time taking care that the instances they examine are representative of the whole range of the phenomenon. They must also guard against overgeneralization, which requires a careful definition and analysis of what it is they have examined.

Fulfilling all these responsibilities does not guarantee completely defensible interpretations or conclusions. But it will earn the academic writer the academic reader's respect. It shows the reader that the writer values communication that is as truthful as possible, and is thus respectful of the reader's time.

In an essay opposing the view that morality can only be a private matter in a country where religion is seen as the sole or primary source of morality and where "no one may impose their religious views on others," Condit (1987) argues for a "theory that recognizes collective discourse as the source of an active public morality" (p. 79). Condit believes that morality can be constructed from rational public argument and is not its precondition. I would agree but argue that the academic community is perhaps an alternative and better setting for nourishing the moral and civic thinking that should guide public moral argument. Academic writing is, or should be, the expression of principled and independent critical inquiry. As students engage in the process of writing for academic purposes, they can develop the moral and civic thinking that should underlie public discourse as well. Thus, a greater emphasis on the moral thinking that not only frequently motivates cognitive effort in academic writing but also serves to guide the entire process of academic writing—a moral theory of the writing process, if you will—may help to strengthen the ethical framework for both scholarship and civic participation in a republican form of government.

How can teachers develop their students' understanding and observance of these responsibilities? Undoubtedly, the most effective way for teachers to develop their students' sensitivity and responsiveness to these ethical responsibilities is by an insistence on their observance in their own writing. But other approaches are also helpful. As teachers come across examples of irresponsible writing in anything they read, these passages or texts can be brought to students' attention for class discussion. Students can then be asked to find examples themselves. They might look, for example, at their own textbooks in geography, history, economics, government, or science to note inconsistencies in the application of organizing principles, unsupported generalizations, blanket generalizations, affectively unbalanced terms, and other lapses in responsible writing that might appear in a textbook. Students might also analyze the editorials, op-ed essays, and syndicated essays in their daily newspapers for these lapses in moral thinking.

Teachers might also send for copies of the WETA–TV guide mentioned earlier, or *Arab World Notebook for the Secondary School Level*, edited by Audrey Shabbas and Ayad Al-Qazzaz (1989), a 460-page loose-leaf binder that purports to be social studies curriculum material on the Middle East. Both materials lend themselves to an illuminating discussion on how to distinguish subsidized propaganda from honest academic material; both are replete with different types of lapses in responsible writing. For example, *Arab World Notebook* contains such non-facts as "Yasir Arafat, now President Arafat of the newly declared state of Palestine" (p. 247). Many recently published curricular materials or textbooks on a variety of subjects could provide English and social studies teachers with opportunities for engaging students in critical thinking about the ethical responsibilities that writers owe their readers in academic and public life.

REFERENCES

Alon, D. (1969). *Arab racialism*. Israel: Kater Publications.

Bok, D. (1988, May–June). Ethics, the university, and society. *Harvard Magazine, 90* (5), 39–51.

Bradley Commission on History in Schools. (1988). *Building a history curriculum: Guidelines for teaching history in schools*. Washington, DC: Educational Excellence Network.

Bronowski, J. (1968). Science in the new humanism. *The Science Teacher, 35* (5), 13–16, 72–73.

Chavez, L. (1983, Fall). Teaching about nuclear war. *American Educator*, pp. 16–21.

Clifford, J. (1988, November 30). Remarks quoted in "Anthropologists explore the possibilities, and question the limits, of experimentation in ethnographic writing and research," by Ellen K. Coughlin. *The Chronicle of Higher Education*, pp. A5, A8.

Condit, C. (1987). Crafting virtue: The rhetorical construction of public morality. *Quarterly Journal of Speech, 73*, 79–97.

Daloz, L. (1986). *Effective teaching and mentoring: Realizing the transformational power of adult learning experiences*. San Francisco: Jossey-Bass.

Davis, J. (1986). *Boston and surrounding communities*. Boulder, CO: Graphic Learning.

Derrick, J. (1975). *Africa's slaves today*. New York: Schocken.

Drum, A. (1986). Responding to plagiarism. *College Composition and Communication, 37*, 241–243.

Evans, R. W. (1989). Diane Ravitch and the revival of history: A critique. *The Social Studies, 80*, 85–88.

Friedley, S. (1982). *Ethics and evidence: The ideal*. Paper presented at the Annual Meeting of the Speech Communication Association, Louisville, KY. (ERIC No. ED 224 083)

Gage, N. L. (1989). The paradigm wars and their aftermath: A "historical" sketch of research on teaching since 1989. *Educational Researcher, 18*, 4–10.

Garver, E. (1985). Teaching writing and teaching virtue. *The Journal of Business Communication, 22*, 51–73.

Gilbert, M. (1975). *The Jews of Arab lands: Their history in maps*. London: Furnival.

Giroux, H. (1987). Introduction to *Literacy: Reading the word and the world*, by P. Friere & D. Macedo. South Hadley, MA: Bergin & Garvey.

Gordon, S., & Dawson, G. (1987). *Introductory economics* (6th ed.). Boston: D.C. Heath.

Grindstaff, F. (1987). The context variable of the organic field model. In William Peters (Ed.), *Effective English teaching: Concept, research, practice* (pp. 45–92). Urbana, IL: National Council of Teachers of English.

Harrington, D. (1979). Encouraging honest inquiry in student writing. *College Composition and Communication, 30,* 182–186.

Harrington, D. (1981). Teaching ethical writing. *Freshman English News, 10,* 13–16.

Hunkins, F., & Armstrong, D. (1987). *World geography: People and places.* Grades 7–10. Columbus, OH: Merrill.

Lewis, B. (1986). *Semites and Anti-Semites: An inquiry into conflict and prejudice.* New York: Norton.

Kinneavy, J. (1980). *A theory of discourse.* New York: Norton.

Kroll, B. (1988). How college freshmen view plagiarism. *Written Communication, 5,* 203–221.

Mahoney, M. (1979). Essay writing in a political education. *Teaching Political Science, 7,* 51–72.

McCleary, W. (1986). *Leading students to recognize writing as an ethical act.* Paper presented at the Annual Meeting of the Conference on College Composition and Communication, New Orleans, LA. (ERIC No. ED 271 788)

McCormick, S. (1989). Effects of previews on more skilled and less skilled readers' comprehension of expository texts. *Journal of Reading Behavior, 21,* 219–240.

McGinley, W., & Tierney, R. (1989). Traversing the topical landscape: Reading and writing as ways of knowing. *Written Communication, 6,* 243–269.

Mitchell, W. J. T. (1989, April 19). Scholars need to explore further the links and dissonance between post-colonial culture and post-imperial criticism. *The Chronicle of Higher Education,* pp. B1–B3.

Pabst, W., Munsterman, G. T., & Mount, C. H. (1977). The value of jury duty: Serving is believing. *Judicature, 61* (1), 38–42.

Parini, J. (1988, December 7). Academic conservatives who decry 'politicization' show staggering naivete about their own biases. *The Chronicle of Higher Education,* pp. B1–B2.

Paul, R. (1988). Ethics without indoctrination. *Educational Leadership, 45,* 10–19.

Ravitch, D. (1989). The revival of history: A response. *The Social Studies, 80,* 89–91.

Ryerson, A. (1989). China's untold story. *American Educator, 13,* 10–15.

Scheffler, I. (1976). Philosophical models of teaching. In R. S. Peters (Ed.), *The concept of education* (pp. 120–134). London: Routledge & Kegan Paul.

Shabbas, A., & Al-Qazzaz, A. (1989). *The Arab World Notebook for the Secondary School Level.* Berkeley, CA: Najda: Women Concerned About the Middle East.

Sledd, A., & Sledd, J. (1989). Success as failure and failure as success: The *Cultural Literacy* of E. D. Hirsch, Jr. *Written Communication, 6,* 364–389.

Stotsky, S. (1990). On planning and writing plans—Or beware of borrowed theories! *College Composition and Communication, 41,* 37–57.

Taylor, D. (1989). The many keys to literacy. *Phi Delta Kappan, 71,* 185–193.

Thurow, L. (1990, March 6). History is far from over. *Boston Globe,* p. 28.

Warnock, J. (1987). Review of *Cultural literacy: What every American needs to know,* by E. D. Hirsch, Jr. *College Composition and Communication, 38,* 486–489.

WETA–TV. (1989). Curriculum guide for *Arab and Jew: Wounded spirits in a promised land,* based on the book by David Shipler.

Winsor, D. (1989). An engineer's writing and the corporate construction of knowledge. *Written Communication, 6,* 270–285.

Witte, S. (1987). Pre-text and composing. *College Composition and Communication, 38,* 397–425.

Young, R. (1987). Recent developments in rhetorical invention. In G. Tate (Ed.), *Teaching composition: Twelve bibliographic essays* (pp. 1–38). Fort Worth: Texas Christian University Press.

6 Language Education and Civic Education

Recovering Past Traditions, Reassessing Contemporary Challenges

LISA EDE

Conscientious educators can only praise the goals of a book such as this, which endeavors, as Sandra Stotsky notes in the Introduction, to encourage language arts and English teachers at all levels in their "efforts to shape those ways of thinking that contribute to their students' capacity for promoting the common good." But those familiar with the history of rhetoric—the art of effective communication first developed in the West by such Greek and Roman rhetoricians as Isocrates (436–338 B.C.), Aristotle (384–322 B.C.), Cicero (106–43 B.C.), and Quintilian (A.D. 35–95)—must experience a moment of deep irony on reading words such as these. For they know that for centuries in Western culture, language education and civic education were so fundamentally and deeply intertwined as to be inseparable.

HISTORY OF RHETORIC

Rhetoric as it developed in the fifth century B.C. in Greece grew out of *public* concerns. Corax of Syracuse, often described as the first formulator of the art of rhetoric, is said to have developed his art to enable ordinary citizens to argue effectively in court about conflicting property claims—private concerns made, of necessity, public. Like Corax, Plato (429–347 B.C.) viewed rhetoric as inherently connected with public discourse. But Plato also emphasized that rhetoric must be motivated solely by a concern for the common civic good and informed by genuine, not spurious, knowledge. For Plato, rhetoric could not be separated from ethics: to discuss rhetoric, he asserted in the *Gorgias* (1960), is "nothing less [than to discuss] how a man should live" (p. 106). And any public discourse that did not meet Plato's rigorous standards was nothing less than "pandering . . .

because it makes pleasure its aim instead of good, and . . . because it has no rational account to give of the nature of the various things which it offers" (p. 46). Later rhetoricians, such as Aristotle, Cicero, and Quintilian, modified Plato's rigidly philosophical approach. But these rhetoricians maintained that rhetoric could not be studied—and should not be practiced—separately from ethics. They saw rhetoric as linked with both the development of knowledge and the quest for public justice and harmony.

Rhetoric in Greece and Rome was not only an art of public discourse, one linked firmly to ethics and politics; rhetoric was also a primary means of educating future citizens. Plato and Aristotle were teachers as well as philosophers; both founded schools (the Academy and the Lyceum) where they lectured to students. But it was the Romans who systematized rhetorical educational practice. Particularly influential in this respect was Quintilian, whose *Institutes of Oratory* (A.D. 95) informed educational practice for centuries. In "Rhetorical History as a Guide to the Salvation of American Reading and Writing: A Plea for Curricular Courage," James J. Murphy (1982) describes how Quintilian's vision of the coordinated teaching of language through reading, writing, speaking, and listening was passed from age to age. Quintilian's methods were used throughout the Middle Ages even though his complete text had been lost. Its recovery in 1416 was, as Murphy notes, a major occurrence.

> When Poggio Bracciolini rediscovered the complete text in the monastery at St. Gall, Switzerland, in 1416, the book electrified humanists. One friend wrote to Poggio, "Send me a copy so that I may see it before I die." The Italian example inspired English writers like Roger Ascham and Sir Thomas Elyot, so that by the time of Queen Elizabeth Quintilian's educational methods were well established in English schools. Shakespeare as a schoolboy studied in a way that would have been familiar to Cicero, Seneca, Tacitus, Horace, and Vergil. In the next century the poet John Milton did the same. When, in Milton's century, the citizens of New Town on the Charles River in Massachusetts desired to open a school, they looked back to the only educational pattern they had known and brought masters from Cambridge University. The boys in the school to which John Harvard left part of his estate studied much the same way Shakespeare and Milton had, and much the same way boys had studied for the preceding millennium and a half. (pp. 5–6)

In his essay, Murphy argues that the most important feature of this centuries-long pedagogical tradition is its integration of reading, writing, speaking, and listening. Edward P. J. Corbett (1971), in his

Classical Rhetoric for the Modern Student, comments on another feature, the connection among rhetoric, ethics, and civic virtue.

> Quintilian insisted that in addition to being intellectually fortified for his office [a point emphasized by Cicero, who, with Marcus Cato, characterized the perfect orator as "a good man skilled in speaking"] the orator must be a man of strong moral character. It was this insistence on the intellectual and moral training of the aspiring orator that made Cicero and Quintilian the two most potent classical influences on rhetorical education in England and America. (p. 602)

Rhetoric did not of course pass from classical to modern times unaltered. Corbett notes, for instance, that in the Middle Ages "rhetoric ceased to be pursued primarily as a practical art and became rather a scholastic exercise" (p. 603). Such changes in the art of rhetoric inevitably influenced its teaching. But the connection among rhetoric, ethics, and civic education was never entirely broken, though in certain periods rhetoric as stylistic display did take precedence over rhetoric as the invention and communication of substantive discourse.

Too few language arts and English educators are aware of the history that I have briefly sketched here. They are also largely unaware of the history of rhetorical instruction in American colleges, which "flowered briefly in the eighteenth century as the art of communication in the conduct of human affairs, [but] had withered by the end of the nineteenth" (Connors, Ede, & Lunsford, 1984, p. 5; see also Berlin, 1984). Language arts and English educators need to know this history: Rhetoric still has a great deal to offer those who teach the art of effective communication—an art that should be studied and practiced, rhetoricians have asserted for centuries, conjoined with, not separated from, ethical and civic concerns.

Though I have argued strongly for the relevance of rhetoric (now studied and taught in a variety of disciplines, including speech communication, English and composition studies, and philosophy) for contemporary language arts and English teachers, I cannot fully defend this assertion here. Such a defense would require a lengthy analysis, one full of contentious definitions, elaborate descriptions, and complex scholarly and pedagogical arguments. Instead, I would like to provide an example that may help readers understand what it means to have a rhetorical perspective on communication and the implications of this perspective for teachers of writing, particularly those concerned with fostering the development and expression of a civic ethic.

AN ANALYSIS OF CONTEMPORARY PUBLIC DISCOURSE

Rhetoric and Public Discourse

Before offering readers an example of what it means to have a rhetorical perspective on communication, I should more clearly describe what I mean by rhetoric, for this discipline's extensive history and the term's multiple connotations make defining it far from easy. Arguments about the scope or province of rhetoric abound in recent scholarship, for example, as do arguments about the relationship of classical to modern or "new" rhetoric and that of rhetoric and philosophy. With Michael Halloran (1975), however, I would argue that "the one feature of discourse that has remained a constant emphasis of rhetorical theories from ancient Greece to the present is that it is addressed" (p. 621). Rhetoricians from Aristotle to Chaim Perelman and Lucia Olbrechts-Tyteca (1969), authors of the influential volume, *The New Rhetoric: A Treatise on Argumentation*, have understood that "it is in terms of an audience that an argumentation develops" (p. 5).

Unlike formal logic, then, which traditionally aspires to decontextualized, mathematical precision, rhetoric embraces the human, the situational. Because rhetoric is situation-based, that is, grounded in what Lloyd Bitzer (1968) calls "the rhetorical situation," it is inevitably concerned with values and beliefs. Rhetoricians from Aristotle to Kenneth Burke (1966) have recognized that to be effective those who wish to persuade others must appeal to the whole human being and must recognize the importance of, in Aristotle's terms, not just logical appeals (*logos*) but emotional appeals (*pathos*). Those who wish to persuade others must also realize that the audience will inevitably be influenced by its evaluation of the credibility (or *ethos*) of the speaker or writer.

During rhetoric's healthiest, most productive periods this recognition of the needs and interests of the audience has been balanced by a commitment to what Wayne Booth and others have called "good reasons." Booth's *Modern Dogma and the Rhetoric of Assent* (1974) grew, he notes in the Introduction to this work, out of his puzzlement in the late 1960s

> by the inability of most protest groups to get themselves heard [i.e., genuinely understood, as opposed to merely listened to, by faculty at the University of Chicago] and by the equal failure of what one of my students called 'establishment protestors' to make their responses intelligible [to student protest groups]. (p. ix)

Throughout his wide-ranging analysis, Booth grapples with two age-old questions.

1. *How should men* [sic] *work when they try to change each other's minds, especially about value questions?*
2. *When should you and I change our minds?*—that is, how do we know a good reason when we see one? (p. 12)

Public Discourse: A Case Study

The much smaller case study that I will describe here grew out of a puzzlement similar to that experienced by Wayne Booth in the 1960s. It involves a controversy in Corvallis, Oregon, catalyzed by the efforts of a local group, the Committee for Quality School Textbooks. On October 18, 1982, the chairperson of this newly formed committee appeared before the Corvallis School Board urging it to adopt a resolution banning what the committee identified as ''secular humanism'' in the schools. The committee's efforts, which included attempts to persuade the board to discontinue the use of a number of texts and resource works, generated considerable debate in this small college town. During the following four months (October, 1982 to January, 1983) the local paper, the *Corvallis Gazette-Times*, published at least 85 letters to the editor on this subject, as well as two editorials, one editorial cartoon, and two guest editorials—one by a member of the school board and one by the chairperson of the committee. On January 22, 1983, the *Gazette-Times* called for a moratorium, noting that ''arguments for and against the committee and its aims have been adequately presented in the many letters published to date'' (p. 4).

As a resident of Corvallis, I was concerned by this controversy and read the letters with care as they appeared. But I increasingly became interested in the letters as possible objects of rhetorical study, particularly because the voluminous debate on the subject clearly not only had failed to resolve the heated conflict but, instead, had perhaps exacerbated it. The *Gazette-Times'* decision not to publish additional letters on the committee's efforts seemed to confirm my sense that in general the letters presented in this public forum had not achieved their implicit purpose of helping to illuminate and resolve an issue of considerable importance to the community. I wanted to learn more about why this exchange of letters did so little to further discussion of the issue at hand that the *Gazette-Times* editor, in apparent exasperation, refused to publish additional comments on this still lively and much-contested topic. I decided to study these letters to see what I could learn about their overall quality and, specifically, their rhetorical effectiveness. Thanks to a grant from the Oregon Council for the Humanities, I was able to devote part of one summer to this project.

The Corvallis Controversy: Logical Analysis

Traditional logical analysis represents one useful way to examine a body of letters such as were generated in response to this local controversy. Such analysis examines texts to determine the degree to which they adhere to the requirements of inductive and deductive logic and manifest common logical fallacies, such as begging the question (circular reasoning), proposing a false analogy, or arguing *ad hominem* (name-calling or attacking the person, rather than analyzing the issue).

An analysis of the 85 letters printed in the *Gazette-Times*, excerpts of which are presented in this chapter, revealed much to absorb the professional energies of logicians, for, unfortunately, many of the letters do not meet generally accepted logical standards. To begin with, logical fallacies appear with discouraging frequency in letters supporting and opposing the Committee for Quality School Textbooks. The letters abound with *ad hominem* attacks and false (simplistic or questionable) analogies, as the following examples show:

> The inconsiderate amount of space the *Gazette-Times* continues to devote to the writing of zealots on the subject they call "secular humanism" is the mark of a newspaper which fails to distinguish between contemporary issues and anachronous tracts of religion. (November 20, 1982)

> The "new right" began with men like George Washington in 1776. He said in his farewell address, "reason and experience both forbid us to expect that national morality can prevail in exclusion of religious principle." (December 6, 1982)

The author of the first excerpt attempts to discredit all those supporting the committee by employing the *ad hominem* strategy of labeling them as zealots. Critical readers will question the unsupported analogy by the author of the second excerpt comparing George Washington with the "new right."

Many letter writers also made highly generalized assertions, rather than specific and concrete arguments. Given the necessary brevity of letters to the editor, writers simply cannot clarify or support such statements as the charge that "secular humanism is a philosophy. It is espoused mainly by theists, agnostics, and atheists. It is a political belief in the value of a socialist one-world government as a cure all" (December 4, 1982). Even when an attempt is made to provide some evidence, a few examples cannot support broad generalizations, as the following letter illustrates:

> Each time someone takes a stand for high-quality education, every American Civil Liberties Union-type liberal comes warping on the eastern wind, proclaiming himself to be a moderate and crying "radical religious right" and "censorship."
>
> The truth of the matter is that textbooks were long ago censored by those who write and publish them. They have censored out decency, reverence, modesty, integrity, trustworthiness, unselfishness, courage, pride, goodness and all the civic virtues.
>
> Besides the obvious affronts to decency and decorum—blasphemy and obscenity—we find death education, a clear invasion of religion by the same schools that exclude prayer and Gideon Bibles. We find that socially unacceptable language in ordinary conversation is tolerated and even encouraged. We also find substandard vocabulary and a preoccupation with unhappy home situations, anti-social behavior and sad or disgusting events.
>
> For example, how do you like this piece from a textbook called "Focus" by Scott, Foresman —"The Kitten," page 68: "I found a piece of rope, made a noose, slipped it about the kitten's neck, pulled it over a nail, then jerked the animal clear of the ground. It gasped, sloppered, spun, doubled, clawed the air frantically; finally its mouth gaped and its pink-white tongue shot out stiffly. I tied the rope to a nail and went to find my brother."
>
> We consumer advocates [must] demand books worthy of our children. They must not be robbed of the inspiration and knowledge they need to become worthy American citizens. (December 11, 1982)

Although this letter does offer some general examples, such as the inclusion of death education and the tolerance of "unacceptable" language in the schools, it relies primarily on a single out-of-context example from a novel (not a district-wide textbook) as evidence. This single and questionable example can hardly support assertions such as that "textbooks were long ago censored by those who write and publish them. They have censored out decency, reverence, modesty, integrity, trustworthiness, unselfishness, courage, pride, goodness and all the civic virtues."

Many letters also demonstrate the fallacy of "begging the question"—asserting as a premise or fact what is actually a debatable question. The following excerpt is from a guest editorial by the chair-person of the Committee for Quality School Textbooks:

> What can be done about it [the trend away from basic educational and traditional values]? The Committee for Quality School Textbooks has not asked for censorship. But it is asking for changes in policies set up by the Corvallis School Board. The board is an appropriate channel for this action. It can establish guidelines for selection of textbooks and curriculum that give us the highest quality for our educational dollar. The board can increase time devoted to academics, abolish social promotion, upgrade graduation requirements and reinforce the traditional values of the community.
>
> In short, the board can stop using our children as guinea pigs in the educational experiments of the day and return to a no-nonsense education in basic, fundamental skills and questions. (December 20, 1982)

The use of "in short" in this example implies that the final assertion follows logically from the preceding suggestions. In fact, however, the statement that "the board can stop using our children as guinea pigs in the educational experiments of the day" is an assertion that many readers of the *Corvallis Gazette-Times* would debate vigorously.

The Corvallis Controversy: Rhetorical Analysis

A rhetorician analyzing the collection of letters to the editor and the editorials generated by this local controversy would certainly not ignore any of the logical failings demonstrated above. But additional questions would guide such an analysis. As mentioned earlier, rhetoric traditionally has emphasized the rhetorical situation. A rhetorical analysis of these letters, consequently, would (in addition to considering logical and stylistic issues) focus on the rhetorical situation and the ways in which letter writers responded to their current situation (the local controversy) and attempted through their letters to influence that situation. Such an analysis would pay particular attention to the writer–reader relationship established by these letters, and it would attempt to evaluate their overall rhetorical impact.

My own rhetorical reading of these letters caused me to note a pervasive and significant problem (one not uncovered by logical analysis): the failure, in rhetorical terms, of writers to establish any common ground—some shared value or belief, for instance, or some fact or generalization that writer and reader could agree on—as a basis for communication. The following pair of letters demonstrates this problem:

> The Corvallis School Board is again being assailed by the high priests of ignorance and superstition. The country is currently going through a rebirth of popularity and interest in conservative philosophy and fundamentalist theology.
>
> Whether this is a permanent change in direction (I sincerely doubt that it is) or the backward swing of the pendulum of history (which would seem more likely), these merchants of fear and doom must be allowed to have their say and present their arguments. But their "true faith" and "missionary zeal" must not be allowed to slip into "witch hunts" and "holy crusades." These attacks upon the textbooks and the "humanistic values" that are presented to so many school boards around the country today have at last, after some initial successes, been addressed and refuted—quite handily, I might add—by an overwhelming number of scientists and educators.
>
> The elected school board members are to be congratulated for their patient stance in the face of these very organized and vocal groups. (November 2, 1982)

> It is evident from reading recent letters in the *Gazette-Times* that there is much confusion as to what "secular humanism" is and what effects, if any, it is having on the public schools.
>
> Many have questioned whether its antagonists even know what it is. The answer is, "yes we do."
>
> The New Webster's Dictionary gives a limited and purely humanistic definition. I am convinced that it is impossible for the non-Christian to really understand the meaning of humanism thus the perplexity among most educators. Consequently, they feel threatened and that their abilities and sincerity as teachers are under attack.
>
> For the Christian, humanism is anything which does not place God at the center of it. Therefore, the public school system is humanistic in nature. This negative philosophy is the basis of all public education today—a philosophy which ignores God and exalts man. This has had a devastating effect on our children and on the quality of education they are receiving.
>
> . . . One wonders about the implications of this philosophy [secular humanism] on moral behavior. I believe the evidence is already in. Young people are discontented and apathetic. Suicide, drug addiction and alcoholism are on the rise, and more children are giving birth to children outside of marriage than anytime in our history. Even the educators would agree that literacy is on the decline.
>
> What is their solution to the problem? More tax dollars, of course! I

say the whole system is sick unto death and in bad need of a "heart" transplant. (November 3, 1982)

As with the letters presented earlier, these two letters manifest a number of logical problems. What I find most striking, however, is the complete nonintersection of these writers' assumptions and views. Each writer is clearly thinking and writing in the context of an entirely different value and belief system. These systems are so strong—their boundaries are so tightly and rigidly drawn—that the writers hold their beliefs with a conviction that ranges from near certainty (in the case of the first writer, who notes confidently that attacks on textbooks have been "addressed and refuted—quite handily, I might add—by an overwhelming number of scientists and educators") to absolute conviction (in the case of the second writer, whose religious values preclude uncertainty in issues relating to God and religion). The first letter both privileges and appeals to readers' faith in science, technology, and social institutions; the second, to readers' belief in God and to traditional Christian values. Perhaps most important (and discouraging), neither writer is willing to concede that there is anything to argue about, any shared mutual concern to explore, any issue to analyze, much less anywhere to compromise.

In a sense, then, the second letter writer is at least partially correct when she states that she is "convinced that it is impossible for the non-Christian to really understand the meaning of humanism." Her own sense of the gulf between her views and those of many of her readers led her to abandon all hopes of a public resolution of this controversy. Instead, she urged the chairperson of the Committee for Quality School Textbooks to work for the establishment of a private Christian school, one reflecting the values of the committee: "Stop trying to salvage something good from today's educational system. You are wasting your time. Why not direct your energies and resources into beginning a really fine Christian academy here—one that is established on the word of God?"

The writers of these two letters have, in effect, positioned themselves so that they can communicate effectively only with those who already share their values and beliefs. Readers firmly in the writer's "camp" would read their advocate's letter not as an argument or a contribution to public discussion of a debatable issue (one about which reasonable persons might disagree), but as confirmation of their own established, if not entrenched, viewpoints. Readers holding opposing values and beliefs would find little in these letters to encourage discussion of shared concerns and issues—and much to polarize and inflame.

Fortunately, not all the letters written in response to this controversy fit the above description. Consider the following letter, written by a college student attending a Christian university:

> I am glad to see that our community is so interested in the quality of the education of students in the Corvallis School District. Personally, I would like to commend the School Board for a job well done. I have been attending Pacific Lutheran University since graduating from Crescent Valley in 1981 and have found my high school education quite adequate for the academic challenges I have faced. College definitely is not easy, but Crescent Valley was an excellent source of preparation for university life.
>
> I would also like to note that situation ethics and values clarification should not necessarily be condemned by the Committee for Quality School Textbooks. Depending on the context in which these two educational tools are used, they can be very useful and are really quite harmless in helping the concerned citizen establish his or her priorities.
>
> I go to a university that proudly claims its students receive a "quality education in a Christian context"; yet in several of my classes, situation ethics have been used. All of the students in my "Leadership for Outdoor Ministries" class used values clarification.
>
> Contrary to [the chairperson's] beliefs, values clarification does not demand that you reject the values of your parents, church or anyone else. Rather, values clarification teaches you to think through your own values and standards and to decide what demands priority in your life.
>
> I believe this is what God wants us to do. I believe God does not want us to have certain values because our parents, pastor or even the Bible says they are right. God wants us to believe in him, and in his ways, because we know what is right.
>
> I once heard a pastor say, "we don't need to park our brains outside the church before we enter." To that I say "Amen!" (January 5, 1983)

This letter manifests a number of strengths. Unlike many letter writers, who charged the committee with being religious "zealots," this writer presents herself as a Christian, one who thus at least partly shares the religious values of those who support the committee. Her affirmation that "God does not want us to have certain values because our parents, pastor, or even the Bible says they are right. God wants us to believe in him, and in his ways, because we know what is right" may not convince members of the committee—but they cannot so easily discount her views either. And her explanation of the importance of values education in her own "Leadership for Outdoor Ministries" class represents an implicit argument in favor of this method, not just for the committee and its supporters, but for many other members of this small-town community as well. Finally, the specificity of this letter and the writer's obvious personal involvement with her subject represent another strength. To use a term favored by rhetoricians, this writer effectively uses language to create a strong and convincing sense of *ethos*—she persuades as much by the image of herself that she creates in her letter as by her specific arguments.

Another writer begins her letter, excerpted below, in a productive and conciliatory manner by recognizing the complex and emotionally charged nature of the issues being debated in the letters to the editor column. She affirms the legitimacy of many parents' fears about secular influences on their children, while also indicating her own opposition to the proposals advocated by some critics of the schools.

> I have been reading the letters on the secular humanism issue with great interest. It is an emotional issue in which few remain objective, but many remain silent. I cannot be totally objective, but I feel I can no longer be silent. . . .
>
> I understand that any caring parent is genuinely concerned about the daily influences upon his children. The unhealthy pressures on today's child via television, movies, books, and music are enormous. It behooves all of us to watch the schools, but there seems to be a movement afoot to . . . solve social ills by instituting school prayer, teaching creationism, or censoring textbooks.

She goes on to appeal to shared religious values by commenting on her own sense of loss that secular songs have replaced traditional religious hymns in Christmas celebrations.

> I value prayer and religious education, but not in the public schools. The potential for abuse is too great. We should be zealously guarding the separation of church and state as vital to our way of life, as witnessed by the excesses of the theocracy in Iran today. I personally feel a sense of loss when Frosty the Snowman replaces our beautiful traditional Christmas music at the schools' winter programs, but I do understand the reasons. . . . (November 30, 1982)

These two letters successfully appeal to shared values and assumptions, making a genuine effort to establish a common ground for public discussion of a controversial issue. Why did so few of the

85 letters written in response to this local controversy demonstrate the rhetorical "goodwill" characterized in these letters? There are, of course, many possible answers to this question. I would like to focus here, however, on one issue particularly relevant to a rhetorical understanding of these letters, the fragmentation of modern and post-modern culture into competing communities and the resulting loss of a genuine sense of public discourse.

Rhetoric, Post-Modern Culture, and Public Discourse

As Michael Halloran (1975) notes in "On the End of Rhetoric, Classical and Modern," during the classical period those citizens who formed the *polis* or community (and it is important to remember how limited this citizenry was) shared " . . . certain assumptions about the world, namely that it is knowable, that values are coherent, that wisdom is public" (p. 622). In our own post-modern culture, speakers and listeners, writers and readers inhabit not a single, homogeneous communal world, but many worlds. And, as Halloran notes, "when speaker and audience inhabit different worlds, it becomes possible for both to hear without listening. . . . In Sartrean terms, both speaker and audience are liable to the rhetorical equivalent of bad faith" (pp. 626–627).

Rhetoric offers no easy solutions to this dilemma. A rhetorical perspective on communication can, however, help language arts and English teachers better understand the challenges and opportunities facing those who wish to contribute, in Stotsky's words, "to the development of the moral framework for public discourse and public behavior in this country." As noted earlier, rhetoric has always emphasized the importance of responding to the values and beliefs of the audience and of establishing a common ground that can serve as a starting point for argument.

In the *Rhetoric*, Aristotle argues vigorously for the importance of what he calls enthymematic reasoning as a means of establishing a common ground. (In the two letters just discussed, for instance, shared religious values provide a crucial enthymematic bridge between writer and readers.) Enthymemes, Aristotle explains, are rhetorical syllogisms. Unlike logical syllogisms, enthymemes address questions involving probable truth. Perhaps even more important, enthymemes' premises are, as John Gage (1984) notes, "derived from, or contributed by, an audience which does not already share the conclusion. The enthymeme . . . is, in one sense, a necessary compromise between what one who wishes to persuade may want to say and what an audience will allow to be said'' (p. 157). Enthymematic reasoning—reasoning that entails acknowledging or indicating that one shares the audience's values—is thus one of the most important ways that writers can establish a common ground for discussion.

A number of modern rhetoricians share Aristotle's and other classical rhetoricians' emphasis on the importance of recognizing the values and beliefs of the audience and of establishing a common ground for argument. Perelman and Olbrechts-Tyteca (1969), for instance, argue that

> The unfolding as well as the starting point of the argumentation presuppose indeed the agreement of the audience. This agreement is sometimes on explicit premises, sometimes on the particular links used in the argument or on the manner of using these links. (p. 65)

Part Two of their analysis in *The New Rhetoric: A Treatise on Argumentation* focuses appropriately on ''The Starting Point of Argument.''

The basic insight of Aristotle, Perelman and Olbrechts-Tyteca (1969), and others (such as Stephen Toulmin, 1958, and Wayne Booth, 1974)—that writers and speakers cannot ignore the values and beliefs of those with whom they wish to communicate—is hardly esoteric or profound. Effective communicators know instinctively that to change others' minds or to explore an issue critically with others, they must in some way establish a starting point, a space where they can agree, in effect, to stand together. The process of negotiating—and maintaining—this space is hardly simple, however. It involves, as Toulmin, Rieke, and Janik (1979) note,

> dealing with claims with an eye to their contexts, to competing claims, and to the people who hold them. It calls for the critical evaluation of these ideas by shared standards; a readiness to modify claims in response to criticism; and a continuing critical scrutiny both of the claims provisionally accepted and of any new ones that may be put forward subsequently. (p. 9)

As Toulmin, Rieke, and Janik's comment indicates, ethical and effective argumentation poses formidable challenges for those who wish to engage in public debate over controversial issues. And the constraints inherent in the format of letters to the editor, particularly their mandated brevity, only add to these challenges. In reading the 85 letters to the editor defending or criticizing the efforts of the Committee for Quality School Textbooks, however, I was discouraged to note how few writers even attempted to take into consideration the necessarily diverse values and beliefs of their readers. Instead, as noted earlier, most letters tended to inflame and polarize—to address, implicitly, only the limited audience of those already in agreement with the writer—rather than to seek consensus or explore potential compromises.

SUGGESTIONS FOR CLASSROOM PRACTICE

With its emphasis on the rhetorical situation, on the necessity of establishing some common ground with readers, and on enthymematic reasoning, rhetoric can help students develop the sensitivity necessary to engage in public discussions of controversial issues in our post-modern world. Teachers can help students increase their sensitivity to the values and beliefs of readers who may disagree with them, by encouraging students to develop a broadly rhetorical understanding of language and communication. I have found that students can most easily understand concepts such as the rhetorical situation if discussion is grounded in their personal experience. When I introduce this concept, for instance, I often ask students to tell me how they decide what clothes to wear in different situations. In the resulting conversation—one punctuated with laughter at my ignorance of current styles and mores—students realize that they have a highly articulated understanding of the appropriateness of specific clothes for specific situations.

We then discuss how students know what kind of language is appropriate in various situations. Why do students speak differently to a close friend and a teacher or minister, to a neighbor and a prospective employer? Students discover in the course of these and other discussions that they know a great deal about the ''rhetoric'' of dress and everyday conversation. They realize that, almost without thinking, they make rhetorical choices every day by considering such factors as the nature and status of the person with whom they are speaking, the constraints inherent in the situation, and their own goals.

Once students have gained a rhetorical perspective on their everyday experience and use of oral language, they can more easily understand how rhetoric functions in written discourse. Such a perspective encourages students to look at writing not as a series of rules to be followed or forms to be filled out, but as a means of communication between writer and reader, even when—as often is the case—writer and reader may never meet. Teachers can use a variety of means to heighten students' awareness of the role rhetorical concerns play in written communication. They might begin by asking students to analyze the junk mail that arrives at their homes, for instance. How do advertisers and fund-raisers use language to persuade recipients to respond positively to their messages? What "etiquette" do they follow, and what, in the students' experience, differentiates successful from unsuccessful junk mail? Students can also easily understand discussions based on personal letter writing. In analyzing how a letter to an aunt thanking her for a birthday present would differ from a note to a close friend or an entry in a diary, students can recognize the ways in which they as writers already use language to respond appropriately to a variety of different rhetorical situations.

Teachers can move from this experience-based focus on the mail that we all write and receive to a variety of written texts, not just traditional literary or educational materials. In my freshman composition classes, for instance, I regularly ask students to analyze three different articles on the same subject written by John Flavell, a noted cognitive psychologist. The first article (1986b) was published in the general interest magazine *Psychology Today;* the second (1986a), in *American Psychologist,* a scholarly journal published by the American Psychological Association, whose 60,000 members include psychologists and other behavioral and social scientists with quite a broad range of interests; the third, co-authored with colleagues (1983), in *Cognitive Psychology,* a specialized academic journal for researchers in that field. By looking at how the same author varies his language and approach for different audiences, even when discussing the same subject, students can understand what it means to respond sensitively and effectively to varying rhetorical situations.

Once students have a rich awareness of how rhetoric functions in a variety of oral and written communication situations, they can understand the commonsense rhetorical reasons why a citizen writing a letter to the editor about a controversial subject cannot ignore the values and assumptions of readers if he or she hopes genuinely to communicate with those whose beliefs differ markedly from his or her own. Students in middle school or junior and senior high school can analyze letters as they appear in newspapers. They can also gain experience writing real letters to the editor on subjects currently being debated in their community.

As these examples indicate, rhetoric offers teachers a number of specific strategies that they can use to help their students become sensitive, effective, and ethical communicators—whatever the rhetorical situation to which they are responding. (For further examples of a rhetorical approach to writing, consult my own textbook, *Work in Progress: A Guide to Writing and Revising*, 1989, or the textbooks by Corbett, 1971; Gage, 1987; and Horner, 1988.) Knowledge of the rhetorical tradition also enables teachers to evaluate recently developed pedagogical methods and determine those that can best prepare students to function as effective citizens and communicators in our increasingly complicated world.

As noted earlier, rhetoric, unlike formal logic, embraces the human and the situational. Rhetoricians have understood for centuries that language use engages the *whole* person. Efforts to improve the quality of public discourse that depend on rote learning—whether of grammar rules or lists of historical figures and events—thus contradict rhetoric's traditional emphasis on intention, context, meaning, and response. In his *Institutes of Oratory* Quintilian argued strongly for coordinated, contextualized instruction in reading, writing, speaking, and listening. Current approaches to the teaching of reading and writing reflect—though in general they do not acknowledge—the wisdom of Quintilian's advice. Rhetoric, I have argued here, has a rich tradition that can empower both teachers and students. It is time not just to acknowledge, but to revive that tradition.

REFERENCES

Aristotle. (1932). *The rhetoric of Aristotle*. (L. Cooper, Trans.) New York: Appleton-Century-Crofts.

Berlin, J. A. (1984). *Writing instruction in nineteenth-century American colleges*. Carbondale: Southern Illinois University Press.

Bitzer, L. (1968). The rhetorical situation. *Philosophy and Rhetoric, 1,* 1–14.

Booth, W. C. (1974). *Modern dogma and the rhetoric of assent*. Chicago: University of Chicago Press.

Burke, K. (1966). *Language as symbolic action: Essays on life, literature, and method*. Berkeley: University of California Press.

Connors, R. J., Ede, L. S., & Lunsford, A. A. (1984). The revival of rhetoric in America. In R. J. Connors, L. S. Ede, & A. A. Lunsford (Eds.), *Essays on classical rhetoric and modern discourse* (pp. 1–15). Carbondale: Southern Illinois University Press.

Corbett, E. P. J. (1971). *Classical rhetoric for the modern student* (2nd ed.). New York: Oxford University Press.

Corvallis Gazette-Times. (October 1982–January 1983). [Letters to the editor].

Ede, L. (1989). *Work in progress: A guide to writing and revising*. New York: St. Martin's Press.

Flavell, J. H. (1986a). The development of children's knowledge about the appearance–reality distinction. *American Psychologist, 41,* 418–425.

Flavell, J. H. (1986b). Really and truly. *Psychology Today, 20,* 38–44.

Flavell, J. H., Flavell, E. R., & Green, F. L. (1983). Development of the appearance–reality distinction. *Cognitive Psychology, 15,* 95–120.

Gage, J. T. (1984). An adequate epistemology for composition. In R. J. Connors, L. S. Ede, & A. A. Lunsford (Eds.), *Essays on classical rhetoric and modern discourse* (pp. 152–169). Carbondale: Southern Illinois University Press.

Gage, J. T. (1987). *The shape of reason: Argumentative writing in college.* New York: Macmillan.

Halloran, S. M. (1975). On the end of rhetoric, classical and modern. *College English, 36,* 621–631.

Horner, W. B. (1988). *Rhetoric in the classical tradition.* New York: St. Martin's Press.

Murphy, J. J. (1982). Rhetorical history as a guide to the salvation of American reading and writing: A plea for curricular courage. In J. J. Murphy (Ed.), *The rhetorical tradition and modern writing* (pp. 3–12). New York: Modern Language Association.

Perelman, C., & Olbrechts-Tyteca, L. (1969). *The new rhetoric: A treatise on argumentation* (J. Wilkinson & P. Weaver, Trans.). Notre Dame: University of Notre Dame Press.

Plato. *Gorgias.* (1960). W. Hamilton (Trans.). New York: Penguin.

Toulmin, S. (1958). *The uses of argument.* Cambridge: Cambridge University Press.

Toulmin, S., Rieke, R., & Janik, A. (1979). *An introduction to reasoning.* New York: Macmillan.

7 The Uses of Argument in Civic Education

A Philosophy and Practices for Our Time

RICHARD A. KATULA

The philosopher Karl Jaspers (1970) writes,

> I do not know which impulse was stronger in me when I began to think: the original thirst for knowledge or the urge to communicate with others. Knowledge attains its full meaning only through the bond that unites human beings; however, the urge to achieve agreement with another was so hard to satisfy I was shocked by the lack of understanding, paralyzed, as it were, by every reconciliation in which what had gone before was not fully cleared up. Early in my life and then later again and again I was perplexed by people's rigid inaccessibility and their failure to listen to reasons, their disregard of facts, their indifference which prohibited discussion, their defensive attitude which kept you at a distance and at the decisive moment buried any possibility of a close approach. . . . No urge seemed stronger to me than that for communication with others. If the never completed movement of communication succeeds with but a single human being, everything is achieved. It is a criterion of this success that there be a readiness to communicate with every person encountered, and that grief is felt whenever communication fails. (p. 147)

Jaspers' words describe as succinctly as any the essential value of communication: to bring those in society closer to what Kenneth Burke calls "consubstantiality," a sense of identification with and belonging to one another. That is, after all, the meaning of citizenship. Jaspers' comments also point out the frustration we feel when communication consists of little more than shouting, whining, or conspiring to win or end a conversation rather than engaging in it for constructive purposes.

SPEECH AND DEMOCRACY

Speaking constitutes our very essence as human beings. It is the way each of us calls our world into existence. Every thought we articulate orients us in a world that is not given, but is rather constructed word by word. Speech and reality go together. One of my favorite expressions, which I dwell on in public speaking classes, is "I am taking you at your word." It is a critical point for it implies that what you say indicates what you have thought, which indicates, therefore, who you are. And yet students are often surprised by the notion, perhaps because they have yet to be held strictly accountable for their own ideas, or perhaps because students are not unlike the rest of us, who, unless constantly on guard, tend to take our talk lightly, remaining insouciantly unaware of how our words are defining us as persons.

Speech is the most revealing form of human action. If I speak ignorantly, spouting opinion after opinion, others will think me ignorant. If my speech is laced with obscenities, or sexist or racist remarks, I will be thought by others to be obscene, sexist, or racist. If I speak continually (and about myself), refusing to listen or to yield to others, I will be seen by them as an egocentric bore. Such truisms are little more than common sense, but they catch us by surprise because we often forget that what we say is who we are.

Speech is serious business. It is our most basic form of encounter with the world and with others. It is through speech that we express our existential need for sociality. Philosopher Georges Gusdorf states this as follows:

> Humanness is not contained within itself. The contours of one's body are a line of demarcation, but never an absolute limit. The existence of others doesn't appear as a delayed result of experience and reason. Intellectually and materially the other is for each of us a condition of existence. The plurality of individuals, the fragmentation of being, appears thus as an original presupposition of lived consciousness. . . . In essence, language itself is not of one, but of many, it is *between*. . . . Through communication, it makes a new world, a real world. (1965, p. 48)

We need to pay attention to more than just the multitude of voices, however. The quality of our speaking also demands attention. Associated activity is a condition of existence, but true communal life is moral; that is, emotionally, intellectually, and purposefully sustaining and fulfilling with some view toward a common good. In fact, it is axiomatic in any democracy that the quality of the community is determined by the quality of each person's speaking. Plato long ago observed an isomorphic relationship between the individual and the polis, and has Socrates express this in his *Republic*.

> The individual is wise in the same way, and in the same part of himself, as the city. And the part which makes the individual brave is the same as that which makes the city brave, and in the same manner; and everything which makes for virtue is the same in both. . . . A person is just in the same way as the city is just. (Moline, 1978, p. 4)

Democratic society is distinctive in that civic, or public, talk plays a determinative role. When public discussion is properly articulated, it serves first as a guide to social, educational, and political policy making; and later as a legitimizing agent for those policies. However, when public discussion is characterized by personal attacks and rude, insulting speech, it subverts policy making. Discussion veers from its intended focus on resolving the issues of the day to a new focus on personal or group supremacy, or, at its very worst, becomes a forum for cheap-shot artistry. An example of contemporary discourse will illuminate this latter phenomenon.

A recent controversy concerning the appropriate curriculum for America's elementary and secondary schools, sparked by the best-selling book, *Cultural Literacy: What Every American Needs to Know*, by E. D. Hirsch (1987), has given those interested in education much to debate. The text is intended as a focal point for public and academic discussion concerning what students should know and what they actually learn. And, clearly, somewhere between Hirsch's vision of the curriculum and the vision of others may be an answer to the question. But reviews of Hirsch's text have too often centered on the list of terms and concepts at the end of the book, or on Hirsch himself, especially his being a white, male, academic from an "elite" institution (the University of Virginia), rather than on his thesis that all literate persons need to possess certain basic information about their world in order to live in it successfully. James Sledd and Andrew Sledd (1989), for instance, offer the following paragraph in a generally scathing critique of the book:

> We happily quote Hirsch's promising entry in the frenetic competition to devise the century's silliest sentence: "Only a few hundred pages of information stand between the literate and the illiterate, between dependence and autonomy" (p. 143). Though wishful academics may be bamboozled by such nonsense, Hirsch should be required to debate

the proposition with the literate unemployed—with skilled workers who have no work because profit-seeking executives have destroyed their jobs by forced technological innovation or have exported those jobs to exploited laborers in other nations. But we refuse to argue the self-evident. A nation of fully enfranchised, autonomous citizens cannot be built by cataloguing, in a few hundred pages, the items that newspaper readers are said to know or believe, sprinkled with the grammatical and scientific terms that three Virginia academics think newspaper readers ought to learn. Our question is different. Why did the distinctive bad-ness, the gross absurdity, of *Cultural Literacy* guarantee its success in the newspaper reader's marketplace? (pp. 378–379)

In another passage, Sledd and Sledd assert, ''a plausible conclu-sion is that the tradition which Hirsch speaks for [sic] is a gerontoc-racy of the white middle class (a regime comparable to that of the regents of some state universities—elderly, affluent Anglo males)'' (p. 367). Sledd and Sledd conclude that Hirsch is simply another expositor of ''middle American rhetoric,'' in the most pejorative sense of that phrase.

The question is not whether Hirsch or the Sledds are correct (even though one might criticize the Sledds for quoting only half of the first statement above as it is actually written in Hirsch's text and for taking the half sentence out of the context of the paragraph in which it appears). The question is, Does such speech advance the debate? Or does the sarcasm dripping from the Sledds' pen shift the focus from what may or may not be a cogent refutation of Hirsch's position to a personal attack on Hirsch's genealogy and professional position? Sledd and Sledd may be reputable academicians, but they do not know how to argue. Their words are more likely to yield a response in kind, and soon the issue itself might be lost in a flurry of *ad hominem* attacks. Most important, the Sledds' approach to argu-ment is not one we would want our students to emulate because it evokes a personal, emotional response rather than an analytical, objective one.

It is because examples such as the one just cited abound, if not predominate, in contemporary public discussion that this chapter is written. Purely disputatious speech that is rude, insulting, emotion-ally laden, and person-centered has always lurked as a convenient medium of public exchange—and it always will. But to counter its destructive tendencies we have had a tradition of training in rhetoric, the art of effective and ethical communication, especially in public speaking, which has given people an alternative model with which to articulate reasonably their positions on matters of public concern.

This chapter calls for a reinvigoration of that kind of training in speech in our schools so that public discussion can authorize and legitimate social, political, and educational policy making. The chapter first suggests that when training in rhetoric has been present in the curriculum, democracies have risen to the challenges presented to them. I then offer a philosophy of argument on which a renewed tradition of training in rhetoric may be based. I conclude with some practical suggestions for implementing that philosophy through speech instruction in the elementary and secondary schools.

THE RHETORICAL TRADITION IN TIMES PAST

Ancient Greece

There is a long tradition of civic talk—public talking—in Western democratic civilization. In fact, all the great Western civilizations reached their zenith when the chorus of reasoned voices was at its fullest, when speaking, both formal and informal, was given free reign. And in every case, training in rhetoric was at the heart of the educational system, serving the society by preparing its members for full participation in civic affairs.

In the sixth and fifth centuries B.C., Athens became the first democracy. Decimated by war and subjugated by tyranny, Athenians were challenged to create a new type of society based on the concept of law and the will of the people. Once that democratic framework was in place, all those who could participate as citizens were expected, indeed required, to participate in it. The great statesman, Pericles, spoke to this principle of pure democracy in his *Funeral Oration*.

> Each individual is interested not only in his own affairs, but in the affairs of the state as well; even those who are mostly occupied with their own businesses are extremely well informed on general politics—this is a peculiarity of ours—we do not say that a man who takes no interest in politics is a man who minds his own business; we say that he has no business here at all. (Corbett, 1971, p. 232)

Affairs of the state, for the Athenian citizen, were affairs of the heart, and democracy was more than a political system; it was a spiritual bond. As G. L. Dickinson (1960) notes, ''public life as we call it was not a thing to be taken up and laid aside at pleasure, but a necessary and essential phase of the existence of a complete person" (p. 72).

According to accounts of the day, Athenian streets were alive with speech. George Willis Botsford (1924) tells us that Athenian assemblies rang with oratory and that the fundamental motive to right conduct was the good of the state (p. 299). In their courtrooms, the true social center of Athenian life, the entire community participated in the maintenance of justice. Juries numbered from 500 to 2000, and litigants spoke for themselves. On a given day, fully one-third of the citizens would serve as jurors, listening to fellow citizens charge and defend themselves on crimes ranging from dog bites to desertion on the battlefield to murder. Kathleen Freeman (1963) tells us that to come before the court was "like addressing a public meeting" (p. 16).

The ability to speak in this oral society was a necessity. Indeed, life and death might hinge on one's words. In the assembly, one's ability to speak might prevent or instigate a war; in the courtroom, the ability to speak might save or cost a life. Little wonder, then, that training in rhetoric, the art of effective and ethical persuasion, was at the very heart of Athenian education, constituting the entire curriculum of what we would regard as the secondary school and much of what we think of as advanced education (Kennedy, 1964, p. 7).

In an academy such as that headed by the celebrated teacher Protagoras, known as the Father of Debate, students were required to speak first on one side of an issue or principle and then on the other. Of course these were schoolroom exercises, but through them and the discussions that followed, Athenian youngsters investigated the controversies and the values of the day, and they learned that reason usually exists on both sides of an argument. Protagoras provided for his pupils a lesson in didacticism as well as in persuasion. "He will learn," Protagoras wrote, "what he came to learn: and that is prudence in affairs private as well as public; he will learn to order his own house in the best manner, and he will be able to speak and act for the best in the affairs of the state" (Botsford, 1924, p. 280).

Colonial America

The roots of Athenian thinking are set deeply in our own democracy, although our form of self-government is republican rather than purely democratic. While it fell to the citizens of Athens to invent self-government for their tiny city-state, those who colonized the

American continent had to address the building of small, local self-governing communities, even though they were subjects of a distant monarch and were frequently ruled by aristocratic governors in their colonies. They did so through the active participation of each citizen.

Drawing primarily from Greek and English traditions, colonial American life was, at its best, a life of discussion and debate. To live in colonial America, perhaps in Boston or Philadelphia, was to be engaged in one continuous civic conversation. No people thrived more on the give-and-take of public dialogue, and to shrink from it was thought to be against nature's very intent. As James Carey (1987) notes, life in colonial America opened into the streets, creating a unity in everyday life that would lead to the unity necessary to secure independence from England. According to historian Samuel Bass Warner, cited in Carey's text, each day merchants and artisans would gather at the coffee houses to read incoming newspapers and discuss prices. Indeed, throughout the founding years until the 1840s, public life in America was ''a life of incessant talk and, above all, questioning in the public houses that were the dominant institutions of early American cities'' (Carey, 1987, p. 9).

In the quest for independence, it was oratory that led the way. We did, indeed, wage war for our right to self-determination, but it was reasoned, ringing debate that led to the Declaration of Independence, and that gathered the leaders of the 13 colonies together for their signatures. Our very Constitution was a document forged on the anvil of debates such as those joined by James Madison and Patrick Henry at the Virginia Convention in 1788. The American system, then, is indissolubly linked with the process of civic argument begun in our colonial founding period.

In the colonial schools, oratory and debate were also at the core of the curriculum. Twenty-five years before the Declaration of Independence, students at Harvard and Yale presented original orations on a regular basis. In 1764, at the College of New Jersey (Princeton University), seniors presented orations at monthly meetings designed for this purpose, and that same year the commencement program for Rhode Island College (Brown University) included forensic debates in both Latin and English (Guthrie, 1954, p. 68). Societies such as Phi Beta Kappa utilized debate as a major part of their agendas. In 1779 and 1780, for instance, the William and Mary Chapter of Phi Beta Kappa debated the following topics: The Justice of American Slavery; Whether an Agrarian Law Is Consistent with the Principles of a Wise Republic; and Is Public or Private Education More

Advantageous? (Potter, 1954, p. 249). It was because of this attention to speaking, both formal and informal, that the Framers could begin building a new nation on persuasion rather than violence.

The Nineteenth Century

After the revolution, the challenge for America was to become a self-governing people. As Malcolm Knowles notes, "The first educational task of the new nation was to transform an entire people from subjects to citizens—from a people used to being governed by an aristocracy to a people able to govern themselves" (Antczak, 1985, p. 56). Oratory and debate served that purpose in several ways.

First, instruction in both public and private schools emphasized speech as the key to individual participation in republican self-government. The legendary William McGuffey himself declared in 1836 that unless every child were able to

> think without embarrassment in any situation in which he may probably be placed . . . express his thoughts on any subject with which he is acquainted with accuracy, and without hesitation . . . generalize his knowledge with rapidity, so as to construct an argument, or a defense, he is not educated, at least he is not educated suitably for this country, and especially for the West. (Borchers & Wagner, 1954, p. 289)

Many biographies of the period attest to the personal and public gain achieved through training in rhetoric in the schools. One young man wrote the following:

> There was one thing I could not do. I could not speak before the school. Many a piece did I commit to memory and rehearse it in my own room, over and over, yet when the day came when the school collected to hear declamations, when my name was called, and I saw all eyes turned to my seat, I could not raise myself from it. When the occasion was over, I went home and wept bitter tears of mortification.

And yet, after joining the debating society at Dartmouth this young man became the prized speaker and debater of the institution, and indeed of the nation. His name—Daniel Webster.

While instruction in oratory developed individual competence and self-confidence in public speaking, exposure to mature oratory served an equally important purpose in the transformation of a people from subjects to citizens: it developed their civic identity. Even more than the fledgling public school system and the universities of the time, it was civic talk on the public speaking lecture circuit, begun in the nineteenth century, that molded the people who inhabited America into "the American people." Frederick Antczak (1985) notes that "as the democratic audience emerged, institutions of popular education were developed, the most successful of which was the circuit of public speech" (p. 7). Through such popular educational movements as the Lyceum and the Chautauqua, he proposes, America discovered itself.

Both the Lyceum, founded by Josiah Holbrook in 1826, and the Chautauqua, founded in 1873 by Reverend John Heyl Vincent and Lewis Miller, served as forums for public discourse. Their goals were to diffuse knowledge, especially practical knowledge, exert a healthy moral and political influence, serve as a thrifty form of education, and have a beneficial effect on the public schools. During their heyday from 1830 to 1920, these two public lecture circuits served to widen the area of shared public concerns and hone the personal capacities of the audience. They served further to break down barriers of class and region by defining an agenda common to all members of the national community. An entire nation was made relevant to its citizens. On a given night, under the Chautauqua tent, sheltering perhaps 1,000 Pennsylvanians or New Yorkers, might come such luminaries as William Jennings Bryan, Thomas Edison, Eugene Debs, and Carrie Nation, each to deliver his or her own sense of American life. Ralph Waldo Emerson might engage the audience on the sacredness of private integrity, while Governor E. W. Hoch might bring them a "Message from Kansas." As Antczak suggests, it was through this congeries of ideas that the American people became connected by an identifiable thought and character—not necessarily agreeing, but for the first time recognizing that they were an audience for one another. They had reached a point, identified by Emerson, where to address others was to address a part of themselves.

Reasoned public debate was as instrumental in shaping national values and public policy as oratory was in shaping a collective identity. Perhaps the finest example of a typical scene in nineteenth-century America is the Lincoln–Douglas debates, carried on in seven cities along the Illinois prairie during 1858. Through live speeches delivered to large audiences of farmers, merchants, and traders, these two political foes raised the consciousness of an entire community on issues such as slavery, the place of the Supreme Court in the system of government, and states versus federal rights.

While both Abraham Lincoln and Stephen Douglas delighted their audiences with occasional witty barbs directed at each other, the debates are much more notable as models of clear reasoning on the issues of the day. Historian George Fort Milton (cited in Crawford, 1958), for example, assigns the success of the debates to the debaters' predominant appeal to reason, as in the following assessment of Douglas's style:

> In beginning his speeches, Douglas nearly always sought to check demonstrations, and would say, much as at Ottawa, "Silence will be more acceptable to me in this discussion of these questions than applause. I desire to address myself to your judgments, your understanding and your consciences, and not to your passions or your enthusiasm." Nor did he employ devices such as anecdote and shady humor. His presentation was a business-like recital of the facts as he saw them, a making-up of the issues and a relentless hammering upon them. (p. 332)

As David Zarefsky (1986) notes, the Lincoln–Douglas debates embody the best of the rhetorical tradition in America in their presentation of competing arguments in the public forum to a citizenry seeking to make an electoral decision. For Zarefsky, public debates such as those engaged in by the two giants of the prairie were "as likely a path to practical wisdom as any" (p. 181).

Rhetorical practices of the nineteenth-century resulted, finally, in more than the constitution of individuals into a collective, and they accomplished more than the shaping of the American value system. Their ultimate accomplishment was to free the individual from his or her own ignorance in order that he or she might participate in the freedoms guaranteed by the Constitution, the first of which is freedom of speech. It was through the communal building of selves and the drawing of each individual into a distinctively American community through civic talking that the ultimate success of nineteenth-century public education was achieved: to set the pursuit of self-interest within the dynamics of a civic ethic, or, as Frederick Antczak (1985) quotes Tocqueville, to encourage "self-interest, rightly understood" (p. 205).

But we need not idealize or romanticize these eras to advance the point of this chapter. As with Athenian society, both colonial and nineteenth-century America were fraught with purely disputatious speech, with public talk that sundered rather than strengthened the bonds of democratic life. Fallacious reasoning, deceit, sarcasm, and coercion weave their way through the pages of democratic history. The Athenian courtroom, mentioned earlier as the site of some of history's finest reasoning and oratory, also witnessed the crude and the pathetic. Poorly trained defendants would often beat their breasts and wail loudly for mercy, even going so far as to bring their children into the arena to garner sympathy with the assembled jurors. Americans have often settled for, even revered, the use of satirical frontal attacks to expose the follies and vices of the day. Who can resist a chuckle, even if silent, when pomposity or arrogance are nakedly revealed with a neat turn of phrase, like the famous line by Senator John Randolph of Virginia characterizing his political foe, Edward Livingston: "He is a man of splendid abilities, but utterly corrupt. Like a mackerel rotting in the moonlight, he both shines and stinks."

The point intended in this chapter, however, is that a strong rhetorical tradition existed in these earlier times, serving to moderate the tendency toward the purely pathetic or disputatious, and allowing debate and discussion to proceed beyond the witty retort or the pointed personal attack to the issue at hand. This rhetorical tradition prepared Americans to engage in and listen to enlightened public debates such as those involving Alexander Hamilton and James Madison (on the Constitution in the *Federalist Papers*), Henry Clay and John C. Calhoun (on the Compromise of 1850), and Lincoln and Douglas. However, as I shall discuss later, this rhetorical tradition has declined in the twentieth century. We need to revitalize that tradition today in the face of a major challenge to our sense of a collective identity.

THE RHETORICAL TRADITION AND THE CONTEMPORARY CHALLENGE

We have a serious problem in America today, one as serious as that faced in any period of our past. William Pfaff (1989) refers to it as "the broken connections of modern America," in which the various segments of our diverse society seem to be, as he puts it, "no longer connected to a culture deeper or more responsible than that provided by the mass entertainment industry, a people for too many of whom 'fun' is what life is all about" (p. 3).

The long-term consequence of our problem may be what Sidney Bernstein (1988), columnist for *Advertising Age*, refers to as the "balkanizing" of the United States, "into dozens of satrapies having their own customs, in many cases their own language, their own interests, their own patterns of life, their own living and voting credos" (p. 16). Is America becoming, as one Census Bureau official called it, "a confederation of minorities that places a priority on social identification, dual language ability, and cultural isolationism'' (Gutierrez, 1989, p. 5)? Today, the question is whether there is such an entity as ''the public'' or whether we have become simply a loose aggregation of self-interest groups concerned with our own group's rights rather than with the common good.

The unique challenge we face as Americans today is to celebrate and thrive on our pluralism while simultaneously subscribing to, as Sandra Stotsky calls it in Chapter 1, a ''civic ethic'' that promotes ''responsibility to and for others.'' The heart of our problem is that we engage too often in polarizing, purely disputatious speech when we communicate with one another across racial, sexual, economic, and political lines. As Robert Bellah and his associates (1985) suggest, ''A public philosophy does exist in our common life, but it is both often badly expressed and only partially realized'' (p. 22).

We engage too often in power speaking and we talk *at* one another rather than *with* one another. While in earlier times, a speaker such as Lincoln or Webster might use satire or a sharply pointed but witty line, speakers today resort to sarcasm or name-calling. Lacking other resources and skills with which to articulate our views, we rely on the ''sound bite'' or the ''word bite'' to bring an opponent down. Such tactics, when operating as the exclusive medium of exchange, only exacerbate the problem.

This chapter, it is important to note, is not concerned with the existence of disagreement, which is a healthy and constant phenomenon in democratic society. At issue is the *quality* of our disagreement, the way we talk and argue with one another in America today. Another example from the world of education will help make the point.

In a recent edition of *The Chronicle of Higher Education*, the headline reads: ''SCHOLARS IN THE HUMANITIES ARE DISHEARTENED BY THE COURSE OF DEBATE OVER THEIR DISCIPLINES.'' And well they should be, since reasoned discourse concerning the role of the humanities in higher education has given way largely to political, economic, racial, and gender name-calling. In one recent article, for instance, the author, a professor, asserted that

> The main function of education in most societies, especially at the primary and secondary levels, is the conservative one of inculcating in children the ideology of the established social order. In the United States, that order is overwhelmingly biased in support of American ethnocentrism; a capitalist economy; organized religion; and a white, male, middle- to upper-class view of the world. (Lazere, 1988, p. A52)

In a letter to the editor in a subsequent issue of *The Chronicle*, another professor asserted in response to the above essay that

Professor Lazere's assault upon "conservatives," advocates of the status quo, and—inevitably—William J. Bennett, is so oversimplified and equivocal that it is hard to accept at face value. If the fallacies and confusion were inadvertent, so much the worse for the English language. If they were deliberate, then, like Jonathan Swift's "Modest Proposal" for reducing poverty by eating the infants of the poor, his Point of View must really be against the "leftist" position he ostensibly supports. (Clayton, 1988, p. B3)

Regardless of who is right or wrong in this debate concerning the role of the humanities in higher education, or even if there is a "right" or "wrong," the tactics used to articulate the various positions will surely shift the argument away from the issue and toward the personal, or worse, to the gamesmanship of style, that is, which person can make the most sarcastic remark or cite more literary allusions than the other. Of one thing we can be certain: Such polemics will not advance the debate; at most, they will succor those who already agree with one position or the other.

Is the way we disagree, the quality of our disagreement, a symptom or a cause of our broken connections? Perhaps it is both, but whichever it is, there is reason for concern that our young people see too much of the polarizing style of speech in public life, and that it can only lead to further breaks in the connections or wider breaches in those that already exist. I would like to describe a philosophy of speech that might serve us well as we teach our students to talk with one another.

BECOMING CITIZENS OF THE NARROW RIDGE

Most public discourse takes place in the context of disagreement, that is, the context of argument, where discussants share differing points of view on a matter, or where a message is being sent in order to try to change someone's point of view. How people resolve disagreement or seek to effect change in others critically influences the nature of their political relationships to each other. There is cause for concern, then, that our young people see only one model of argument at work, the purely disputative model exemplified twice earlier in this essay from the world of academic discourse. If we could help our students understand the components of purely disputative speech in its contemporary form, and then give them another model, one that is reformative in nature, then both through description and comparison we might illuminate for them another tradition of argument that could serve them and us equally well in our public talking.

The Morton Downey Model

The first model of argument, the disputative, I call the Morton Downey model because Mr. Downey's television show is its most visible nonacademic example. It is not possible to capture the venomous nature of the program in written form alone, since a large part of the show relies on hooting from the audience, continuous interruptions by one speaker of others, obscenities screamed into the faces of guests by Mr. Downey, and occasional fisticuffs such as those engaged in one evening by two guests who were discussing the case of a young black girl who claimed to have been gang-raped by a group of white adults in upstate New York. In one segment devoted to the issue of capital punishment, Mr. Downey told one speaker who disagreed with him that murderers ought to be "fried" or made to "suck my armpit," while at the same time flapping his opened arm at the other speaker. The show is laced with invectives and sexist remarks, as in Mr. Downey's general tendency to refer to female guests as "honey." Regardless of one's position on the issues discussed, the approach to the issue is clearly disheartening and frustrating. In both its style and its substance, the Morton Downey show represents much that we often observe in argumentative speech and much that is wrong with it.

The Downey model is marked by an effort to bury one's opponent in a weltering rage of verbal epithets and nonverbal threats. Disputants are characterized by their unalterable polarity on the issue under discussion. The argument unfolds, perhaps unravels is a better term, as a series of questions on which horns are locked until one arguer is either shouted down by the other or by the "big mouths," as members of the studio audience are called.

Are such confrontations entertaining? For a time, perhaps. Is such argument cathartic? There may be something soothing about the release of one's emotions, but the pleasure is probably momentary, as one soon feels failure at having convinced no one of anything. The Downey model is the tradition of unilateral argument, as Douglas Ehninger (1970) defines it, in which lines of influence flow in only one direction. Entertainment and catharsis aside, as a method of argument, the Downey model is not intended to heal the broken connections of modern America.

First, in the classic Aristotelian sense, the Downey model signals the triumph of emotion over reason. It reminds one of those sadder moments in the original Athenian courtrooms when guilt or innocence was determined by which litigant could wail the loudest or beat his breast most demonstrably. It is a tradition that was partly responsible for Socrates' condemnation of democracy, his argument being that the courtroom was one of the most observable signs that the human community was composed mostly of a bleating herd of sheep that, as I. F. Stone (1988) puts it, "had to be ruled by a king or kings as a sheep by a shepherd" (p. 38).

Second, the Downey model is characterized by pure contentiousness. There is little attempt to reach agreement or even secure compliance. Looking at and listening to the disputants, one does not see the look of conversion or hear accommodating tones or expressions. This is argument intended to serve only the individual or his or her special interest or political ideology. It pursues selfish ends, the ends of the individual or his or her enclave.

Equally worrisome is the third characteristic of Downey-style speech: the use of labeling that accompanies a person's argument. Mr. Downey often dismisses guests as "guilt-ridden, left-wing, limousine liberals," or "tight-necked geek conservatives." In the academic world, writers describe others as members of a "white gerontocracy," or as "black activists," or simply as "ideologues." It is as though a statement is no longer either reasonable or unreasonable on its own, but only insofar as it represents an ideological position. Neither Lincoln nor Jefferson needed such tactics to press their position; no responsible speaker should. The trend toward obligatory labeling has become a special variation of the personal attack—the *ad hominem* argument, a fallacy in argumentation that places the emphasis not on what the person has said but on the person himself or herself.

The Downey model represents disputatious speech in its worst and most polarized form. I shout at you, you shout back, and we both walk away angrier than before. It is such rhetorical practices that are largely responsible for what Ronald Arnett (1986) has called the most serious crisis facing us today, the crisis of polarized positions (p. 15).

Does the widespread occurrence of this kind of disputatious argument mark a pathology in the nation's voice? Do examples such as those cited above point to the reign of ideological warfare? In our highly diverse and pluralistic society, is the disputative model of argument the inevitable approach to power and control in the battle for the supremacy of vested interests? Was Socrates correct? Or is there another model of argument that can help us go beyond ideological divisiveness and regenerate the rhetorical tradition in a way that is appropriate for our time. Even though argument as pure disputation has always existed and will continue to manifest itself in public discourse, I believe we can teach, nurture, and practice a second language of argument—one that reverberates with the words of John Stuart Mill, Thomas Jefferson, and Martin Luther King and that represents the finest in the rhetorical tradition of Western civilization. This second language of argument, I believe, can best be captured in the writings of Martin Buber, most imaginatively in his vivid metaphor of "The Narrow Ridge," a detailed discussion of which appears in Arnett (1986).

The Narrow Ridge Model

The narrow ridge is the position between polarized alternatives. It requires the arguers to embrace a position while remaining open to the other points of view. A citizen of the narrow ridge does not take relativistic, nonjudgmental positions; he or she looks at the multiple facets of an issue and learns from the opposition. Polarized arguments are often characterized by one-sidedness, and, when questioned, polarized arguers often do not know the position of the other side. Nor do they acknowledge even the possibility of more than one opposing position, or of intermediary positions. Public hearings, for instance, are often characterized by speakers who present their point of view and then leave the hearing having heard no other position. The consequence of this practice is that when a third party makes a decision that is binding on the arguers, no common ground has been reached, the result being simply another battle in another hearing room of another town. No conviction has resulted, no public consensus has been generated. Narrow ridgers live by the words of John Stuart Mill: "He who knows only his own side of the case, knows little of that."

Narrow ridgers always say, "The other person has some chance of persuading me. I am convinced of my position only until a better one is available." Freedom and individualism are tempered by a philosophy that contraries can be bridged. If I know that I might actually persuade someone to do something or to take a position I favor, I proceed more cautiously because I now have a great responsibility. If I am open to the views of others, I proceed more cautiously because I realize that I might have to change my mind in the public eye. Reason has a chance to prevail in such a situation, simply because reason is my best chance for success.

Citizens of the narrow ridge avoid the easy tactics of Downey-style argument: name-calling, sarcasm, invective, and labeling. They are concerned less with the withering turn of phrase than with the articulation of a clear position on an issue. For citizens of the narrow ridge, style is the servant of substance, and while a person's position on an issue may be attacked, the person is treated with integrity. Citizens of the narrow ridge understand that even though one makes a better case, if the opposition is treated poorly during the debate, little has been accomplished.

The narrow ridge is difficult to walk. It is easy to stumble or fall. Emotional excess, the ambiguities of language, lack of motivation to listen, specious reasoning, fear of the loss of image, and a host of other pitfalls mar the path. And yet there is value in the effort. Douglas Ehninger (1970) comments on the sanguine ends of this reformative model of argument:

> The ultimate justification of [reformative] argument lies not in any pragmatic test of results achieved or disasters avoided. Rather, it lies in the fact that by introducing the arguer into a situation of risk in which open-mindedness and tolerance are possible, it paves the way toward personhood for the disputants, and through them, and millions like them, opens the way to a society in which the values and commitments requisite to personhood may some day replace the exploitation and strife which now separates man from man and nation from nation. (p. 110)

This second tradition of argument may appear somewhat idealistic as it is described here, but there are examples of it readily available to teachers. The MacNeil/Lehrer Report on public television is one example of a program that provides a balanced perspective on issues and requires advocates to speak civilly and listen to one another. The Emmy-award-winning Chicago Tonight is the archetype of many local interview programs, usually on public television, that attempt to look at issues reasonably. There are, then, examples to which we can turn to demonstrate to our students a model of argument squarely within the rhetorical traditions that have served us successfully in times past.

Two models of argument operate in the public arena today. The Morton Downey model is alluring because it is easy and sometimes gratifying to simply shout down one's opponent. The model of the narrow ridge, as with all things of worth, is more difficult because arguers must articulate their position reasonably, avoiding rude, insulting speech, and holding to the courage of their convictions while remaining open to persuasion. Training in speech communication that is based on the philosophy of the narrow ridge can serve to ameliorate the tendency to argue disputatively, and it can help us to address the broken connections of modern America.

CLASSROOM PRACTICES FOR OUR TIME

The civic world is a rhetorical world, in which little is given us as certain and in which we must choose even if we cannot know, a world Chaim Perelman and Lucia Olbrechts-Tyteca (1969) describe as the domain of the probable and the contingent, where the psychological, the logical, and the ideological seek to merge. Students must learn that a democracy is a "messy" form of government, where there are few axioms and more interpretations, and where issues must be debated toward some common resolution. Every American must understand the system of inquiry and advocacy on which our nation was built. From there citizens can proceed to the forms and structures they need—ways to argue and discuss that allow them to walk along that narrow ridge. Thus, students need training in language; they need to learn how to articulate their views appropriately without resorting to the fallacies in argumentation so common in public discourse today. In short, we need to give the rhetorical practices of the past new life in the curriculum. But as one surveys the contemporary classroom, resource allocations in most school departments, and teacher preparation for the elementary and secondary schools, there is much cause for alarm.

The twentieth century has witnessed first the demise of a thriving rhetorical tradition and now a continual struggle to include speech training in the curriculum. At the turn of this century, many public school administrators considered speech training to be a "frill of education, not an essential" (Gulley & Seabury, 1954, p. 473). The emphasis at that time was on composition, training in written communication. That, coupled with the "elocutionary movement," a debilitating movement in speech communication that favored oral reading and a highly artificial style of speech and gestures, resulted in the almost complete abandonment of speech training. By 1932, some improvement was noted, but whole regions of the country, such as New England, reported *no* speech training in the public schools (Gulley & Seabury, 1954).

The situation today is somewhat better; however, the speech curriculum in the nation's public schools, almost always connected to an English department, must still be described as little more than a frill. In a 1981 nationwide survey, for instance, only 76 percent of the schools surveyed offered a speech course, and only 32 percent of those schools required the course. Surveys on the speech curriculum show a lack of administrative support for the programs and an unwillingness to shift resources to speech training (Book & Pappas, 1981).

Moreover, speech training is still too often taught by teachers who lack adequate preparation. Four states surveyed in 1981 reported that fewer than 30 percent of the teachers providing speech training were undergraduate majors in speech, while 12 states reported that fewer than 60 percent of their speech teachers held degrees in speech communication. Only 8 percent of all speech teachers surveyed belonged to the national speech communication association (Book & Pappas, 1981). Clearly, while many innovative programs have recently begun, there must be a national movement toward reinvigorating the rhetorical tradition in the schools if we are to address adequately the way we talk to one another today.

A Series of Assignments

One approach to a course of instruction in oral communication is based on the notion that students learn to think more abstractly and analytically through a process of gradual decentering; that is, through speaking assignments that move from the personal and subjective to the analytical and objective (Katula, 1987). Since this approach is a recent innovation in the discipline, I will describe it here, using the assignments I give in my textbook as examples (Katula, 1987).

Students can begin a course on public speaking by telling a favorite story or reading aloud from a fable or fairy tale. The story should have a moral, and the successful speaker is one who communicates this moral to the audience. An experience-based first assignment is easier to deliver for those who have moderate apprehension. And because it is centered on the personal, such an assignment prepares students to see the difference between subjective thinking and the more analytical thinking required to support an argument.

A second assignment can introduce students to the concept of definition. The teacher may provide a list of words that are often troublesome or confusing because of their meaning, such as "euthanasia," "karma," "peace," and "democracy," although students can be allowed to choose their own term if one interests them. This assignment is particularly helpful for discussions about values, many of which are symbolized as abstract nouns, for example, "integrity," "pessimism," "optimism," "diplomacy." Students can be required to think about their own meaning for the term and also to look for research on it, perhaps an essay or a poem written by someone else. They also learn how to conduct etymological research in order to understand how the meaning of a word changes over time. From this assignment students learn that symbols have both a subjective and an objective meaning, that connotations differ among individuals, that words are not things but guides to them, and, most important, that meaning lies somewhere between communicators.

The third assignment can be structured around that most difficult question, "why?" and focus, perhaps, on a cause–effect analysis of a controversial issue. In this assignment, students are not asked to defend a position on the issue, but are required to understand all sides of it. The issue-analysis assignment also works well with groups; for instance, a group of students might decide to do a symposium on AIDS, looking for its causes and effects and presenting suggested solutions to the AIDS crisis. Through such an assignment, students learn how to use library resources and how to gather and assemble information.

The next assignment is based on an analytical pattern such as argument. Argumentative assignments can be organized as debates, group encounters, symposia, or individual speeches. Students must explore an issue, using reasoning and evidence, and must fit their argument into a pattern such as a stock issues system (Katula & Roth, 1980; Sheckels, 1983). The argument must be based on evidence and reasoning, and every argument must anticipate refutation by recognizing opposing points of view and possible disadvantages of the proposition advanced. By following a pattern that requires attention to opposing views and to potential weaknesses in their own position, students can learn to walk the narrow ridge through active listening.

The argumentative assignment can lead directly to class discussions of the language techniques that characterize so much public discourse today. Discussion can center on the use of sarcasm, which one scholar defines as a double-edged message that can have both positive and negative consequences depending on the context (Mehrabian, 1971). Students can be asked to decide whether labeling the speaker affects their interpretation of the speaker's message, and whether student speakers should be required to state their ideological bias before speaking, or if they have one at all. A discussion of the use of obscenities in speech, or of the use of racist or sexist remarks, can be most engaging to young people who have been raised in a language-permissive era. One essential element of training in argument should be coverage of "fallacies of irrelevance," *non sequiturs,* such as the *ad hominem* attack alluded to earlier. The value of a reformative model of argument can go far beyond learning how to advocate effectively and ethically. It may provide students with a forum for discussing their own speech habits as well as the speech behavior they hear and see in public life.

The approach described above is simply one way to organize a course in oral communication. There are many other legitimate assignments and appropriate course procedures. Any reputable speech text will have an instructor's manual filled with sample syllabi and other course suggestions. *In the Appendix to this chapter, readers will find three evaluation forms often used to critique public speeches given in the classroom; these can be used without permission of the author.*

Related Assignments

As a related reading assignment in the English or language arts classroom, students can analyze advertisements as continuing narratives on American life. Students might comb through a complete issue of a magazine, looking at the ads as a single story, much as they would read a feature article that is continued from page to page. They can then engage in class discussion or write an essay discussing the ads from a cultural perspective: Who are the people in the ads? What cultural referents surround them? What are they doing and with whom? Students can then be asked to compare essays based on a magazine such as *Newsweek* with those based on a magazine such as *Ebony.* This is an excellent way for students to observe for themselves such important but abstract notions as "lifestyle enclaves" (Bellah, Madsen, Sullivan, Swidler, & Tipton, 1985, pp. 71–75) and the "balkanizing of America" by the mass communications industry (especially the advertising industry) into small, culturally segmented target groups. Analyzing advertisements in the way suggested here can lead to interesting class discussions on the consequences of group-isolationism.

Students might also be required to listen to speeches on television or in their community and write criticisms of them based on the criteria they have learned in the classroom. Magazines such as *Vital Speeches* provide a ready source of materials for critical analysis, and speech models can be gathered by videotaping them as they are presented on television or by purchasing videotape collections of speeches. By critiquing the speeches or the actual speaking of others, students learn through modeling, and they learn to look past flashy delivery techniques to the substance of a speech.

In addition to using speech exercises in the classroom, elementary and high school teachers can utilize systems for calling on students that ensure each student a chance to speak. Jan Burke, an elementary school teacher in Virginia, developed a system for doing this that involved assigning each student a number and then devising number patterns such as odd–even to use when calling on students. Burke also allows those who desire to speak to do so in addition to the students called on in the number sequence. According to Burke (1987),

> One gifted and talented student commented that this system is "more interesting, because I hear what all students think." I have used this approach in first, third, and sixth grades. It is an excellent way to ensure that all students are called upon frequently. By the end of the year the confidence and detail exhibited by students in their oral comments make this system a hit with students and teachers. (p. 7)

Writing may be the essential tool for thinking through an idea, but speaking is the best way to find out how well that idea has been communicated to a live audience. When a speech is followed by a discussion and then by a written critique, the speaker learns not only that an idea has a life of its own once it has been communicated, but also that he or she has ideas that others will listen to and think about.

The amount of material that must be covered in a class often precludes spending time on oral communication exercises; nevertheless, we badly need to develop oral communication skills. The Speech Communication Association has issued standards for developing a speech curriculum in the schools and for those who teach speech. Included as essentials in any well-balanced speech curriculum are the following:

> Oral communication instruction provides a wide range of speaking and listening experiences, in order to develop effective communication skills appropriate to
> A. a range of purposes; e.g., informing, learning, persuading, evaluating messages, facilitating social interaction, sharing feelings, imaginative and creative expression.
> B. a range of situations; e.g., informal to formal, interpersonal to mass communication.
> C. a range of audiences; e.g., classmates, teachers, peers, employers, family, and community.

D. a range of communication forms; e.g., conversation, group discussion, interview, drama, debate, public speaking, and oral interpretation.

E. a range of speaking styles: impromptu, extemporaneous, and reading from manuscripts.

Standards for those who teach the course are equally important:

1. Oral communication instruction is provided by individuals adequately trained in oral communication and/or communication disorders, as evidenced by appropriate certification.

2. Individuals responsible for oral communication instruction receive continuing education on theories, research, and instruction relevant to communication.

3. Individuals responsible for oral communication instruction participate actively in conventions, meetings, publications, and other activities of communication professionals. (Book & Pappas, 1981, p. 207)

There are also numerous articles and booklets published by the Speech Communication Association and regional speech associations that will aid in the development of a speech curriculum (see O'Keefe, 1986).

CONCLUSION

I believe that our unique contemporary challenge requires rhetorical practices such as those that have served other democracies and our own democracy in times past. It is true that our times are not like any that have gone before, and it is true that old solutions cannot be applied unaltered to new situations. However, there still exist a number of basic similarities between American society today and societies of the past. The individual is still defined through communication with others; we are still a democracy requiring public knowledge and an identifiable audience to authorize decisions and actions. Orators can still heighten public awareness, shape public opinion, and set the social and political agenda. There is still a need for lively debate in our streets and public meeting houses and for speech that adapts ideas to people and people to ideas. Most important, there is still a need for training in speech communication to provide us with the abilities necessary for reasoned argument and civilized speech.

Great societies place high value on rhetorical training. Speech is both our most reflective and our most social act. It is the way we learn most immediately and most frequently who we are in relation to others. Civic discourse, both formal and informal, is essential to the maintenance of a free, democratic society. To understand and participate in this society, the individual must be an articulate speaker. Our challenge as teachers, then, is to produce citizens who are capable of expressing themselves in the public forum, who are ready to take the challenge of inquiry and advocacy, who are prepared to walk the narrow ridge. By so doing, we will be reviving a tradition central to Western civilization, indeed, civilization itself. We will also be giving ourselves and our nation its best chance to meet the challenges of the contemporary world. Ours need not be a world either of lock-step unity or of debilitating opposition. Rather, ours can be an age of articulation, of seeking the common ground. If communication is truly the "meeting of meaning," then ours is a time when communication is more desperately needed than ever before.

REFERENCES

Antczak, F. (1985). *Thought and character: The rhetoric of democratic education.* Ames: Iowa State University Press.

Arnett, R. (1986). *Communication and community.* Carbondale: Southern Illinois University Press.

Bellah, R., Madsen, R., Sullivan, W. M., Swidler, A., & Tipton, S. M. (1985). *Habits of the heart.* Berkeley: University of California Press.

Bernstein, S. (1988, October 18). Our lost melting pot. *Advertising Age*, p. 16.

Book, C., & Pappas, E. (1981). The status of speech communication in secondary schools in the United States. *Communication Education, 30*, 199–209.

Borchers, G., & Wagner, L. (1954). Speech education in nineteenth century schools. In K. Wallace (Ed.), *A history of speech education in America* (pp. 277–300). New York: Appleton-Century-Crofts.

Botsford, G. W. (1924). *Hellenic history.* New York: Macmillan.

Burke, J. (1987, Summer). Using numbers for greater participation. *Speech Communication Teacher*, p. 7.

Carey, J. W. (1987). The press and the public discourse. *The Center Magazine, 20*, 4–15.

Clayton, T. (1988, December 7). "Biases of principle" versus "biases of special interest." *The Chronicle of Higher Education*, p. B3.

Corbett, E. P. J. (1971). *Classical rhetoric for the modern student.* New York: Oxford University Press.

Crawford, P. (1958). *The Lincoln–Douglas Debate at Freeport, Illinois, August 27, 1858.* De Kalb: Northern Illinois University Press.

Dickinson, G. L. (1960). *The Greek view of life.* Ann Arbor: University of Michigan Press.

Ehninger, D. (1970). Argument as method: Its nature, its limitations, and its uses. *Speech Monographs, 37*, 101–110.

Freeman, K. (1963). *The murder of Herodes*. New York: Norton.

Gulley, H., & Seabury, H. (1954). Speech education in twentieth-century public schools. In K. Wallace (Ed.), *A history of speech education in America* (pp. 471–490). New York: Appleton-Century-Crofts.

Gusdorf, G. (1965). *Speaking* (P. T. Brockelman, Trans.). Evanston, IL: Northwestern University Press.

Guthrie, W. (1954). Rhetorical theory in colonial America. In K. Wallace (Ed.), *A history of speech education in America* (pp. 48–59). New York: Appleton-Century-Crofts.

Gutierrez, F. F. (1989, April). *Advertising and the growth of minority markets and media*. Paper presented at a conference on ''Minority Images in Advertising,'' DePaul University, Chicago.

Hirsch, E. D. (1987). *Cultural literacy: What every American needs to know*. New York: Houghton-Mifflin.

Jaspers, K. (1970). Existenzphilosophie. In W. Kaufman (Ed.), *Existentialism from Dostoevsky to Sartre* (pp. 146–147). New York: Meridian.

Katula, R. (1987). *Principles and patterns of public speaking*. Belmont, CA: Wadsworth.

Katula, R., & Roth, R. (1980). A stock issues approach to writing arguments. *College Composition and Communication, 31*, 183–196.

Kennedy, G. (1964). *The art of persuasion in Greece*. Princeton: Princeton University Press.

Lazere, D. (1988, November 9). Conservative critics have a distorted view of what constitutes ideological bias in academe. *The Chronicle of Higher Education*, p. A52.

Mehrabian, A. (1971). *Silent messages*. Belmont, CA: Wadsworth.

Moline, J. (1978). Plato on the complexity of the Psyche. *Archiv Für Geschichte Der Philosophie, 60*, 1–27.

O'Keefe, V. P. (1986). *Affecting critical thinking through speech*. Urbana, IL: ERIC Clearinghouse on Reading and Communication Skills.

Perelman, C., & Olbrechts-Tyteca, L. (1969). *The new rhetoric: A treatise on argumentation* (J. Wilkinson & P. Weaver, Trans.). Notre Dame: University of Notre Dame Press.

Pfaff, W. (1989, May 7). 'Fun' in the park: Modern America's broken connections. *Chicago Tribune*, Section 4, p. 3.

Potter, D. (1954). The literary society. In K. Wallace (Ed.), *A history of speech education in America* (pp. 238–258). New York: Appleton-Century-Crofts.

Schuyler, W. (1900). The orator's training in America. In D. J. Brewer (Ed.), *A library of the world's best orations*. St. Louis: Ferdinand Kaiser.

Sheckels, T. (1983). Three strategies for deliberative discourse: A lesson from competitive debating. *College Composition and Communication, 34*, 31–42.

Sledd, A., & Sledd, J. (1989). Success as failure and failure as success. *Written Communication, 6*, pp. 364–389.

Stone, I. F. (1988). *The Trial of Socrates*. Boston: Little, Brown.

Zarefsky, D. (1986). The Lincoln–Douglas debates revisited: The evolution of public argument. *Quarterly Journal of Speech, 72*, 162–184.

APPENDIX: Evaluation Forms

SPEECH EVALUATION FORM

SPEAKER'S NAME:

ASSIGNMENT:

KEY: + = EXCELLENT
      - = NEEDS IMPROVEMENT
      0 = ADEQUATE

<u>CONTENT</u>:

< > Topic level and choice of topic for assignment
< > Topic adapted to the audience
< > Thesis clearly stated
< > Supporting material
< > Organization of body of speech
< > Introduction
< > Conclusion
< > Preview and transitional material
< > Speech purpose

<u>DELIVERY</u>

< > Naturalness and spontaneity
< > Dynamism and enthusiasm
< > Articulateness
< > Gestures
< > Posture
< > Movement
< > Facial expression
< > Pitch
< > Volume
< > Pause and emphasis
< > Fluency
< > Articulation and pronunciation
< > Eye contact

<u>VERBAL SKILLS</u>

< > Filler speech
< > Oral grammar
< > Word choice

<u>REMARKS</u>   <u>GRADE</u>

NARRATIVE EVALUATION FORM

SPEAKER'S NAME:

YOUR NAME:

1. Were you able to picture the characters in the story?

2. Did the speaker have a consistent story line?

3. What was the speaker's point? Was the point
    made clearly and convincingly?

4. Was this a valuable point? Did it make you think
    about your own experiences?

5. What did you enjoy most about the presentation?

6. What could the speaker do to improve his or her speaking?

7. Provide the speaker with a brief overall evaluation
    of the story. You may use a grade or a number if you
    wish.

ORAL REPORT EVALUATION FORM

SPEAKER'S NAME: _____

ASSIGNMENT: _____

	YES	NO	
INTRODUCTION	____	____	Did the speaker capture the interest and attention of the audience?
	____	____	Did the speaker provide necessary background details?
	____	____	Did the speaker indicate a purpose?
ORGANIZATION	____	____	Did the speaker follow a recognizable organization plan?
	____	____	Did the speaker use effective transitions to move through the parts of the speech?
	____	____	Did the progression of ideas lead naturally to a conclusion?
CONTENT	____	____	Did the speaker have adequate supporting material?
	____	____	Was the supporting material relevant?
	____	____	Was the supporting material up-to-date?
	____	____	Were sources noted for supporting material?
VISUAL AIDS	____	____	Did the speaker use visual aids effectively?
	____	____	Were the visuals carefully prepared?
	____	____	Did the speaker use an appropriate amount of visual material?
CONCLUSION	____	____	Did the speaker review key points?
	____	____	Did the speaker provide a sense of closure for the topic?
	____	____	Did the speaker offer the audience a course of action, if appropriate?
DELIVERY	____	____	Did the speaker use a natural style?
	____	____	Did the speaker seem enthusiastic about the topic?
	____	____	Did the speaker speak clearly?
	____	____	Did the speaker use language accurately?
	____	____	Did the speaker have effective gestures, movement, posture, and expressions?
DISCUSSION	____	____	Did the speaker answer questions accurately and clearly?
	____	____	Did the speaker show respect for the audience?
	____	____	Did the speaker keep answers brief?
	____	____	Did the speaker avoid defensiveness and contentious responses such as personal attacks?

212

About the Editor
and the Contributors

Sandra Stotsky is a research associate at the Harvard Graduate School of Education and director of the Summer Institute on Writing, Reading, and Civic Education. The author of many articles and essays on theory, research, and practice in the field of writing and reading, her research focuses on reading–writing relationships and the uses of writing for intellectual and public purposes. In 1992, she will begin her responsibilities as editor of *Research in the Teaching of English*. Dr. Stotsky received an Ed.D. in reading from the Harvard Graduate School of Education.

Barbara Hardy Beierl has taught literature, writing, and interdisciplinary courses at Harvard University and Wayne State University and in the City and State University of New York systems. She has served as president of the New York College English Association and on the board of directors of the College English Association. She is currently engaged in research and writing on how to read literature from a civic perspective. Dr. Beierl received a Ph.D. in English literature from Wayne State University.

John W. Cameron is head of the English Department at the Dana Hall School in Wellesley, Massachusetts, and has taught secondary school English for more than 30 years. Cameron served as editor of the newsletter of the New England Association of Teachers of English for 13 years and as its president in 1988–89. He was named a Joseph Klingenstein Fellow to Teachers College (Columbia University) in 1982–83, and in 1989–90 he was the National Endowment for the Humanities/*Reader's Digest* Teacher-Scholar from Massachusetts.

Jeanne S. Chall is Professor of Education at the Harvard Graduate School of Education and director of the Reading Laboratory. The author of the classic *Learning to Read: The Great Debate* and *Stages of Reading Development*, Dr. Chall's most recent work is *The Reading Crisis: Why Poor Children Fall Behind* (with Vicki Jacobs and Luke Baldwin). She is a member of the National Academy of Education and the Reading Hall of Fame. Dr. Chall received a Ph.D. in communication from Ohio State University.

Lisa Ede is associate professor of English and director of the Center for Writing and Learning at Oregon State University. Dr. Ede has authored, co-authored, or co-edited three books: *Essays on Classical Rhetoric and Modern Discourse* (with Robert Connors and Andrea Lunsford), *Work in Progress: A Guide to Writing and Revising*, and *Singular Texts/Plural Authors: Perspectives on Collaborative Writing* (with Andrea Lunsford). She has also published numerous articles on the teaching of writing and on rhetorical theory. Dr. Ede received a Ph.D. in English from Ohio State University.

Dorothy Henry is Coordinator of the Harvard Adult Literacy Initiative at the Harvard Graduate School of Education. She received her Ed.M. in Reading and Human Development from the Harvard Graduate School of Education and is an advanced doctoral candidate in Administration, Planning, and Social Policy at that school. She is on a leave of absence from the Massachusetts Department of Education, where she was Regional Director of federal compensatory programs (Chapter 1) in Central Massachusetts.

Richard A. Katula is Professor and Chair of the Department of Speech Communication, Northeastern University, Boston. He has published two books: *Communication: Writing and Speaking* and *Principles and Patterns of Public Speaking*, in addition to numerous articles in the language arts. Dr. Katula is particularly interested in the contribution oral communication training can make to civic education. He received a Ph.D. in speech communication from the University of Illinois, with an emphasis on rhetorical theory and criticism.

Index

Academic scholarship, decline in civic
ethic and, 14–22
Ackerman, John, 105
Adler, Mortimer, 48, 61–62
Adventures of Huckleberry Finn, The
(Twain), 71
Africa's Slaves Today (Derrick), 151
Alcott, Louisa May, 76
Allen, Lee, 100–101, 115–116
Allende, Isabel, 91
Alley Cat, The (Beauchemin), 97
Almond, G., 3
Alon, Dafna, 148
American Federation of Teachers, 25
Anderson, Philip, 62
Angelou, Maya, 71
Anna Karenina (Tolstoy), 76
Antczak, Frederick, 192, 193
Applebee, A., 103, 104
*Arab and Jew: Wounded Spirits in a Promised
Land*, 145, 148
Arab Racialism (Alon), 148
*Arab World Notebook for the Secondary School
Level* (Shabbas and Al-Qazzaz, eds.),
163–164
Arafat, Yassir, 148
Argument, xxiii–xxiv, 185–209
in ancient Greece, 189–190
classroom practices in, 202–207
in colonial America, 190–192
contemporary challenges of, 195–197
democracy and, 186–189
Morton Downey model of, 198–200
"narrow ridge" model of, xxiv, 200–
202
in the nineteenth century, 192–195
Aristotle, ix, 167, 168, 170, 179, 180
Armstrong, D., 154
Arnett, Ronald, 199, 200
Arrington, C. E., 9
At Risk (Hoffman), 92
Audience, research papers and, 118–119

Autobiography of Miss Jane Pittman, The
(Gaines), 95
Awakening, The (Chopin), 71, 76

Baker, Russell, 93
Baldwin, L., 56
Bambara, Toni Cade, 94
Bartleby the Scrivener (Melville), 71, 86
Bates, Katherine Lee, 87
Beagle, Peter, 95–96
Bean Trees, The (Kingsolver), 92
Beauchemin, Yves, 97
Beck, L. J., 56
Beierl, Barbara Hardy, xxi
Bellah, Robert, 2, 9, 11, 12, 196, 205
Bell for Adano, A (Hersey), 87
Bennett, William J., 197
Berg, R., 18
Berlin, J. A., 169
Bernstein, Sidney, 195
Berry, Wendell, 94–95
Betsey Brown (Shange), 92
*Beyond Entitlement: The Social Obligations
of Citizenship* (Mead), 12
Bissex, G., 49
Bitzer, Lloyd, 170
Black Beauty (Sewall), 87
Blacks
ethnic identity of, 27–28
literature on, 68–71, 76
Blodgett, Geoffrey, 15
Bloom, Allan, 143–144, 159
Blue Highways (Least Heat Moon), 95
Bok, Derek, 129–130
Book, C., 203, 207
Boorstin, Daniel, 20
Boorstin, Robert, 9–10
Booth, Wayne, C., 170–171, 180
Borchers, G., 192
Bormuth, J. R., 48
Boston Public Library, 7, 15
Boston Public Schools, 19, 32*n*